Pirkei DeRabbi Eliezer

Chapter of the great Rebbi Eliezer

Rebbi Eliezer Ben Hyrcanus

There is no known book without mistakes. Therefore, I ask in every language of application if anyone has any questions, comments, clarifications, corrections, please send to: **simchatchaim@yahoo.com**

All material used in this section may not be used for commercial purposes, but only for study and teaching.

To get this book or books and information Email me at:

simchatchaim@yahoo.com

Copyright©All Rights Reserved to

www.simchatchaim.com

YB"S©All rights reserved to the Editor

First Edition 2023

Pirkei DeRabbi Eliezer

Content of the book

3.	Introduction on Rebbi Eliezer
11.	Chapter 1
14.	Chapter 2
17.	Chapter 3
24.	Chapter 4
28.	Chapter 5
31.	Chapter 6
37.	Chapter 7
44.	Chapter 8
50.	Chapter 9
54.	Chapter 10
61.	Chapter 11
69.	Chapter 12
74.	Chapter 13
79.	Chapter 14
82.	Chapter 15
85.	Chapter 16
91.	Chapter 17
99.	Chapter 18
106.	Chapter 19
113.	Chapter 20
117.	Chapter 21
122.	Chapter 22
126.	Chapter 23
133.	Chapter 24
138.	Chapter 25
145.	Chapter 26

Pirkei DeRabbi Eliezer

- 149. Chapter 27
- 152. Chapter 28
- 157. Chapter 29
- 168. Chapter 30
- 175. Chapter 31
- 182. Chapter 32
- 189. Chapter 33
- 200. Chapter 34
- 208. Chapter 35
- 214. Chapter 36
- 226. Chapter 37
- 231. Chapter 38
- 245. Chapter 39
- 252. Chapter 40
- 258. Chapter 41
- 267. Chapter 42
- 274. Chapter 43
- 281. Chapter 44
- 287. Chapter 45
- 294. Chapter 46
- 301. Chapter 47
- 307. Chapter 48
- 318. Chapter 49
- 325. Chapter 50
- 336. Chapter 51
- 344. Chapter 52
- 350. Chapter 53
- 355. Chapter 54

Pirke De-Rebbi Eliezer

The chapters of Rebbi Eliezer, read in acronyms: Pedera, is a Midrashic essay attributed to the Tanna of Rebbi Eliezer ben Hyrcanus.

The Midrash was known among Torah scholars in all generations. Rebbi Amram Gaon was quoted, as were Rashi, Maimonides, Ramban and other Rishonim.

A book of Midrashim and legends attributed to Rebbi Eliezer ben Hyrcanus. In a book of legends about the act of Genesis and the days of the world, customs and laws.

Pirke De-Rebbi Eliezer - A book of Midrashim and legends from the beginning and days of the world with customs and laws.

Some call it **Breita Derby Eliezer** or the **Haggadah of Rebbi Eliezer**. The book is attributed to Tanna Rebbi Eliezer ben Hyrcanus, The Great.

Rebbi Amram Gaon says: We have seen that in the chapters of Rebbi Eliezer ben Hyrcanus he commanded to look at his nails in Havdalah.

The Rambam brings his words in the book **The Guide for the Perplexed** and says: I saw that Eliezer the Great speaks in his chapters named after the well-known, chapters of Rebbi Eliezer, etc.

The edited book is brought in by the name of **Breita Divrei Eliezer**.

Rabbeinu Tam brings this book in the Tosafot.

All these Torah scholars attributed the book to Rebbi Eliezer the Great.

Rebbi Eliezer ben Hyrcanus

Rebbi Eliezer ben Hyrcanus, called - Rebbi Eliezer, or Rebbi Eliezer the Great, was one of the greatest Tannaim in the second generation, during and after the destruction of the Second Temple, and a senior disciple of Rabban Yochanan ben Zakkai, who called it a **secret pit that does not lose a drop**. Due to his learning abilities. Was the colleague and brother-in-law of Rabban Gamliel from the city of Yavne, He was his learning partner of Rebbi Yehoshua ben Hanania. He lived in the city of Lod and headed a **yeshiva** and a court there.

In Avot De Rebbi Natan it is narrated that at the age of 28 Rebbi Eliezer began to continue to study the Torah, and against the will of his father Hyrcanus, who was a rich man and a landowner, but ignorant as he did not the value of Torah. Rebbi Eliezer left for Jerusalem to devote himself to Torah study. He entered the yeshiva of Rabban Yochanan ben Zakkai and studied steadily, even though he had to deal with great poverty, without support from his father and without a supportive acquaintance.

The other sons of Hyrcanus were angry that Eliezer had neglected his part in the field work. They pressured their father to evict Eliezer from the inheritance, Hyrcanus heard them and went up to the Sanhedrin in Yerushalayim to evict and exclude his son from all his property.

When Hyrcanus came to Yerushalayim, Rabban Yochanan Ben Zakki invited him to come to the Yeshiva.

Pirkei DeRabbi Eliezer

Rabban Yochanan asked Rebbi Eliezer to give a speech, but the latter was ashamed and modest to speak to the dignitaries. His father, who did not recognize his missing son and did not even understand what was being said.

Rabban Yochanan ben Zakki blessed Rebbi Eliezer and said, praise you Avraham, Yitzhak and Yaakov that this son came from you.

Hyrcanus asked those around him who Rabban Yochanan ben Zakki had blessed. Those around him had said Rebbi Eliezer had been blessed. Hyrcanus stood up and said on his feet and said - first I went up here to evict and exclude Eliezer from my property and leave him with nothing. Hyrcanus saw it was his son Rebbi Eliezer who had been blessed and reconciled with him.

Rebbi Eliezer, who was happy about the reconciliation with his father, refused to accept property intended for his brothers and asked to divide the property equally amongst them.

He continued to study with Rabban Yochanan ben Zakkai, until the beginning of the siege of Yerushalayim, when he and Rebbi Yehoshua helped smuggle their Rebbi out of the city during the Roman siege.

After the destruction of the Temple in Yerushalayim, Rebbi Eliezer Livneh moved there, where he became a member of the Sanhedrin under the presidency of Rabban Gamliel from the city of Yavne, and married Rabban Gamliel's sister, Mother Shalom. Rebbi Eliezer lived in the city of Lod, and headed a court and a yeshiva there, and also owned vineyards in the village of Tabi near Lod to the east.

Pirkei DeRabbi Eliezer

Rebbi Eliezer was sometimes referred to - Rebbi Eliezer the Great, his glory reached its peak when his disciples interpreted the verse - justice will pursue justice, for the sake of living and inheriting the land that the Lord your God gives you. Definitely: Looking for the fair trial, go after Rebbi Eliezer of Lod or after Rabban Yochanan ben Zakkai Berur Chayil.

Although Rebbi Yochanan ben Zakkai was from Beit Hillel, Rebbi Eliezer tended to follow the path of Beit Shamai, and this is one of the explanations for the name given to him. As is the custom of the disciples of Beit Shamai, Rebbi Eliezer was firm and sharp, and gave great weight to tradition over **Hasbra** [explanations]. On the other hand, his Bar-Plugata - Rebbi Yehoshua ben Hananiah belonged to Beit Hillel, which is also a reason why the **Halacha** [The Jewish law]. was usually decided in the opinion of Rebbi Yehoshua, in his disagreements with Rebbi Eliezer.

Rebbi Eliezer endeavored to prove his claims in various ways, and was often found arguing with his friends on the matter, using the measures required by the Torah, as light and material.

Rebbi Eliezer was perceived as both conservative and innovative. On the one hand, he testified to himself: because from time immemorial a man has not been in the Beit Midrash, and I have not slept in the Beit Midrash nor rested there. Nor have I left a person by himself in the Beit Midrash. Nor did I discuss mundane matters at anytime. Or I never spoke about anything I did not hear other than from my Rebbi.

Pirkei DeRabbi Eliezer

Controversy in Achnai's furnace

Achnai is a snake as we known today by the name Python. They used to build an oven back then by putting stones in a circle. Then built layer upon layer till it was completed. Then after that they would put clay between the layers to seal it. The walls of the oven also had clay to seal it.

The argument was between the Rebbi's and Rebbi Eliezer what would happen if a **Sheritz** שרץ [eight creeping thing or vermin that are mentioned in the Torah in Parsha Shemini] that got into the oven before they sealed the up with clay. It the oven **Tameh or not Tameh** [impure or pure].

The Halacha is that we always go according to the **majority of the Rebbis**. In this case all the rebbis were in agreement together except for Rebbi Eliezer. **In** an event that a **Sheritz** went into the oven you had to destroy the oven and rebuild it. This was the only way to make the oven kosher. This applies to any clay utensil.

Rebbi Eliezer held that even you didn't put the clay and **Sheritz** went inside the oven you need to destroy it, and all the Rebbi's held the even not need to be destroy.

Rebbi Eliezer was at the center of the famous controversy over Achnai's furnace. According to the Babylonian Talmud, in this controversy Rebbi Eliezer endeavored to prove his claims in various ways, even by decrees deviating from the laws of nature. The sages stood firm in their opinion and refused to accept the opinion of Rebbi Eliezer, despite the supernatural evidence that aided him. This ended in the act of the **Excommunication** of Rebbi Eliezer.

They said the same day, they brought all the purities that Rebbi Eliezer and Sharfom purified by fire and they counted him and blessed him. Akiva, dressed in black and wrapped in black and sat in front of him for four amot. Rebbi Eliezer Akiva told him what day it was, Rebbi told him, it seems to me that friends are in deals with you.

His greatness is the theory of Kabbalah

In a new Zohar it is stated that Rebbi Eliezer was a reincarnation of Reuven the firstborn of Yaakov, and for this reason, the decree of ten martyrs who according to the Kabbalah was sentenced to the ten sages for being equal against the ten tribes who threw Yosef into the pit, did not apply to Rebbi Eliezer but only ordered to throw Yosef into the pit, and therefore threw Rebbi Eliezer into the pit but raised him afterwards and did not kill him.

In the book of **Bnei Yissachar** it is stated that since Reuven was the one who always dealt with repentance for his sin that confused his father's performance, it is appropriate to rule like him when it comes to repentance, and because Rebbi Eliezer rules that the witnesses handed over This year - the time of writing, Yom Kippur - the time of signing, and Hoshana Rabba - which is the time of handing over the notes to the emissaries, it should be ruled that the time of repentance exists until Hoshana Rabba, and until then it is possible to repent, and

Pirkei DeRabbi Eliezer

change the sentence. He connects these things, to the reason by which Moshe Rabbeinu prayed that Rebbi Eliezer came out of his loins as quoted in the ruling in the name of Rebbi Acha.

Years passed during which Rebbi Eliezer was prevented from reaching the Beit Midrash. Sages lost his teachings, and the many of his traditions he had. Specially in particular Rebbi Akiva who was his special student. He lost the controversy the of Achnai's furnace. He did not compromise with the sages, even though the halacha [the Jewish law] is - singular and plural halacha as plural. But he did not give up his mind, without which there is no point in life, but what are years, even decades, in the face of eternity.

Before the death of Rebbi Eliezer, Rebbi Akiva and his friends stood next to him, and stood four amot [about two meters, 8 fit] away because of the excommunication imposed upon him, after the affair of the oven of Achnai. Rebbi Eliezer was very sorry for all the many words of the Torah he knew and no one came to learn from him because of the excommunication, and even foresaw the death of the sages of the generation in general, and the death in the torments of Rebbi Akiva, and he told to him, yours will be harder than all of the ten sages. As soon as he died Rebbi Yehoshua said the vow was allowed.

Rebbi Eliezer died on Friday, and after the departure of Shabbat the journey began and passed through Lod, and he was buried in Alma. Rebbi Akiva praised him from Elisha's words about

Pirkei DeRabbi Eliezer

Eliyahu, the same things that Elisha my father said, the chariot of Israel and its riders.

Before his death, Rebbi Eliezer regretted much of the Torah he had, and did not pass it on to Rebbi Akiva.

I heard from the one of the greatest Kabbalistic Rabbi in our generation that Rebbi Eliezer returned in the incarnation of our Ar"i Z"L, and his disciple Rebbi Akiva returned in the incarnation of Rebbi Chaim Vital, as explained in the **Shar Hagiguliim** [Gate of the Incarnations], who was the clearly the disciple of the Holy Ar"i Z"L, and received from him all Internals of Kabbalah, and wrote it for generations.

Despite his boycott, Rebbi Eliezer was quoted many times in the Mishnah, Breita and the Talmud. The sages of future generations deal extensively with his laws.

In this book we have opened all the acronyms. We corrected all the verses in order, and scored them. We have recorded the exact sources on each verse or quote from the words of Chazal.

His right and the right of all sacred conditions. Will stand for you and all the children of Israel.

Chapter 1

Following befell Rabbi Eliezer, son of Hyrḳanos. His father had many ploughmen who were ploughing gravel ground, whereas he was ploughing a stony plot; he sat down and wept. His father said to him: O my son! Why dost thou weep? Art thou perchance distressed because thou dost plough a stony plot? In the past thou hast ploughed a stony plot, now behold thou shalt plough with us arable soil. He sat down on the arable ground and wept. His father said to him: But why dost thou weep? Art thou perchance distressed because thou art ploughing the arable land? He replied to him: No. Hyrḳanos said to him: Why dost thou weep? He answered him: I weep only because I desire to learn Torah. Hyrḳanos said to him: Verily thou art twenty-eight years old yet dost thou desire to learn Torah? Nay, go, take thee a wife and beget sons and thou wilt take them to the school. He fasted two weeks not tasting anything, until Eliyahu - may he be remembered for good - appeared to him and said to him: Son of Hyrḳanos! Why dost thou weep? He replied to him: Because I desire to learn Torah. [Eliyahu] said to him: If thou desirest to learn Torah get thee up to Jerusalem to Rabban Yoḥanan ben Zakkai. He arose and went up to Jerusalem to Rabban Yoḥanan ben Zakkai and sat down and wept. Rabban Yoḥanan ben Zakkai said to him: Why dost thou weep? He answered him: Because I wish to learn Torah. Rabban Yoḥanan ben Zakkai said to him: Whose son art thou? But he did not tell him.

Pirkei DeRabbi Eliezer 1

Rabban Yohanan ben Zakkai asked him: Hast thou never learnt to read the Shema, or the Tefilla, or the Grace after meals? He replied to him: No. He arose and Rabban Yohanan ben Zakkai taught him the three prayers. Again, he sat down and wept. Rabban Yohanan ben Zakkai said to him: My son, why dost thou weep? He replied: Because I desire to learn Torah. He thereupon taught him two rules of the Law every day of the week, and on the Sabbath Eliezer repeated them and assimilated them. He kept a fast for eight days without tasting anything until the odour of his mouth attracted the attention of Rabban Yohanan ben Zakkai ben Zakkai, who directed him to withdraw from his presence. He sat down and wept. Rabban Yohanan ben Zakkai said to him: My son, why dost thou weep? He rejoined: Because thou didst make me withdraw from thy presence just as a man makes his fellow withdraw, when the latter is afflicted with leprosy. Rabban Yohanan ben Zakkai said to him: My son, just as the odour of thy mouth has ascended before me, so may the savour of the statutes of the Torah ascend from thy mouth to Heaven. He said to him: My son! Whose son art thou? He replied: I am the son of Hyrkanos. Then said Rabban Yohanan ben Zakkai: Art thou not the son of one of the great men of the world, and thou didst not tell me? By thy life! he continued, this day shalt thou eat with me. Eliezer answered: I have eaten already with my host. Rabban Yohanan ben Zakkai asked: Who is thy host? He replied: Rabbi Yehoshua ben Hananiah and Rabbi Yosef the Ha-Kohen.

Pirkei DeRabbi Eliezer   1

Rabban Yohanan ben Zakkai sent to inquire of his hosts, saying to them: Did Eliezer eat with you this day? They answered: No; moreover, has he not fasted eight days without tasting any food? Rabbi Yehoshua ben Hananiah and Rabbi Yosef the Ha-Kohen went and said to Rabban Yohanan ben Zakkai ben ḳakkai: Verily during the last eight days Eliezer has not partaken of any food.

Chapter 2

The sons of Hyrkanos said to their father: Get thee up to Jerusalem and vow that thy son Eliezer should not enjoy any of thy possessions. He went up to Jerusalem to disinherit him, and it happened that a festival was being celebrated there by Rabban Yohanan ben Zakkai. All the magnates of the district were dining with him; such as Rabban Yohanan Ben Zizith Hakkeseth, Nicodemus ben Gorion, and Ben Kalba S'bu'a.

Why was his name called Ben Zizith Hakkeseth? Because he reclined at table in a higher position than the other magnates of Jerusalem. Concerning Nicodemus ben Gorion, people said that he had [stored] provisions containing 3 S'ah of fine flour for every inhabitant of Jerusalem. When the zealots arose and burnt all the storehouses, they measured and found that he had had provisions for three years for every inhabitant in Jerusalem. Concerning Ben Kalba S'bua it was told that he had a house measuring 4 Kors with roofs covered with gold. The people said to Rabban Yohanan ben Zakkai: Behold, the father of Rabbi Eliezer has arrived. He bade them saying: Prepare a place for him, and seat him next to us. Rabban Yohanan ben Zakkai fixed his gaze on Rabbi Eliezer, saying to him, Tell us some words of the Torah. Rabbi Eliezer answered him saying: Rabbi! I will tell thee a parable. To what is the matter like? To this well which cannot yield more water than the amount which it has drawn

Pirkei DeRabbi Eliezer 2

[from the earth]; likewise, am I unable to speak words of the Torah in excess of what I have received from thee.

Rabban Yohanan ben Zakkai said to him, I will also tell thee a parable. To what is the matter like? To this fountain which is bubbling and sending forth its water, and it is able to effect a discharge more powerful than what it secretes; in like manner art thou able to speak words of the Torah in excess of what Moses received at Sinai. Rabban Yohanan ben Zakkai continued: Lest thou shouldst feel ashamed on my account, behold I will arise and go away from thee. Rabban Yohanan ben Zakkai arose and went outside. Thereupon Rabbi Eliezer sat down and expounded. His face shone like the light of the sun and his effulgence beamed forth like that of Moses, so that no one knew whether it was day or night. They went and said to Rabban Yohanan ben Zakkai: Come and see Rabbi Eliezer sitting and expounding, his face shining like the light of the sun and his effulgence beaming like that of Moses, so that no one knows whether it be day or night. He came from his place behind him and kissed him on his head, saying to him: Happy are ye, Abraham, Isaac, and Jacob, because this one has come forth from your loins.

Hyrḳanos his father said: To whom does Rabban Yohanan ben Zakkai speak thus? The people answered: To Eliezer thy son. He said to them: Rabban Yohanan ben Zakkai should not have spoken in that manner, but in this wise, "Happy am

I because he has come forth from my loins." Whilst Rabbi Eliezer was sitting and expounding, his father was standing upon his feet. When Eliezer saw his father standing upon his feet, he became agitated and said to him: My father! be seated, for I cannot utter the words of the Torah when thou art standing on thy feet. Hyrḳanos replied to him: My son, it was not for this reason that I came, but my intention was to disinherit thee. Now that I have come and I have witnessed all this praise; behold thy brothers are disinherited and their portion is given to thee as a gift.

Eliezer replied: Verily I am not equal to one of them. If I had asked the Holy One, blessed be He, for land, it would be possible for Him to give this to me, as it is said, "The earth is the Lord's, and the fulness thereof" [Psalms 24:1]. Had I asked the Holy One, blessed be He, for silver and gold, He could have given them to me, as it is said, "The silver is mine, and the gold is mine" [Haggai 2:8]. But I asked the Holy One, blessed be He, that I might be worthy to learn the Torah only, as it is said, "Therefore I esteem all precepts concerning all things to be right; and I hate every false way" [Psalms 119:128].

Chapter 3

Rabbi Eliezer Ben Hyrkanos opened his discourse with the text, "Who can utter the mighty acts of the Lord, or shew forth all his praise?" [Psalms 106:2]. Is there any man who can utter the mighty acts of the Holy One, blessed be He, or who can shew forth all His praise? Not even the ministering angels are able to narrate, the Divine praise. But to investigate a part of His mighty deeds with reference to what He has done, and what He will do in the future is permissible, so that His name should be exalted among His creatures, whom He has created, from one end of the world to the other, as it is said, "One generation to another shall laud thy works" [Psalms 145:4].

Before the world was created, the Holy One, blessed be He, with His Name alone existed, and the thought arose in Him to create the world. He began to trace, the foundations of the world before Himself, but it would not stand. They told a parable. To what is the matter like? To a king who wishes to build a palace for himself. If he had not traced in the earth its foundations, its exits and its entrances, he does not begin to build. Likewise, the Holy One, blessed be He, was tracing the plans of the world before Himself, but it did not remain standing until He created repentance.

Seven things were created before the world was created. They are: The Torah, Gehinnom, the

Pirkei DeRabbi Eliezer 3

Garden of Eden, the Throne of Glory, the Temple, Repentance, and the Name of the Messiah.

Whence do we know that this applies to the Torah? Because it is said, "The Lord possessed me in the beginning of his way, before his works of old " [Proverbs 8:22]. "Of old" means before the world was created. Whence do we know this with regard to the Garden of Eden? Because it is said, "And the Lord God planted a garden of old" [Genesis 2:8]. "Of old," whilst as yet the world had not been created. Whence do we know this with reference to the Throne of Glory? Because it is said, "Thy throne is established of old" [Psalms 93:2]. "Of old," whilst as yet the world had not been created. Whence do we know that Repentance was premundane? Because it is said, "Before the mountains were brought forth, or ever thou hadst formed the earth and the world" [Psalms 90:2]; and then in close proximity we read, "Thou turnest man to contrition" [Psalms 90:3]. "Before," [i.e. before the world was created]. Whence do we know this with regard to the Temple? Because it is said, "A glorious throne, set on high from the beginning, is the place of our sanctuary" [Jeremiah 17:12]. "From the beginning," whilst as yet the world had not been created. Whence we do know that the name of the Messiah was premundane? Because it is said, "His name shall endure for ever; before the sun Yinnon was his name" [Psalms 72:17]. "Yinnon," before the world had been created. Another verse says, "But thou, Bethlehem Ephrathah, which art to be least among the thousands of Judah, from thee shall he come forth

Pirkei DeRabbi Eliezer 3

unto me who is to be ruler over Israel; whose ancestry belongs to the past, even to the days of old" [Micah 5:1]. "The past," whilst as yet the world had not been created.

Forthwith the Holy One, blessed be He, took counsel with the Torah whose name is Tushijah [Stability or Wisdom] with reference to the creation of the world. The Torah replied and said to Him: Sovereign of the worlds! if there be no host for the king and if there be no camp for the king, over whom does he rule? If there be no people to praise the king, where is the honour of the king? The Holy One, blessed be He, heard this and it pleased Him. The Torah spake: The Holy One, blessed be He, took counsel with me concerning the creation of the world, as it is said, "Counsel is mine, and sound knowledge; I am understanding; I have might" [Proverbs 8:14]. Hence, they say, every government which has no counsellors is not a proper government. Whence do we know this? From the government of the House of David which employed counsellors, as it is said, "And Jonathan David's uncle was a counsellor, a man of understanding, and a scribe" [Chronicles-A 27:32]. If the government of the House of David had counsellors, how much more so should other people act likewise. This is of benefit to them, as it is said, "But he that hearkeneth unto counsel is wise" [Proverbs 12:15], and Scripture says, "But in the multitude of counsellors there is safety" [Proverbs 11:14].

Eight things were created on the first day, namely,

Pirkei DeRabbi Eliezer 3

Heaven, Earth, Light, Darkness, Tohu [Chaos], Bohu [Void], Wind [or Spirit], and Water, as it is said, "And the wind of God was moving upon the face of the waters" [Genesis 1:2].

Whence were the heavens created? From the light of the garment with which He was robed. He took of this light, and stretched it like a garment and the heavens, began to extend continually until He caused them to hear, "It is sufficient." Therefore, is He called God Almighty [El Shaddai], who said to the world: "It is sufficient," and it stood firm. Whence do we know that the heavens were created from the light of His garment? Because it is said, "Who coverest thyself with light as with a garment; who stretchest out the heavens like a curtain" [Psalms 104:2].

Whence was the earth created? He took of the snow [or ice] which was beneath His Throne of Glory and threw it upon the waters, and the waters became congealed so that the dust of the earth was formed, as it is said, "He saith to the snow, Be thou earth" [Job 37:6].

The hooks of the heavens are fixed in the waters of the ocean. The waters of the ocean are situated between the ends of the heavens and the ends of the earth. The ends of the heavens are spread out over the waters of the ocean, as it is said, "Who layeth the beams of his chambers in the waters" [Psalms 104:3].

The dome [or inside shape] of the heavens ascends

Pirkei DeRabbi Eliezer 3

upwards like a tub, that is to say like a tent [denda] which is spread out with its extremities fixed downwards and its dome stretching upwards so that people can sit beneath it and their feet stand on the earth, whilst all of them are inside the tent; in like wise are the heavens, their extremities are fixed downwards and their dome stretches upwards and all creatures dwell beneath them as in a tent, as it is said, "And he spreadeth them out as a tent to dwell in" [Isaiah 40:22].

Four quarters have been created in the world; the quarter facing the east, that facing the south, that facing the west and that facing the north. From the quarter facing the east the light goeth forth to the world. From the quarter facing south the dews of blessing and the rains of blessing go forth to the world. From the quarter facing west where are the treasuries of snow and the treasuries of hail, and thence come forth into the world cold and heat and rains. From the quarter facing north darkness goeth forth into the world. The quarter facing north He created, but He did not complete it, for He said, anyone who says: I am a God, let him come and complete this quarter which I have left incomplete and all will know that he is a God.

There in the north, is the abode of the destroying spirits, earthquakes, winds, demons, lightnings and thunders; thence evil issues forth into the world, as it is said, "Out of the north evil shall break forth upon all the inhabitants of the earth" [Jeremiah 1:14]. Some say by ten Sayings was the world created and

Pirkei DeRabbi Eliezer 3

in three [Divine attributes] are these [ten Sayings] comprised, as it is said, "The Lord by wisdom founded the earth:

God said, "Let there be light". [Genesis 1:3].

God said, "Let there be an expanse in the midst of the water" [Genesis 1:6].

God said, "Let the water below the sky" [Genesis 1:9].

And God said, "Let the earth sprout vegetation". [Genesis 1:11].

God said, "Let there be lights". [Genesis 1:14]

God said, "Let the waters bring forth swarms of living creatures" [Genesis 1:20].

God said, "Let the earth bring forth" [Genesis 1:24].

And God said, "Let us make man" [Genesis 1:26].

God said, "See, I give you every" [Genesis 1:29].

The LORD God said, "It is not good for man to be alone; I will make a fitting helper for him" [Genesis 2:18].

By understanding he established the heavens, by his knowledge the depths were broken up" [Proverbs 3:19-20]. By these three [attributes] was the Tabernacle made, as it is said, "And I have filled him with the spirit of God, with wisdom, with understanding, and with knowledge" [Exodus 31:3].

Pirkei DeRabbi Eliezer 3

Likewise with these three [attributes] was the Temple made, as it is said, "He was the son of a widow woman of the tribe of Naphtali, and his father was a man of Tyre, a worker in brass; and he was filled with wisdom and understanding and knowledge" [Kings-A 7:14]. By these three attributes it will be rebuilt in the future, as it is said, "Through wisdom is a house builded; and by understanding it is established; and by knowledge are the chambers filled" [Proverbs 24:3, 4].

With these three attributes will the Holy One, blessed be He, give three good gifts to Israel in the future, as it is said, "For the Lord will give wisdom, out of his mouth cometh knowledge and understanding" [Proverbs 2:6]. It is not said, "The Lord has given wisdom." These three attributes will be given to King Messiah, as it is said, "And the spirit of the Lord shall rest upon him, the spirit of wisdom and understanding, the spirit of counsel and might, the spirit of knowledge and of the fear of the Lord" [Isaiah 11:2].

Chapter 4

The second day the Holy One, blessed be He, created the firmament, the angels, fire for flesh and blood, and the fire of Gehinnom. Were not heaven and earth created on the first day, as it is said, "In the beginning God created the heaven and the earth" [Genesis 1:1], Which firmament was created on the second day? Rabbi Eliezer said: It was the firmament which is above the heads of the four Chajjoth [living creatures], as it is said, "And over the head of the Chajjoth there was the likeness of a firmament, like the colour of the terrible crystal" [Ezekiel 1:22]. What is the meaning of [the expression], "like the colour of the terrible crystal"? It means like precious stones and pearls; it illuminates all the heavens like a lamp which is illuminating the whole house and like the sun which is shining with maximum intensity at noonday, as it is said, "The light dwelleth with him" [Daniel 2:22]; and like this in the future will the righteous shed light, as it is said, "And they that be wise shall shine as the brightness of the firmament" [Daniel 12:3]. Were it not for that firmament the world would be engulfed by the waters above it and below it; but the firmament divides the waters above from the waters below, as it is said, "And God said, Let there be a firmament in the midst of the waters, and let it divide the waters from the waters" [Genesis 1:6], it illuminates between the waters above and the waters below.

As for the angels created on the second day, when

Pirkei DeRabbi Eliezer 4

they are sent as messengers by His word they are changed into winds, and when they minister before Him they are changed into fire, as it is said, "Who maketh his angels winds; his ministers a flaming fire" [Psalms 104:4].

Four classes of ministering angels minister and utter praise before the Holy One, blessed be He: The first camp led by Michael on His right. The second camp led by Gabriel on His left. The third camp led by Uriel before Him. And the fourth camp led by Raphael behind Him; and the Shekhinah [The divine revelation in the world] of the Holy One, blessed be He, is in the centre. He is sitting on a throne high and exalted. His throne is high and suspended above in the air. The appearance of His Glory is like the colour of amber. And the adornment of a crown is on His head, and the Ineffable Name is upon His forehead. One half of His glory is fire the other half is hail, at His right hand is life and at His left is death. He has a sceptre of fire in His hand and a veil is spread before Him, and His eyes run to and fro throughout the whole earth, and the seven angels, which were created first, minister before Him within the veil, and this veil is called Pargod. His footstool is like fire and hail. Fire is flashing continually around His throne, righteousness and judgment are the foundation of His throne. And the likeness of His throne is like a sapphire throne with four legs, and the four holy Chajjoth are fixed to each leg, each one has four faces and each one has four wings, as it is said, "And every one had four faces and four wings" [Ezekiel 1:6], and these Chajjoth are the Cherubim

Pirkei DeRabbi Eliezer 4

[type of angels].

And when he speaks towards the East, He speaks between the two cherubim the face of **Man**. And when he speaks towards the south, He speaks between the two cherubim the face of a **Lion**. And when he speaks towards the West, He speaks between the two cherubim the face of an **Ox**. And when he speaks towards the north, he speaks between the two cherubim the face of an **Eagle**.

Over against them are the Ophanim [Wheels] and the Whirling Wheels of the Chariot, and when He looketh upon the earth His chariots are upon the Ophanim, and owing to the noise caused by the whirling wheels of the Chariot - lightnings and thunder go forth into the world. When He dwells in heaven, He rideth upon a swift cloud. When He hastens, He flies upon the wings of the wind, as it is said, "And he rode upon a cherub, and did fly; yea, he flew swiftly upon the wings of the wind" [Psalms 18:10].

The Chajjoth stand next to the throne of His glory and they do not know the place of His glory. The Chajjoth stand in awe and dread, in fear and trembling, and from the perspiration of their faces a river of fire arises and goes forth before Him, as it is said, "A fiery stream issued and came forth from before him…"[Daniel 7:10]. And the wings of Gallizur the angel, who stands next to the Chajjoth, are spread forth, so that the fire which consumes the fire of the angels should not burn them. Two Seraphim

Pirkei DeRabbi Eliezer 4

stand, one on His right and one on His left, each one has six wings, with twain they cover their face so as not to behold the presence of the Shekhinah, with twain they cover their feet so that they should not be seen before the presence of the Shekhinah, so that the standing of the foot of the calf might be forgotten. With twain do they fly, praising and reverencing, and they sanctify. One answers and another calls, one calls and another answers, and they say, "Holy, Holy, Holy, is the Lord of Hosts; the whole earth is full of his glory" [Isaiah 6:3].

The Chajjoth stand at the side of the throne of His glory and they do not know the place of His glory; they respond and say in every place where His glory is, "Blessed be the glory of the Lord from his place" [Ezekiel 3:12]. Israel, a nation unique on the earth, declares daily the unity of His great Name, saying, "Hear, O Israel: The Lord is our God, the Lord is one" [Deuteronomy 6:4]. He answers His people Israel and says to them, I am the Lord your God who has delivered you from every trouble.

Chapter 5

The third day all the earth was flat like a plain and the waters covered the surface of all the earth. When the word of the Almighty was uttered, "Let the waters be gathered together" [Genesis 1:9], the mountains and hills arose from the ends of the earth and they were scattered over the surface of all the earth, and valleys were formed over the inner parts of the earth; and the waters were rolled together and gathered into the valleys, as it is said, "And the gathering together of the waters he called seas" [Genesis 1:10]. Forthwith the waters became proud and they arose to cover the earth as at first, when the Holy One, blessed be He, rebuked them and subdued them, and placed them beneath the soles of His feet, and measured them with the hollow of His hand that they should neither decrease nor increase. He made the sand as the boundary of the sea, just like a man who makes a fence for his vineyard. When they rise and see the sand before them, they return to their former place, as it is said, "Fear ye not me? saith the Lord: will ye not tremble at my presence, which have placed the sand for the bound of the sea?" [Jeremiah 5:22].

Before the waters were gathered together the depths were created. These are the depths which are beneath the earth; for the earth is spread upon the water like a ship which floats in the midst of the sea, so likewise is the earth spread out over the water, as it is said, "To him that spread forth the earth above

Pirkei DeRabbi Eliezer 5

the waters..." [Psalms 136:6]. He opened an entrance to the Garden of Eden because thence were planted upon the face of all the earth all kinds of trees yielding fruit according to their kind, and all kinds of herbs and grass thereof, and in them [was seed], as it is said, "Wherein is the seed thereof, upon the earth" [Genesis 1:11]. He prepared a table for the creatures whilst as yet they were not created, as it is said, "Thou preparest a table before me" [Psalms 23:5]. All the fountains arise from the depths to give water to all creatures.

Rabbi Yehoshua said: The diameter of the earth is equal to a journey of sixty years, and one of the depths which is near to Gehinnom bubbles with water and produces water for the delight of the sons of man.

Rabbi Yehuda said: Once every month ducts rise from the depths to irrigate the face of all the earth, as it is said, "And there went up a mist from the earth and watered the whole face of the ground" [Genesis 2:6]. The clouds cause the seas to hear the sound of their waterspouts, and the seas cause the depths to hear the sound of their waterspouts, and the deep calls to the deep to bring up waters to give them to the clouds, as it is said, "Deep calleth unto deep at the sound of thy waterspouts" [Psalms 42:7].

The clouds draw water from the depths, as it is said, "He causeth the vapours to ascend from the ends of the earth" [Psalms 135:7], and in every place where the King commands them, there they cause rain to fall,

Pirkei DeRabbi Eliezer 5

and forthwith the earth becomes fruitful and yields produce like a widow who becomes pregnant through debauchery. But when the Holy One, blessed be He, desires to bless the produce of the earth, and to give provision to the creatures, He opens the good treasuries in heaven and sends rain upon the earth, namely, the fructifying rain, and forthwith the earth becomes fruitful like a bride who conceives from her first husband and produces offspring of blessing, as it is said, "The Lord shall open unto thee his good treasury the heaven" [Deuteronomy 28:12].

Chapter 6

The fourth day He connected together the two luminaries, of which one was not greater in size than the other. They were equal as regards their height, qualities, and illuminating powers, as it is said, "And God made the two great lights" [Genesis 1:16]. Rivalry ensued between them, one said to the other, I am bigger than thou art. The other rejoined, I am bigger than thou art.

What did the Holy One, blessed be He, do, so that there should be peace between them? He made the one larger and the other smaller, as it is said, "The greater light to rule the day, and the lesser light to rule the night and the stars he also made" [Genesis 1:16]

All the stars minister to the seven planets, and their names are: Sun, Venus, Mercury, the Moon, Saturn, Jupiter, Mars. The mnemonic of their service is KZNSh ChLM, by night; ChLM KZNSh by day and KLSh ZMChN for the hours of the night; ChNKL ShZM for the hours of the day.
On the first day Mercury and the Sun.
On the second day Jupiter and the Moon.
On the third day Venus and Mars.
On the fourth day Saturn and Mercury.
On the fifth day the Sun and Jupiter.
On the sixth day the Moon and Venus.
On the seventh day Mars and Saturn.

All of them minister to the twelve constellations

Pirkei DeRabbi Eliezer 6

which correspond to the twelve months. The constellations are: Aries, Taurus, Gemini, Cancer, Leo, Virgo, Libra, Scorpio, Sagittarius, Capricornus, Aquarius, and Pisces. All the constellations minister to the days of the sun. Now the days of the solar month are 30 days, 10 hours and a half, and each constellation ministers to the days of the solar month for two days and a half, so that two constellations minister for five days. The chief which begins at the beginning of the solar month is the same chief which completes at the end of the solar month; the one which opens is the one which closes.

The great cycle of the sun is 28 years, and therein are seven small cycles each of four years. The number of days of the solar year is 365 and a quarter of a day. The seasons of the solar year are four, each season consisting of 91 days 7½ hours. The beginnings of the cycles of the seasons are the 4th, 2nd, 7th, 5th, 3rd, 1st, and 6th days. Between each cycle there are 5 days and 6 hours.

The Teḳuphoth [seasons] of the small cycle are four in each year, some of them last 91 days 7½ hours and some last 92 days. The first year of the cycle of four years has its Teḳuphah in Nisan at 6 p.m.; in the second year at 12 p.m.; in the third year at 6 a.m.; in the fourth year at 12 a.m.

The four beginnings of the Teḳuphah of the four months of Nisan commence at the beginning of the night, at midnight, at the beginning of the day, and

Pirkei DeRabbi Eliezer 6

at noon respectively. The rest of the other days of the Teḵuphoth are as follows: ZCh; GYCh; VACh; TDCh.

The first Teḵuphah of Nisan took place at the beginning of the hours of Saturn. The Teḵuphah of Tammuz took place at the middle of the hours of Saturn. The Teḵuphah of Tishri occurred at the beginning of the hours of Jupiter. The Teḵuphah of Ṭebeth took place at the middle of the hours of Jupiter. And thus, with all the other Teḵuphoth, which occur at the beginning of the hours or at the middle of the hours.

The first cycle took place at the beginning of the hour of Saturn, and the names of the Planets of the hours are Saturn, Jupiter, Mars, the Sun, Venus, Mercury, and the Moon. The second cycle occurred in the hour of the Planet which is in front of it, at the beginning of the hour of Jupiter. The third cycle occurred at the beginning of the hour of Mars. The fourth cycle entered at the beginning of the hour of the Sun. The fifth cycle entered at the beginning of the hour of Venus. The sixth cycle entered at the beginning of the hour of Mercury. The seventh cycle entered at the beginning of the hour of the Moon. [At] the end of seven hours, at the end of seven cycles, at the end of 35 days of the great cycle of 28 years, the Teḵuphah cycle returns [i.e. begins again] at the beginning of the fourth day in the hour of Saturn in the hour when it was created.

In 366 degrees the sun rises and declines, it rises 183

Pirkei DeRabbi Eliezer 6

degrees in the east, and it declines 183 degrees in the west corresponding to the 365 days of the solar year. The sun goes forth through 366 apertures and enters by the east; 90 days it is in the south east quarter, 91 days in the north east quarter and one aperture is in the middle and its name is Nogah.

At the Teḵuphah of Tishri the sun begins from the aperture of Nogah and goes through its revolutions towards the south quarter, through one aperture after another until it reaches the aperture of Bilgah. At the Teḵuphah of Ṭebeth [the sun] begins from the aperture of Bilgah and continues its course, returning backward through one aperture after another until it reaches the aperture of Ta'alumah, through which the light goes forth, as it is said." And the thing that is hid bringeth he forth to light" [Job 28:11]. At the Teḵuphah of Nisan the sun begins from the aperture of Ta'alumah, and it goes to the north quarter through one aperture after another until it reaches the aperture No'aman. At the Teḵuphah of Ṭammuz the sun begins from the aperture No'aman and goes on its course, returning backwards through aperture after aperture until it reaches the aperture Cheder whence the whirlwind goes forth, as it is said, "Out of the chamber cometh the storm and cold out of the scattering winds" [Job 37:9].

Through these apertures which are in the east the sun goes forth and opposite to them in the west the sun sets. The Shekhinah is always in the west. The sun sets and worships before the King of Kings, the Holy One, blessed be He, saying: Lord of all worlds!

Pirkei DeRabbi Eliezer 6

I have done according to all that Thou hast commanded me.

The aperture which is in the midst of the firmament is named M'zarim and the sun does not go forth or set therein except once in its great cycle; thereon it goes through it as on the day when it was created. At night the sun is in the west. At the Teḳuphah of Tishri and at the Teḳuphah of Ṭebeth the sun goes on its course in the south quarter and in the waters of the Ocean which are between the ends of the heavens and the ends of the earth where it is submerged. For the night is long and the way is long until the sun reaches the aperture which is in the east, even the aperture through which it desires to go forth, as it is said, "It goeth toward the south, and turneth about unto the north" [Ecclesiastes 1:6]. It goes to the south at the Teḳuphah of Tishri and at the Teḳuphah of Ṭebeth, and turns to the north at the Teḳuphah of Nisan and at the Teḳuphah of Tammuz. It goes on its course for six months in the south quarter, and for six months in the north quarter, and owing to its circuits the sun returns to the aperture which is in the east. The sun has three letters of God's Name written upon his heart, and the angels lead him; such as lead him by day do not lead him by night, and such as lead him by night do not lead him by day. The sun rides in a chariot and rises, crowned as a bridegroom, as it is said, "Which is as a bridegroom coming out of his chamber, and rejoiceth as a strong man to run his course" [Psalms 19:5]. The sun's rays and face, which are turned downwards to the earth, are of hail; and were it not

Pirkei DeRabbi Eliezer 6

for the hail which quenches the flames of fire the world would be consumed by fire, as it is said, "And there is nothing hid from the heat thereof" [Psalms 19:6]. In winter [the sun] turns the upper half of his face downwards, and were it not for the fire which warms the face of hail the world could not endure because of the ice cold, as it is said, "Who can stand before his cold?" [Psalms 147:17]. These are the ends of the ways of the sun.

Chapter 7

Rabban Yohanan ben Zakkai, Rabban Gamaliel, Rabbi Ishmael, Rabbi Elazar ben Arakh, Rabbi Eliezer ben Hyrḳanos, and Rabbi Aḳiba were expounding the laws of the **Molad** [The precise moment of the appearance of the new moon] of the moon. They said: The Holy One, blessed be He, spake one word and the heavens were created as the residence of the Throne of His Glory, as it is said, "By the word of the Lord were the heavens made" [Psalms 33:6]. But in connection with the creation of the host of heaven He laboured with great labour. Rabbi What did the Holy One, blessed be He, do? He blew with His mouth the wind of the breath of life and all the host of heaven were created, as it is said, "And all the host of them by the breath of his mouth" [Psalms 33:6].

All the stars and constellations were created at the beginning of the night of the fourth day, one luminary did not precede the other except by the period of two-thirds of an hour. Therefore, every motion of the sun is done with deliberation, and every motion of the moon is done quickly. The distance covered by the sun in thirteen days and a fifth is covered by the moon in one day, and the distance covered by the sun all the days of the year, the moon traverses the same distance in forty-one days. All the days serve for the beginning of the Molad of the new moon; for the following series the days are reckoned backward; at the beginning of the

Pirkei DeRabbi Eliezer 7

night of the fourth day the beginning of the Molad new moon was in the hour of Saturn; and the mnemonic is **ShNZ KMLChSh**. After three years of the small cycle the day of the next cycle reverts to the beginning of the night of the third day, and the beginning of the **Molad** [new moon] is in the hour of Venus. After three years of the small cycle the day of the next cycle reverts to the beginning of the night of the second day, the beginning of the Molad is in the hour of Jupiter. After three years of the small cycle the day of the next cycle reverts to the beginning of the night of the first day, the beginning of the Molad is in the hour of Mercury. After three years of the small cycle the day of the next cycle reverts to the beginning of the night of the Sabbath, the beginning of the Molad is in the hour of Mars. After three years of the small cycle the day of the next cycle reverts to the beginning of the night of the sixth day, the beginning of the Molad is in the hour of the Moon. After three years of the small cycle the day of the next cycle reverts to the beginning of the night of the fifth day, the beginning of the Molad is in the hour of the Sun. After three years of the small cycle the day of the next cycle reverts to the beginning of the night of the fourth day, the beginning of the Molad reverts to the hour of Saturn as in the hour when it was created.

The great cycle of the moon is 21 years; it has 7 small cycles each containing 3 years. The total of the days of the lunar month is 29½ days, 40 minutes, and 73 parts. Each constellation serves the days of the lunar month for 2 days and 8 hours; three

Pirkei DeRabbi Eliezer 7

constellations serve for 7 days. The chief which begins on the new moon [of the lunar month] is the same which concludes at the end of the lunar month. The moon becomes new at every Molad, once at night and the next time by day, and this is their sign: "And it was evening and it was morning" [Genesis 1:5]. Between one Molad and the corresponding Molad in the ensuing year there elapse 4 days, 8 hours, and 876 parts.

From one small cycle to the next cycle - elapse 13 days. When the sun goes in the south quarter, the moon goes in the north quarter, and when the sun goes in the north quarter the moon goes in the south quarter. All the hours serve for the beginning of the Molad of the moon in a retrospective order, according to the order "ShLKNChM and Z." In the first year at the beginning of the night of the fourth day the beginning of the **Molad** [conjunction of the moon] is in the hour of Saturn. In the second year the beginning of the conjunction of the moon is in the hour of the Moon. In the third year, in the following hour, the beginning of the conjunction of the moon is in the hour of Mercury. In the fourth year the beginning of the conjunction of the moon is in the hour of Venus. In the fifth year, in the hour following, the beginning of the conjunction of the moon is in the hour of the Sun. In the sixth year the beginning of the conjunction of the moon is in the hour of Mars. In the seventh year, in the hour following, the beginning of the conjunction of the moon is in the hour of Jupiter in the hour following. The third and fifth years are like the seventh. In like

Pirkei DeRabbi Eliezer 7

manner for three times these hours serve at the conjunction of the moon retrospectively until the expiration of the 21 years of the cycle.

All the constellations serve the moon by night from the four corners of the world: Three in the north, three in the south, three in the east, and three in the west. All the hours serve the moon by night from the four corners of the world: Two in the south, two in the north, two in the east, and two in the west. In the hour in which it began to serve in the south, therein it finishes in the west; and so, with all its circuits.

All the great luminaries of the stars are situated in the south except Ursa Major, which is placed in the north. All the **Mazzikin** [spiritual negative strength] which move in the firmament and the angels who fell from their holy place even from heaven, when they ascend to hear the Divine Word behind the veil they are pursued with a rod of fire, and they return to their place.

10 days, 21 hours, and 204 parts are the excess of the days of the solar year over the days of the lunar year; and the intercalation is introduced to equalize the days of the solar year with the days of the lunar year. The sun and the moon begin their courses at the new moon of Nisan, the sun goes before the moon at its **Tekuphah** [period]; and Aries begins to serve before it by day, and all the constellations serve thereafter according to their order. The moon goes in the opposite direction and Aries begins to serve before it by night, and all the constellations

Pirkei DeRabbi Eliezer 7

serve thereafter according to their order, until the year of the small cycle, until the year of intercalation comes round. When the intercalated month comes round it supersedes or thrusts aside the new moon [of Nisan] and remains at the new moon of Shebat, and so on until the twelve intercalated months come round when the sun and the moon are equal again at the commencement of the eve of the fourth day in the hour of Saturn in the hour when they were created. Between each Molad conjunction of the moon and sun there are only 86 hours, 40 minutes, and 73 minims [parts].

The moon does not disappear from the firmament save for the twinkling of an eye; even though there were a full thread of light surrounding it in the east and in the west, the eye has not the power to see the moon until eight large hours have elapsed. The large hours are two hours for each large hour, either at the beginning of the Molad [conjunction] of the moon or at the end of the Molad of the moon.

The number of the days of the lunar year is 354 days, a third of a day, and 876 minims. All the hours of a lunar month are 708 hours and 40 minutes; all the hours of a lunar year are 8504 hours.

All the constellations serve the Molad of the moon and also the generations of the children of men; upon them the world stands, and everyone who is wise and understands, he understands the Molad of the moon and the generations of the children of men, and concerning them the text says, "And let them be for signs, and for seasons" [Genesis 1:14]. The signs of the hours shall not depart from serving the sun by day and the moon by night.

In three cycles of the sun or in four cycles of the moon there are 84 years, which are one hour of the day of the Holy One, blessed be He. When the sun and moon become equal at the beginning of the eve of the fourth day and at the hour of Saturn in the hour when they were created, and in the hour when the flames of the moon reach the sun by day at the degree or ascent of 60 degrees, it passes therein and extinguishes its light; and in the hour when the flames of the sun reach the moon at night in the degree or ascent of 40 degrees, it passes through it and extinguishes its light.

Rabbi Nehorai said: It is the decree of the King that when Israel sins and fails to intercalate the year as is becoming, the Holy One, blessed be He, acts in His mercy at the time when the flame of the sun reaches the moon by night at 40 degrees or ascents, then the Holy One, blessed be He, makes the moon dim and hides one of the Synhedrion. When Israel does the will of the Holy One, blessed be He, in His great mercy He makes the sun dim and He sends forth His anger upon the nations of the world, as it is said, "Thus saith the Lord, Learn not the way of the nations, and be not dismayed at the signs of heaven, for the nations are dismayed at them" [Jeremiah 10:2]. Just as the moon's light does not rule over the sun's light by day, nor does the sun's light rule over the moon's light by night, likewise the calculation of the

Pirkei DeRabbi Eliezer 7

moon does not rule by day nor does the calculation of the sun obtain by night, and the one does not trespass on the boundary of the other.

The dwelling of the moon is between cloud and thick darkness made like two dishes turned one over the other, and when it is the conjunction of the moon these two clouds turn in the east quarter and the moon goes forth from between them like a ram's horn. On the first night is revealed one measure of light, on the second night the second measure, and so on until the half of the month when the moon is fully revealed, and from the middle of the month these two clouds turn their faces in the west quarter. The corner [i.e. crescent] of the moon with which it comes forth first, the same-begins to enter and is covered therein by the two clouds on the first night by one measure, on the second night by a second measure, and so on to the end of the month until it is entirely covered. And whence do we know that it is placed between two clouds? Because it is said, "When I made the cloud the garment thereof, and thick darkness a swaddling band for it" [Job 38:9]. And whence do we know that it becomes entirely covered? Because it is said, "Blow ye the trumpet in the new moon, at the covering, on our solemn feast day" [Psalms 81:8]. "At the covering," on the day when it is entirely covered, blow ye the trumpet in the new moon.

Chapter 8

On the 28th of Ellul the sun and the moon were created. The number of years, months, days, nights, terms, seasons, cycles, and intercalation were before the Holy One, blessed be He, and He intercalated the years and afterwards He delivered the calculations to the first man in the garden of Eden, as it is said, "This is the calculation for the generations of Adam" [Genesis 5:1], the calculation of the world is therein for the generations of the children of Adam.

Adam handed on the tradition to Enoch, who was initiated in the principle of intercalation, and he intercalated the year, as it is said, "And Enoch walked with God" [Genesis 5:22]. Enoch walked in the ways of the calculation concerning the world which God had delivered to Adam. And Enoch delivered the principle of intercalation to Noah, and he was initiated in the principle of intercalation, and he intercalated the year, as it is said, "While the earth remaineth, seed-time and harvest, and cold and heat, and summer and winter" [Genesis 8:22]. "Seed-time" refers to the Tekuphah of Tishri, "harvest" refers to the Tekuphah of Nisan, "cold" refers to the Tekuphah of Tebeth, and "heat" refers to the Tekuphah of Tammuz; "summer" is in its season and "winter" is in its season.

The counting of the sun is by day and the counting of the moon is by night, "they shall not cease." [Genesis 8:22].

Pirkei DeRabbi Eliezer 8

Noah handed on the tradition to Shem, and he was initiated in the principle of intercalation; he intercalated the years and he was called a Ha-Kohen, as it is said, "And Melchizedek king of Salem [Jerusalem]… was a Ha-Kohen of God Most High" [Genesis 14:18]. Was Shem the son of Noah a Ha-Kohen? But because he was the first-born, and because he ministered to his God by day and by night, therefore was he called a Ha-Kohen. Shem delivered the tradition to Avraham; he was initiated in the principle of intercalation and he intercalated the year, and he also was called Ha-Kohen, as it is said, "The Hashem hath sworn, and will not repent, Thou art a Ha-Kohen for ever after the order of Melchizedek" [Psalms 110:4]. Whence do we know that Shem delivered the tradition to Avraham? Because it is said, "After the order of Melchizedek" [ibid]. Avraham delivered the tradition to Yitzhak, and he was initiated in the principle of intercalation, and he intercalated the year after the death of our father Avraham, as it is said, "And it came to pass after the death of Avraham, that God blessed Yitzhak his son" [Genesis 25:11], because he had been initiated in the principle of intercalation and had intercalated the year [therefore] He blessed him with the blessing of eternity. Yitzhak gave to Yaakov all the blessings and delivered to him the principle of intercalation. When Yaakov went out of the [Holy] Land, he attempted to intercalate the year outside the [Holy] Land. The Holy One, blessed be He, said to him: Yaakov! Thou hast no authority to intercalate the year outside the land [of Israel]; behold, Yitzhak thy father is in the [Holy] Land, he will intercalate

Pirkei DeRabbi Eliezer 8

the year, as it is said, "And God appeared unto Yaakov again, when he came from Paddan-Aram, and blessed him" [Genesis 35:9]. Why "again"? Because the first time He was revealed to him, He prevented him from intercalating the year outside the [Holy] Land; but when he came to the [Holy] Land the Holy One, blessed be He, said to him: Yaakov! Arise, intercalate the year, as it is said, "And God appeared unto Yaakov again… and blessed him" [Genesis 35:9], because he was initiated in the principle of the intercalation, and He blessed him [with] the blessing of the world. Thus were the Israelites wont to intercalate the year in the Holy Land. When they were exiled to Babylon they intercalated the year through those who were left in the Holy Land. When they were all exiled and there were not any [Jews] left in the Holy Land, they intercalated the year in Babylon. When Ezra and all the community with him went to the Holy Land, Ezekiel wished to intercalate the year in Babylon; then the Holy One, blessed be He, said to him: Ezekiel, thou hast no authority to intercalate the year outside the Land; behold, Israel thy brethren, they will intercalate the year, as it is said, "Son of man, when the house of Israel dwell in their own land" [Ezekiel 36:17]. Hence the Sages have said, Even when the righteous and the wise are outside the Land, and the keeper of sheep and herds are in the Land, they do not intercalate the year except through the keeper of sheep and herds in the Land. Even when prophets are outside the Land and the ignorant are in the Land they do not intercalate the year except through the ignorant who are in the land of Israel, as it is said,

Pirkei DeRabbi Eliezer 8

"Son of man, when the house of Israel dwell in their own land" [Ezekiel 36:17].it is their duty to intercalate the year.

Yaakov delivered to Yosef and his brethren the principle of intercalation, and they intercalated the year in the land of Egypt. When Yosef and his brethren died, the intercalations ceased from Israel in Egypt, as it is said, "And Yosef died, and all his brethren, and all that generation" [Exodus 1:6]. Just as the intercalations were diminished from the Israelites in the land of Egypt, likewise in the future will the intercalations be diminished at the end of the fourth kingdom until Eliyahu, be he remembered for good, shall come. Just as the Holy One, blessed be He, was revealed to Moshe and Aharon in Egypt, likewise in the future will He be revealed to them at the end of the fourth kingdom, as it is said, "And the Hashem spake unto Moshe and Aharon in the land of Egypt saying, This month shall be unto you the beginning of months" [Exodus 12:1-2]. What is the significance of the word "saying"? Say to them, Till now the principle of intercalation was with me, henceforth it is your right to intercalate thereby the year.

The intercalation takes place in the presence of three; Rebbi Eliezer says that ten men are required, as it is said, "God standeth in the congregation of God" [Psalms 82:1], and if they become less than ten, since they are diminished they place a scroll of the Torah before them, and they are seated in a circle in the court-room, and the greatest among them sits first, and the least sits last; and they direct their gaze downwards to the earth and then they stand and spread out their hands before their Father who is in heaven, and the chief of the assembly proclaims the name of God, and they hear a **Bat Ḳol** [voice from heaven] saying the following words, "And the Hashem spake unto Moshe and Aharon… saying, This month shall be unto you" [Exodus 12:1-2].

If, owing to the iniquity of the generation, they do not hear anything at all; then, if one may say so, He is unable to let His glory abide among them. Happy were those who stood in that place in that hour, as it is said, "Happy is the people who know the joyful sound: they walk, O Hashem, in the light of thy countenance" [Psalms 89:15]; in the light of the countenance of the Holy One, blessed be He, they walk.

On account of three things is the year intercalated, on account of trees, grass, and the seasons. If two of these signs be available and not the third, they do not intercalate the year, that is to say neither because of the trees nor because of the grass. If one sign be available and the other two be absent, they do not intercalate the year on account of the Seasons. If the Season of Ṭevet had occurred on the 20th day of the month or later, they intercalate the year; but till the 20th day of the month Tevet or earlier they do not intercalate the year.

The cycle of intercalation is 19 years, and there are seven small cycles therein; some of these are

Pirkei DeRabbi Eliezer 8

separated by three years, some by two years, and others are separated by three or two years, or by three, three, and three years, the order of the cycles being: 3rd, 6th, 8th, 11th, 14th, 17th, and 19th years. There are two sets of three years cycles.

On the New Moon of **Nissan** the Holy One, blessed be He, was revealed to Moshe and Aharon in the land of Egypt, and it was the 15th year of the great cycle of the moon, the 16th year of the cycle of intercalation, and He said: henceforward the counting devolves on you.

Chapter 9

On the fifth day He caused the waters to bring forth abundantly all kinds of winged fowls, male and female, unclean and clean. By two signs are they declared to be clean, by the crop, and by the craw peeling off? Rebbi Eliezer said: Another sign was also by the projecting toe of the claw. Two kinds of birds have been chosen for the offering of a burnt sacrifice, namely, the turtle-dove and the young pigeon.

On the fifth day He caused the waters to bring forth abundantly all kinds of fish, male and female, unclean and clean. By two signs are they declared to be clean, by the fins and by their scales; and if they do not have them [i.e. both signs] they are unclean.

On the fifth day He caused the waters to bring forth abundantly all kinds of locusts, male and female, clean and unclean. By two signs are they declared to be clean: by their long legs with which they jump, and by the wings which cover the entire body, such are clean? Such living things as were brought forth from the water, namely, fish and locusts, are eaten without being subject to the laws of **Shechiṭah** [with the ritual slaughtering], but the bird cannot be eaten unless it be killed, by the method of Shechiṭah. Such creatures which have been created from the earth have their blood covered with earth, and such as have been created from the water must have their blood poured out like water.

Pirkei DeRabbi Eliezer 9

Rebbi Eliezer said: Not only concerning the water does the Scripture say that "the waters should bring forth abundantly" [Genesis 1:20], but also concerning the birds which are compared with water, as it is said, "And the uproar of many peoples, which roar like the roaring of the seas" [Isaiah 17:12], and just as the waters brought forth abundantly on the fifth day, likewise in the future will the nations of the world swarm in the fifth world, and they will fight one another to destroy one another, as it is said, "And they were broken in pieces, nation against nation, and city against city; for God did vex them with all adversity" [Chronicles-B 15 6]. What is written immediately afterwards? The Salvation of Israel is mentioned, as it is said, "But be ye strong; and your hands shall not be slack" [Chronicles-B 15 7].

All rivers flowing on the earth, as soon as they flow on the earth, they are blessed and good and sweet. There is some benefit to the world through them; [when] they flow into the sea they are bad, cursed, and bitter, and they are of no benefit to the world. Why are they similar to Israel? For when the Israelites rely upon the protection of their Creator and do His will, they are blessed and good and sweet, and there is some benefit to the world through them, and for their sake the world stands. When the men of Israel depart from their Creator and trust in the statutes of the nations, they are bad, accursed, and bitter, and there is no benefit in them for the world. Just as the waters of the rivers are the food of the waters of the sea, so are the sinners destined to be fuel for Gehinnom. All the rains that descend into

Pirkei DeRabbi Eliezer 9

the sea are as seed for all creatures in them, and thereby the fish are fed.

On the fifth day the waters in Egypt were changed into blood. On the fifth day our forefathers went forth from Egypt. On the same day the waters of the Jordan stood still before the ark of the Covenant of God. On the same day Hezekiah stopped the fountains which were in Jerusalem, as it is said, "This same Hezekiah also stopped the upper spring of the waters of Gihon" [Chronicles-B 32 80].

On the fifth day He brought forth from the water the Leviathan, the flying serpent, and its dwelling is in the lowest waters; and between its fins rests the middle bar of the earth. All the great sea monsters in the sea are the food for the Leviathan. Every day it opens its mouth, and the great sea monster destined to be eaten that day tries to escape and flee, but it enters the mouth of the Leviathan; and the Holy One, blessed be He, plays with it, as it is said, "This is the Leviathan, whom thou hast created to play with him" [Psalms 104:26].

Rebbi Mana said: Such creatures which have been created from the earth increase and multiply on the earth, and such which have been brought forth from the water increase and multiply in the water, except all kinds of winged birds, for their creation was from the water, yet they increase and multiply on the earth, as it is said, "And let the fowl multiply in the earth" [Genesis 1:22]. Such as were brought forth from the water increase and multiply by the egg; and such

Pirkei DeRabbi Eliezer 9

as were created from the earth increase and multiply by fetus [living offspring].

Chapter 10

On the fifth day Yonah fled before his God. Why did he flee? Because on the first occasion when God sent him to restore the border of Israel, his words were fulfilled, as it is said, "And he restored the border of Israel from the entering in of Hamath" [Kings-B 14:25]. On the second occasion God sent him to Jerusalem to prophesy that He would destroy it. But the Holy One, blessed be He, did according to the abundance of His tender mercy and repented of the evil decree, and He did not destroy it; thereupon they called him a lying prophet. On the third occasion God sent him against Nineveh to destroy it. Yonah argued with himself, saying, I know that the nations are nigh to repentance, now they will repent and the Holy One, blessed be He, will direct His anger against the children of. And is it not enough for me that Israel should call me a lying prophet; but shall also the nations of the world do likewise? Therefore, behold, I will escape from His presence to a place where His glory is not declared. If I ascend above the heavens, it is said, "Above the heavens is his glory" [Psalms 113:4]. If above the earth, it is said, "The whole earth is full of his glory" [Isaiah 6:8]; behold, I will escape to the sea, to a place where His glory is not proclaimed. Yonah went down to Yaffo, but he did not find there a ship in which he could embark, for the ship in which Yonah might have embarked was two days journey away from Yaffo, in order to test Yonah. What did the Holy One, blessed be He, do? He sent against it a mighty

Pirkei DeRabbi Eliezer 10

tempest on the sea and brought it back to Yaffo. Then Yonah saw and rejoiced in his heart, saying, Now, I know that my ways will prosper before me.

He said to the sailors, we will embark with you. They replied to him, Behold, we are going to the islands of the sea, to Tarshish. He said to them, we will go with you. Now this is the custom on all ships that when a man disembarks therefrom, he pays his fare; but Yonah, in the joy of his heart, paid his fare in advance, as it is said, "But Yonah rose up to flee unto Tarshish from the presence of the Hashem; and he went down to Yaffo and found a ship going to Tarshish; so, he paid the fare thereof, and went down into it, to go with them" [Yonah 1:3].

They had travelled one day's journey, and a mighty tempest on the sea arose against them on their right hand and on their left hand; but the movement of all the ships passing to and fro was peaceful in a quiet sea, but the ship into which Yonah had embarked was in great peril of shipwreck, as it is said, "But the Hashem sent out a great wind into the sea, and there was a mighty tempest in the sea, so that the ship was like to be broken" [Yonah 1:4].

Rebbi Chanina said: Men of the seventy languages were there on the ship, and each one had his god in his hand, each one saying: And the God who shall reply and deliver us from this trouble, He shall be God. They arose and every one called upon the name of his god, but it availed nought. Now Yonah, because of the anguish of his soul, was slumbering and asleep. The captain of the ship came to him, saying, Behold, we are standing betwixt death and life, and thou art slumbering and sleeping; of what people art thou? He answered them, "I am a Hebrew" [Yonah 1:9]. The captain said to him, have we not heard that the God of the Hebrews is great? Arise, call upon thy God, perhaps He will work salvation for us according to all His miracles which He did for you at the Reed Sea. He answered them, it is on my account that this misfortune has befallen you; take me up and cast me into the sea and the sea will become calm unto you, as it is said, "And he said unto them, take me up, and cast me forth into the sea; so, shall the sea be calm unto you" [Yonah 1:12].

Rebbi Shimon said: The men would not consent to throw Yonah into the sea; but they cast lots among themselves and the lot fell upon Yonah. What did they do? They took all their utensils which were in the ship, and cast them into the sea in order to lighten it for their safety, but it availed nought. They wanted to return to the dry land, but they were unable, as it is said, "Nevertheless the men rowed hard to get them back to the land; but they could not" [Yonah 1:13]. What did they do? They took Yonah and they stood on the side of the ship, saying, God of the world! O Hashem! Do not lay upon us innocent blood, for we do not know what sort of person is this man; and he says deliberately, on my account has this misfortune befallen you.

They took Yonah and cast him into the sea, up to his

Pirkei DeRabbi Eliezer 10

knee-joints, and the sea-storm abated. They took him up again to themselves and the sea became agitated again against them. They cast him in again up to his neck, and the sea-storm abated. Once more they lifted him up in their midst and the sea was again agitated against them, until they cast him in entirely and forthwith the sea-storm abated, as it is said, "So they took up Yonah, and cast him forth into the sea: and the sea ceased from her raging" [Yonah 1:15].

Rebbi Ṭarphon said: That fish was specially appointed from the six days of Creation to swallow up Yonah, as it is said, "And the Hashem had prepared a great fish to swallow up Yonah" [Yonah 1:17]. He entered its mouth just as a man enters the great synagogue, and he stood therein. The two eyes of the fish were like windows of glass giving light to Yonah.

Rebbi Meir said: One pearl was suspended inside the belly of the fish and it gave illumination to Yonah, like this sun which shines with its might at noon; and it showed to Yonah all that was in the sea and in the depths, as it is said, "Light is sown for the righteous" [Psalms 97:11].

The fish said to Yonah, Dost thou not know that my day had arrived to be devoured in the midst of Leviathan's mouth? Yonah replied, take me beside it, and I will deliver thee and myself from its mouth. It brought him next to the Leviathan. Yonah said to the Leviathan, on thy account have I descended to

Pirkei DeRabbi Eliezer 10

see thy abode in the sea, for, moreover, in the future will I descend and put a rope in thy tongue, and I will bring thee up and prepare thee for the great feast of the righteous. Yonah showed it the seal of our father Avraham saying, Look at the Covenant seal, and Leviathan saw it and fled before Yonah a distance of two days' journey. Yonah said to it the fish, Behold, I have saved thee from the mouth of Leviathan, show me what is in the sea and in the depths. It showed him the great river of the waters of the Ocean, as it is said, "The deep was round about me" [Yonah 2:5], and it showed him the paths of the Reed Sea through which Israel passed, as it is said, "The reeds were wrapped about my head" [Yonah 2:5]; and it showed him the place whence the waves of the sea and its billows flow, as it is said, "All thy waves and thy billows passed over me" [Yonah 2:3]; and it showed him the pillars of the earth in its foundations, as it is said, "The earth with her bars for the world were by me" [Yonah 2:6]; and it showed him the lowest Sheol, as it is said, "Yet hast thou brought up my life from destruction, O Hashem, my God" [Yonah 2:6]; and it showed him Gehinnom, as it is said, "Out of the belly of Sheol I cried, and thou didst hear my voice" [Yonah 2:2]; and it showed him what was beneath the Temple of God, as it is said, "I went down to the bottom of the mountains" [Yonah 2:6]. Hence, we may learn that Jerusalem stands upon seven [hills], and he saw there the **Eben Shethiyah** [Foundation Stone] fixed in the depths. He saw there the sons of Korach standing and praying over it. They said to Yonah, behold thou dost stand beneath the Temple of God,

Pirkei DeRabbi Eliezer 10

pray and thou wilt be answered. Forthwith Yonah said to the fish, stand in the place where thou art standing, because I wish to pray. The fish stood still, and Yonah began to pray before the Holy One, blessed be He, and he said: Sovereign of all the Universe, Thou art called "the One who kills" and "the One who makes alive," behold, my soul has reached unto death, now restore me to life. He was not answered until this word came forth from his mouth, "What I have vowed I will perform" [Yonah 2:9], namely, I vowed to draw up Leviathan and to prepare it before Thee, I will perform this on the day of the Salvation of Israel, as it is said, "But I will sacrifice unto thee with the voice of thanksgiving" [Yonah 2:9]. Forthwith the Holy One, blessed be He, hinted [to the fish] and it vomited out Yonah upon the dry land, as it is said, "And the Hashem spake unto the fish, and it vomited out Yonah upon the dry land" [Yonah 2:10].

The sailors saw all the signs, the miracles, and the great wonders which the Holy One, blessed be He, did unto Yonah, and they stood and they cast away everyone his God, as it is said, "They that regard lying vanities forsake their own shame" [Yonah 2:8]. They returned to Yaffo and went up to Jerusalem and circumcised the flesh of their foreskins, as it is said, "And the men feared the Hashem exceedingly; and they offered a sacrifice unto the Hashem" [Yonah 1:16]. Did they offer sacrifice? But this sacrifice refers to the blood of the covenant of circumcision, which is like the blood of a sacrifice. And they made vows everyone to bring his children and all

Pirkei DeRabbi Eliezer 10

belonging to him to the God of Yonah; and they made vows and performed them, and concerning them it says, "Upon the proselytes, the proselytes of righteousness."

Chapter 11

On the sixth day God brought forth from the earth all kinds of animals, male and female, clean and unclean. By two signs are they declared to be clean: the signs are chewing the cud, and dividing the hoof. Three kinds of animals were chosen for the sacrifice of a burnt-offering, namely, the ox, the lamb, and the goat. Every kind of clean animal which is neither **Nevelah** [which has not been slaughtered according to the rules of Shechitah] nor **Ṭreif** [internal blemishes that are found in the body of the animal] in the field is permitted to be eaten, except with regard to three parts, namely, the fat, the blood, and the sinew of the thigh, as it is said, "As the green herb have, I given you all" [Genesis 9:3].

On the sixth day God brought forth from the earth seven clean beasts; their slaughter and the method of consumption are similar to the rules observed with a bird; and all the rest of the beasts in the field are entirely unclean.

He brought forth from the earth all kinds of abominations and creeping things, all of them are unclean. Such creatures which have been created from the earth, their life or soul and body are from the earth, and when they return, they touch their dust at the place whence they were created, as it is said, "Thou takest away their breath, they die, and return to their dust" [Psalms 104:29]; and it is written, "And the spirit of the beast goes downward to the earth"

Pirkei DeRabbi Eliezer 11

[Ecclesiastes 3:21].

On the sixth day He brought forth from the earth a beast [**Behemoth**] which lies stretched out on a thousand hills and every day has its pasture on a thousand hills, and overnight [the verdure] grows of its own account as though he had not touched it, as it is said, "Surely the mountains bring him forth food" [Job 40:20]. The waters of the Jordan give him water to drink, for the waters of the Jordan surround all the earth, half thereof flow above the earth and the other half below the earth, as it is said, "He is confident, though Jordan swell even to his mouth" [Job 40:23]. This creature is destined for the day of sacrifice, for the great banquet of the righteous, as it is said, "He only that made him can make his sword to approach unto him" [Job 40:19].

The Holy One, blessed be He, spake to the Torah: "Let us make man in our image, after our likeness" [Genesis 1:26]. The Torah spake before Him: Sovereign of all the worlds. The man whom Thou wouldst create will be limited in days and full of anger; and he will come into the power of sin. Unless Thou wilt be long-suffering with him, it would be well for him not to have come into the world. The Holy One, blessed be He, rejoined: And is it for nought that I am called "slow to anger" and "abounding in love"? He began to collect the dust of the first man from the four corners of the world; red, black, white, and "pale green," which refers to the body. Why did He gather man's dust from the four corners of the world? Thus, spake the Holy One,

Pirkei DeRabbi Eliezer 11

blessed be He: If a man should come from the east to the west, or from the west to the east, and his time comes to depart from the world, then the earth shall not say, the dust of thy body is not mine, return to the place whence thou wast created. But this circumstance teaches thee that in every place where a man goes or comes, and his end approaches when he must depart from the world, thence is the dust of his body, and there it returns to the dust, as it is said, "For dust thou art, and unto dust shalt thou return" [Genesis 3:19].

The day had twelve hours; in the first hour He collected the dust for the body of **Adam**, in the second hour He formed it into a mass, in the third hour He gave it its shape, in the fourth hour He endowed it with breath, in the fifth hour he stood on his feet, in the sixth hour he called the animals by their names, in the seventh hour Eve was joined to him in wedlock, in the eighth hour they were commanded concerning the fruits of the tree, in the ninth hour they went up to their couch as two and descended as four, in the tenth hour they transgressed His commandment, in the eleventh hour they were judged, in the twelfth [hour] they were driven forth, as it is said, "So he drove out the man" [Genesis 3:24].

And He formed the lumps of the dust of the first man into a mass in a clean place, it was on the navel of the earth. He shaped him and prepared him, but breath and soul were not in him. What did the Holy One, blessed be He, do? He breathed with the breath

Pirkei DeRabbi Eliezer 11

of the soul of His mouth, and a soul was cast into him, as it is said, "And he breathed into his nostrils the breath of life" [Genesis 2:7].

Adam stood and he began to gaze upwards and downwards. He saw all the creatures which the Holy One, blessed be He, had created; and he was wondering in his heart, and he began to praise and glorify his Creator, saying, "O Hashem, how manifold are thy works!" [Psalms 104:24]. He stood on his feet and was adorned with the Divine Image. His height was from east to west, as it is said, "Thou hast beset me behind and before" [Psalms 139:5]. "Behind" refers to the west, "before" refers to the east. All the creatures saw him and became afraid of him, thinking that he was their Creator, and they came to prostrate themselves before him.

Adam said to them: What is this, ye creatures, Why are ye come to prostrate yourselves before me? Come, I and you, let us go and adorn in majesty and might, and acclaim as King over us the One who created us. If there be no people to acclaim the king as king, the king acclaims himself. If there be no people to praise the king, the king praises himself. In that hour Adam opened his mouth and all the creatures answered after him, and they adorned in majesty and might and acclaimed their Creator as King over themselves, and they said, "The Hashem reigneth, he is apparelled with majesty" [Psalms 93:1].

Ten kings ruled from one end of the world to the other. The first king was the Holy One,

Pirkei DeRabbi Eliezer 11

blessed be He, who rules in heaven and on earth, and it was His intention to raise up kings on earth, as it is said, "And he changeth the times and the seasons; he removeth kings, and setteth up kings" [Daniel 2:21].

The second king was **Nimrod**, who ruled from one end of the world to the other, for all the creatures were dwelling in one place and they were afraid of the waters of the flood, and Nimrod was king over them, as it is said, "And the beginning of his kingdom was Babel" [Genesis 10:10].

The third king was **Yosef**, who ruled from one end of the world to the other, as it is said, "And all the earth came into Egypt to Yosef" [Genesis 41:57]. It is not written here "Egypt came," but "they came into Egypt," for they brought their tribute and their presents to Yosef to buy corn; for forty years he was second to the king, and for forty years he was king alone, as it is said, "Now there arose a new king over Egypt" [Exodus 1:8].

The fourth king was **Solomon**, who reigned from one end of the world to the other, as it is said, "And Solomon ruled over all the kingdoms" [Kings-A 4:21]; and it says, "And they brought every man his present, vessels of silver, and vessels of gold, and raiment, and armour, and spices, horses, and mules, a rate year by year" [Kings-A 10:25].

The fifth king was **Ahab**, king of Israel, who ruled from one end of the world to the other, as it is said,

Pirkei DeRabbi Eliezer 11

"As the Hashem thy God liveth, there is no nation or kingdom, whither my Hashem hath not sent to seek thee" [Kings-A 18:10]. All the princes of the provinces were controlled by him; they sent and brought their tribute and their presents to Ahab. Are not all the princes of the provinces of the world two hundred and thirty-two? As it is said, "Then he mustered the young men of the princes of the provinces, and they were two hundred and thirty-two" [Kings-A 20:15].

The sixth king was **Nebuchadnezzar**, who ruled from one end of the world to the other. Moreover, he ruled over the beasts of the field and the birds of heaven, and they could not open their mouth except by the permission of Nebuchadnezzar, as it is said, "And wheresoever the children of men dwell, the beasts of the field and the fowls of the heaven hath he given into thine hand" [Daniel 2:88].

The seventh king was **Koresh**, who ruled from one end of the world to the other, as it is said, "Thus saith Koresh king of Persia, All the kingdoms of the earth hath the Hashem, the God of heaven, given me" [Chronicles-B 36:23]. Ahasuerus ruled over half the world. Is not half the world but 116 provinces, as it is said, "This is Ahasuerus, who reigned from India unto Ethiopia" [Esther 1:1].

The eighth king was **Alexander of Macedonia**, who ruled from one end of the world to the other, as it is said, "And as I was considering, behold, a he-goat came from the west over the face of the whole earth" [Daniel 8:5]. "Over the earth" is not written here, but "over the face of the whole earth." And not only that, but he wished to ascend to heaven in order to know what is in heaven, and to descend into the depths in order to know what is in the depths, and not only that, but he attempted to go to the ends of the earth in order to know what was at the ends of the earth. The Holy One, blessed be He, divided his kingdom among the four corners [or winds] of the heavens, as it is said, "And when he shall stand up, his kingdom shall be broken, and shall be divided towards the four winds of the heaven" [Daniel 11:4].

The ninth king is King **Mashiach**, who, in the future, will rule from one end of the world to the other, as it is said, "He shall have dominion also from sea to sea" [Psalms 72:8]; and another Scripture text says, "And the stone that smote the image became a great mountain, and filled the whole earth" [Daniel 2:35].

The tenth king will restore the sovereignty to its owners. He who was the first king will be the last king, as it is said, "Thus saith the Hashem, the King… I am the first, and I am the last; and beside me there is no God" [Isaiah 44:6]; and it is written, "And the Hashem shall be king over all the earth" [Zechariah 14:9]. And the kingdom shall return to her heirs, and the idols will pass away altogether, Man's haughty look shall be brought low, And the pride of mortals shall be humbled. None but the LORD shall be Exalted in that day [Isaiah 2:11]. And he will shepherd his flock and lay them down I Myself will graze My flock, and I Myself will let them lie down

Pirkei DeRabbi Eliezer 11

[Ezekiel 34:15]. As one they shout for joy; For every eye shall behold The LORD's return to Zion [Isaiah 52:8]. Amen.

Chapter 12

With love abounding did the Holy One, blessed be He, love the first man, inasmuch as He created him in a pure locality, in the place of the Temple, and He brought him into His palace, as it is said, "And the Hashem God took the man, and put him into the garden of Eden to dress it and to keep it" [Genesis 2:15]. From which place did He take him? From the place of the Temple, and He brought him into His palace, which is Eden, as it is said, "And he put him into the Garden of Eden to dress it" [Genesis 2:15]. Perhaps thou wilt say: To plough [the fields] and cast out the stones from the ground. But did not all the trees grow up of their own accord?

Perhaps thou wilt say, there was some other work to be done in the Garden of Eden, such as to water the garden. But did not a river flow through and issue forth from Eden, and water the garden, as it is said, "And a river went out of Eden to water the garden" [Genesis 2:10].

What then is the meaning of this expression: "to dress it and to keep it"[Genesis 2:15]. The text does not say "to dress it and to keep it" except in the sense of being occupied with the words of the Torah and keeping all its commandments, as it is said, "to keep the way of the tree of life" [Genesis 3:24]. But the "tree of life" signifies only the Torah, as it is said, "It is a tree of life to them that lay hold upon it" [Proverbs 3:18].

Pirkei DeRabbi Eliezer 12

And Adam was at his leisure in the Garden of Eden, like one of the ministering angels. The Holy One, blessed be He, said: I am alone in my world and this one [**Adam**] also is alone in his world. There is no propagation before me and this one [**Adam**] has no propagation in his life; hereafter all the creatures will say: Since there was no propagation in his life, it is he who has created us. It is not good for man to be alone, as it is said, "And the Hashem God said, It is not good for man to be alone; I will make him a helper corresponding to him ..." [Genesis 2:18].

Rebbi Yehuda said: If he be worthy, she shall be a help for him; if not, she shall be against him and fight him.

When the earth heard this expression thereupon it trembled and quaked, crying before its Creator: Sovereign of all worlds, I have not the power to feed the multitude of mankind. The Holy One, blessed be He, replied: I and thou will together feed the multitude of mankind. They agreed to divide [the task] between themselves: the night was for the Holy One, blessed be He, and the day was apportioned to the earth. What did the Holy One, blessed be He, do? He created the sleep of life, so that man lies down and sleeps whilst He sustains him and heals him and gives him life and repose, as it is said, "I should have slept: then had I been at rest" [Job 3:18]. The Holy One, blessed be He, supports [man] with the earth, giving it water; and it yields its fruit and food for all creatures - but the first man's food "in toil shalt thou eat of it all the days of thy life" [Genesis 3:17].

Pirkei DeRabbi Eliezer 12

The Holy One, blessed be He, had compassion upon the first man [**Adam**], and, in order that he should not feel any pain, He cast upon him the sleep of deep slumber, and He made him sleep whilst He took one of his bones from his side and flesh from his heart and made it into a help meant for him and placed her opposite to him. When he awoke from his sleep, he saw her standing opposite to him. And he said, "Bone of my bones and flesh of my flesh" [Genesis 2:28]. As long as he was alone, he was called Adam.

Rebbi Yehuda said: Because of the name **Adamah** [ground] whence he was taken, his name was called Adam. Rebbi Yehoshua ben Karha said: He was called **Adam** because of his flesh and blood [**Dam**]. He said to him: Adam, Adam, And when a helpmate had been built for him, his name was called **Ish** [fire], and she was called **Ishshah** [fire].

What did the Holy One, blessed be He, do? He put His name יה between their names, saying: If they go in My ways and keep all My precepts, behold My name is given to them, it will deliver them from all distress. If they do not walk in My ways, behold I will take away My name from their names, and they will become **Ish** [fire]. And fire consumes fire, as it is said, "For it is a fire that consumeth unto destruction" [Job 31:12].

The Holy One, blessed be He, made ten wedding canopies for Adam in the Garden of Eden. They were all made of precious stones, pearls, and gold. Is it not a fact that only one wedding canopy is made

Pirkei DeRabbi Eliezer 12

for every bridegroom, whilst three wedding canopies are made for a king? But in order to bestow special honour upon the first man, the Holy One, blessed be He, made ten wedding canopies in the garden of Eden, as it is said, "Wast thou in Eden the garden of God; was every precious stone thy covering, the sardius, topaz, and the diamond, the beryl, the onyx, and the jasper, the sapphire, the emerald, and the carbuncle, and gold?" [Ezekiel 28:13]. Behold these are the ten canopies. The angels were playing upon timbrels and dancing with pipes, as it is said, "The workmanship of thy tabrets and of thy pipes was with thee" [Ezekiel 28:13].

On the day when the first man was created, as it is said, "In the day when thou wast created they were prepared" [Ezekiel 28:13], the Holy One, blessed be He, said to the ministering angels: Come, let us descend and render loving service to the first man and to his help-mate, for the world rests upon the attribute of the service of loving-kindness. The Holy One, blessed be He, said: More beloved is the service of loving-kindness than the sacrifices and burnt-offerings which Israel will bring in the future upon the altar before Me, as it is said, "For I desire love, and not sacrifice" [Hosea 6:6].

The ministering angels were going to and fro and walking before him like friends who guard the wedding canopies, as it is said, "For he shall give his angels charge over thee, to keep thee in all thy ways" [Psalms 91:11]. The word "Way" here means only the way of bridegrooms. The Holy One, blessed be He,

Pirkei DeRabbi Eliezer 12

was like a precentor. What is the custom observed by the precentor? He stands and blesses the bride in the midst of her wedding chamber. Likewise, the Holy One, blessed be He, stood and blessed Adam and his help-mate, as it is said, "And God blessed them" [Genesis 1:28].

Chapter 13

Envy, cupidity, and ambition remove man from the world. The ministering angels spake before the Holy One, blessed be He, saying: Sovereign of all Worlds! "What is man, that thou shouldst take note of him?" [Psalms 144:3]. "Man is like unto vanity" [Psalms 144:4], upon earth there is not his like. God answered them: Just as all of you praise me in the heights of heaven so he professes My Unity on earth, nay, moreover, are you able to stand up and call the names for all the creatures which I have created? They stood up, but were unable [to give the names]. Forthwith Adam stood up and called the names for all His creatures, as it is said, "And the man [**Adam**] gave names to all cattle" [Genesis 2:20]. When the ministering angels saw this, they retreated, and the ministering angels said: If we do not take counsel against this man so he will sin before his Creator, we cannot prevail against him.

Sammae"l [The angel of death] was the great prince in heaven; The beasts and animals had four wings and the Seraphim had six wings, and Sammae"l had twelve wings. What did Sammae"l do? He took his band and descended and saw all the creatures which the Holy One, blessed be He, had created in His world and he found among them none so skilled to do evil as the serpent, as it is said, "Now the serpent was more subtil than any beast of the field" [Genesis 3:1]. Its appearance was something like that of the camel, and he mounted and rode upon it.

Pirkei DeRabbi Eliezer 13

The Torah began to cry aloud, saying, why, O Sammae"l, now that the world is created, is it the time to rebel against the Omnipresent? Is it a time when thou shouldst lift up thyself on high? The Lord of the world "will laugh at the horse and its rider" [Job 39:18].

To understand this part, you need to know that there are ten different names of Angels, as it is explained in the Rambam, The Book of knowledge Chapter 2:7 - The variation in the names of the angels is based upon their degrees; they are therefore called: Holy Living Creatures, which are above all others, Wheels, Valiant Ones, Electrum, Flying Serpent, Angels, Gods, Sons of Gods, Chariot Bearers, and Men. All these ten names by which the angels are called designate their respective ten degrees; the degree which has nothing higher than itself, save only the degree of God, blessed is He! Is the degree of the form which is called Living Creatures; Thus, it is spoken of in prophecy as being beneath the Throne of Glory. And the tenth degree is the degree of the form known as Men, which are the angels who speak with the prophets and appear to them in the vision of prophecy. Therefore, they are called Men, as their degree approaches the degree of the intellect of the sons of man.

A parable, to what is the matter like? To a man in whom there was an evil spirit. All the deeds which he does, or all the words which he utters, does he speak by his own intention? Does he not act only according to the idea of the evil spirit, which rules

Pirkei DeRabbi Eliezer   13

over him? So was it with the serpent. All the deeds which it did, and all the words which it spake, it did not speak except by the intention of Sammae"l. Concerning him, the Scripture says, "The wicked is thrust down in his evil-doing" [Proverbs 14:32].

A parable, to what is the matter like? To a king who married a woman and made her supreme over all that he had. He said to her: All that I have shall be in thy hands, except this house, which is full of scorpions. A certain old man visited her; he asks, for instance, for vinegar. He said to her: Wilt thou argue that he deals kindly with thee? He deals with me thus: over all that he possesses has he made me supreme. Thus, said he to her: Behold, all that I have is given into thy hands except this house, which is full of scorpions. The first man [**Adam**] said to her: Is not all the jewellery of the king indeed in this house? But he wishes to marry another woman, and to give them to her. The king is the first man [**Adam**], the woman is Eve, and the one who asked for vinegar is the serpent; and concerning them the text says, "There are the workers of iniquity fallen, they are thrust down, and shall not be able to rise" [Psalms 36:12].

The serpent argued with itself, saying: If I go and speak to Adam, I know that he will not listen to me, for a man is always hard to be persuaded, as it is said, "For a man is churlish and evil in his doings" [Samuel-A 25:3]; but behold I will speak to Eve, for I know that she will listen to me; for women listen to all creatures, as it is said, "She is simple and

Pirkei DeRabbi Eliezer 13

knoweth nothing" [Proverbs 9:18]. The serpent went and spake to the woman: Is it [true that] you also have been commanded concerning the fruit of the tree? She said to him: Yes, as it is said, "Of the fruit of the tree which is in the midst of the garden" [Genesis 3:8]. And when the serpent heard the words of Eve, he found a way through which he could enter to approach her, so he said to her: This precept is nought else except the evil eye, for in the hour when ye eat thereof, ye will be like Him, a God. Just as He creates worlds and destroys worlds, so will ye be able to create worlds and to destroy worlds. Just as He slays and brings to life, so also will ye be able to kill and to bring to life, as it is said, "For God doth know that in the day ye eat thereof, then your eyes shall be opened" [Genesis 3:5].

The serpent went and touched the tree, which commenced to cry out, saying: Wicked One. Do not touch me. As it is said, "Let not the foot of pride come against me, and let not the hand of the wicked drive me away. There are the workers of iniquity fallen" [Psalms 36:11-12].

The serpent went and said to the woman: Behold, I touched it, but I did not die; thou also mayest touch it, and thou wilt not die. The woman went and touched the tree, and she saw the angel of death coming towards her; she said: Woe is me. I shall now die, and the Holy One, blessed be He, will make another woman and give her to Adam, but behold I will cause him to eat with me; if we shall die, we shall both die, and if we shall live, we shall both live.

Pirkei DeRabbi Eliezer 13

And she took of the fruits of the tree, and ate thereof, and also gave of its fruits to her husband, so that he should eat with her, as it is said, "And she took of the fruit thereof, and did eat; and she gave also unto her husband with her" [Genesis 3:6]. When Adam had eaten of the fruit of the tree, he saw that he was naked, and his eyes were opened, and his teeth were set on edge. He said to her: What is this that thou hast given me to eat, that my eyes should be opened and my teeth set on edge? Just as my teeth were set on edge, so shall the teeth of all generations be set on edge.

Chapter 14

Ten descents upon the earth were made by the Holy One, blessed be He; they were: [1] Once in the Garden of Eden; [2] Once at the time of the generation of the Dispersion; [3] once at Sodom; [4] once at the thorn-bush; [5] once in Egypt; [6] once at Sinai; [7] once at the cleft of the rock; [8-9] and twice in the tent of Assembly; [10] once in the future.

Once in the Garden of Eden; whence do we know, because it is said, "And they heard the voice of the Hashem God walking in the garden in the cool of the day" [Genesis 3:8]. And it is written, "My beloved is gone down to his garden, to the beds of spices" [Song of Songs 6:2]. God sat in judgment, and He judged with judgment. He said to Adam: Why didst thou flee before me? He answered Him: I heard Thy voice and my bones trembled, as it is said, "I heard thy voice in the garden, and I was afraid, because I was naked: and I hid myself" [Genesis 3:10].

What was the dress of the first man? A skin of nail, and a cloud of glory covered him. When he ate of the fruits of the tree, the nail-skin was stripped off him, and the cloud of glory departed from him, and he saw himself naked, as it is said, "And he said, who told thee that thou wast naked? Hast, thou eaten of the tree, whereof I commanded thee?" [Genesis 3:11].

Pirkei DeRabbi Eliezer 14

Adam said before the Holy One, blessed be He: Sovereign of all worlds. When I was alone, I did not sin against Thee. But the woman whom Thou hast brought to me enticed me away from Thy ways, as it is said, "The woman whom thou gavest to be with me, she gave me of the tree, and I did eat" [Genesis 3:12]. The Holy One, blessed be He, called unto Eve, and said to her: Was it not enough for thee that thou didst sin in thy own person? But [also] that thou shouldst make Adam sin? She spake before Him: Sovereign of the world. The serpent enticed my mind to sin before Thee, as it is said, "The serpent beguiled me, and I did eat" [Genesis 3:13]. He brought the three of them and passed sentence of judgment upon them, consisting of nine curses and death.

He cast down Sammae"l [The angel of death] and his troop from their holy place in heaven, and cut off the feet of the serpent, and decreed that it should cast its skin and suffer pain once in seven years in great pain, and cursed it that it should drag itself with its belly on the ground, and its food is turned in its belly into dust and the gall of asps, and death is in its mouth, and He put hatred between it and the children of the woman, so that they should bruise its head, and after all these curses comes death. He gave the woman nine curses and death: the afflictions arising from menstruation and the tokens of virginity; the affliction of conception in the womb; and the affliction of child-birth; and the affliction of bringing up children; and her head is covered like a mourner, and it is not shaved except on account of immorality, and her ear is pierced like the ears of

Pirkei DeRabbi Eliezer 14

perpetual slaves; and like a hand-maid she waits upon her husband; and she is not believed in a matter of testimony; and after all these curses comes death.

He extended pardon to Adam as to a part of the nine curses and death. He curtailed his strength, and He shortened his stature by reason of the impurity connected with issues and with pollution; as well as the impurity arising from sexual intercourse; he was to sow wheat and to reap thistles, and his food was to be the grass of the earth, like that of the beast; and he was to earn his bread in anxiety, and his food by the sweat of his brow; and after all these curses came death.

If Adam sinned, what was the sin of the earth, that it should be cursed, because it did not speak against the evil deed, therefore it was cursed; for in the hour when the sons of man transgress the graver sins God sends a plague to the sons of man; and in the hour when the sons of man transgress sins less vital, He smites the fruits of the earth, because of the sins of the sons of man, as it is said. "Cursed is the ground for thy sake" [Genesis 3:17].

Chapter 15

Rebbi Elezer said: I heard with my ear the Hashem of hosts speaking. What did He speak? He said: "See, I have set before thee this day life and good, and death and evil" [Deuteronomy 30:15]. The Holy One, blessed be He, said: Behold, these two ways have I given to Israel, one is good, the other is evil. The one which is good, is of life; and the one which is evil, is of death. The good way has two byways, one of righteousness and the other of love, and Eliyahu, be he remembered for good, is placed exactly between these two ways. When a man comes to enter one of these ways, Eliyahu, will be remembered for good, cries aloud concerning him, saying, "Open ye the gates, that the righteous nation which keepeth truth may enter in" [Isaiah 26:2]. And there cometh Samuel the prophet, and he places himself between these two byways. He says: On which of these two byways shall I go? If I go on the way of righteousness, then the path of love is better than the former; if I go on the way of love, the way of righteousness is better: but I call heaven and earth to be my witnesses that I will not give up either of them.

The Holy One, blessed be He, said to him: Samuel. Thou hast placed thyself between these two good byways. By thy life. I will give to thee three good gifts. This teaches thee that everyone who doeth righteousness and sheweth the service of love, shall inherit three good gifts, and they are: life,

Pirkei DeRabbi Eliezer 15

righteousness, and glory, as it is said, "He that followeth after righteousness and love, findeth life, righteousness, and glory" [Proverbs 21:21].

Leading to the way of evil, there are four doors, and at each door seven angels are standing - four without, and three within. The angels without are merciful, and those within are cruel. When a man comes to enter, the merciful angels go to meet him and say to him: What hast thou to do with the fire yonder? What hast thou to do with those glowing coals? Listen to us and repent. If he hearken to them and repent, behold it is well, and if not, he says to them: Amongst them yonder let my life [be]. They say to him: Thou hast entered the first door; do not enter the second door. When he comes to enter the second door, the merciful angels go to meet him and say to him: What benefit is it to thee to be erased from the Torah of thy God? Would it not be better to be inscribed in the Torah of thy God? Hearken unto us and repent. If he listens to them and repent, it is well; and if not, he says to them: With them yonder let my life be. They say to him: Behold thou hast entered the second door, do not enter the third door. When he is about to enter the third door the merciful angels go to meet him and say to him: What benefit is to thee that they [The good angels] should flee from thee and call thee "Unclean"? Would it not be better that they should call thee "Pure One" and not "Unclean"? Hearken to us and repent. If he hearken unto them, behold, it is well; and if not, he says unto them: With them [yonder] let my life [be]. They say to him: Behold thou hast entered the third

Pirkei DeRabbi Eliezer 15

door; do not enter the fourth door. When he is about to enter the fourth door the merciful angels go to meet him and say to him: Behold, thou hast entered these doors, and thou hast not hearkened nor returned. Thus far the Holy One, blessed be He, receives the penitent; thus far the Holy One, blessed be He, pardons and forgives, and every day He says: Return, ye children of man, as it is said: "Thou turnest man to contrition" [Psalms 90:8].

The cruel angels say: Since he would not hearken to the first angels, let us cause his spirit to depart, as it is said, "Let his spirit go forth, let him return to his earth" [Psalms 146:4]. And concerning them [the Scripture] says: "Upon the third and upon the fourth generation of them that hate me" [Exodus 20:5]; and another verse says: "Lo, all these things doth God work, twice, yea thrice, with a man" [Job 33:29]. And thus, He calls to Eliezer.

The Holy One, blessed be He, said: Eliezer. Thou hast made thyself like a threefold cord, as it is said, "And a threefold cord is not quickly broken" [Ecclesiastes 4:12]. I also will apply to thee this verse: "Thou shalt be perfect with the Hashem thy God" [Deuteronomy 18:13]. **Do not read thus, but:** "Thou shalt be perfect before the Hashem thy God."

Chapter 16

The world rests upon three things: upon the Torah, upon Divine Worship, and upon the service of loving-kindness.

Upon the Torah, whence do we know this, Because it is written, "If my covenant of day and night stand not" [Jeremiah 33:25]; and another text says, "This book of the Torah shall not depart out of thy mouth, but thou shalt meditate therein day and night" [Yehoshua 1:8]. Whence do we know [that the world rests] upon the service of loving-kindness, because it is said, "For I desired love, and not sacrifice" [Hosea 6:6]. Whence do we know that the world rests upon Divine Worship? Because it is written, "And the prayer of the upright is his delight" [Proverbs 15:8].

Whence do we learn of the service of loving-kindness for bridegrooms? We learn this from the Holy One, blessed be He; for He Himself bestowed loving-kindness upon Adam and his help-mate. The Holy One, blessed be He, said to the ministering angels: Come ye and let us show loving-kindness to Adam and his help-mate. The Holy One, blessed be He, descended with the ministering angels to show loving-kindness to Adam and his help-mate. The Holy One, blessed be He, said: More beloved unto Me is the service of loving-kindness than sacrifices and burnt-offering which Israel, in the future, will bring on the altar before Me, as it is said, "For I desired love, and not sacrifice" [Hosea 6:6].

Pirkei DeRabbi Eliezer 16

Rebbi Yosef said: From whom do we learn of the seven days of banquet? From our father Yaakov. For when our father Yaakov married Leah, he made a banquet with rejoicing for seven days, as it is said, "Fulfill the week of this one" [Genesis 29:27].

Rebbi Shimon said: Our father Avraham wrote [in his will and bequeathed] all that he had as an inheritance to Yitzhak, as it is said, "And Avraham gave all that he had unto Yitzhak" [Genesis 25:5]. He took the document and gave it into the hands of Eliezer, his servant, who said, since the document is in my hand all his money is in my hand, so that he might go and be recommended thereby in his father's house and with his family.

From the city of **Kiryat Arba** unto the city **Haran** was a journey of seventeen days; and in three hours the servant Eliezer came to Haran. He was astonished in his mind and he said: This day I went forth, and this day I arrived, as it is said, "And I came this day unto the fountain" [Genesis 24:42].

Rebbi Abbahu said: The Holy One, blessed be He, wished to show loving-kindness to Yitzhak, and he sent an angel before Eliezer; and the way was shortened for him, so that the servant came to Haran in three hours.

And everything is revealed before the Holy One, blessed be He. A daughter of kings, who in all her life had never gone forth to draw water, went out to draw water in that hour. And the girl, who did not

Pirkei DeRabbi Eliezer 16

know who the man was, accepted the proposal to be married to Yitzhak. Why? Because she had been destined for him from his mother's womb, as it is said, "In the balances they will go up, they are together lighter than vanity" [Psalms 62:9].

Lavan and Bethuel answered: Since this word has come forth from the mouth of the Almighty, we cannot prevent it, as it is said, "Then Lavan and Bethuel answered and said, the thing proceedeth from the Hashem: we cannot speak unto thee bad or good" [Genesis 24:50]. "Behold, Rivkah is before thee; take her and go" [Genesis 24:51].

The Eliezer servant arose early in the morning, and saw the angel standing and waiting for him in the street. He said to them: "Do not hinder me, for the Hashem hath prospered my way" [Genesis 24:56]. For behold, the man who came with me yesterday, he has prospered my way; behold, he is standing and waiting for me in the street, as it is said, "And he said to them. Do not hinder me, for the Hashem hath prospered my way." They ate and drank at Rivkah's [bridal] banquet. Like a precentor, who is standing and blessing the bride in her bridal canopy, so they stood and blessed Rivkah their sister [wedded] to Yitzhak, as it is said, "And they blessed Rivkah, and said unto her, our sister…" [Genesis 24:60].

At six hours of the day the servant went forth from Haran, and he took Rivkah and Devorah her nurse and made them ride upon the camels. So that the servant should not be alone with the maiden Rivkah

Pirkei DeRabbi Eliezer 16

by night, the earth was contracted before him, and in three hours the servant came to Hebron at the time of the prayer of the afternoon-evening. And Yitzhak had gone forth to say the afternoon-evening prayer, as it is said, "And Yitzhak went forth to meditate in the field towards even" [Genesis 24:63].

Rebbi Shimon said: Avraham spake to Yitzhak his son saying. This servant is suspected of all the transgressions of the Torah, and deceit is in this servant, as it is said, "He is a Canaanite, the balances of deceit are in his hand; he loveth to defraud" [Hosea 12:7]. See, lest he has defiled her, therefore bring the girl into the tent and examine her tactually; and if she be undefiled, behold, she is destined for thee from her mother's womb. He brought her into the tent and examined her tactually, and he showed the result to Avraham his father, and afterwards he took her to be his wife, as it is said, "And Yitzhak brought her into the tent of Sarah his mother… And Yitzhak was comforted after his mother's death" [Genesis 24:67]; for the deeds of Rivkah were like unto those of Sarah. Hence the Israelites have the custom of producing the tokens of the damsel's virginity, as it is said, "Then shall the father of the damsel, and her mother, take and bring forth the tokens of the damsel's virginity" [Deuteronomy 22:15].

The steward of Avraham's household was his servant Eliezer, and whence was his servant? When Avraham went forth from Ur of the Chaldees all the magnates of the kingdom came to give him gifts; and Nimrod took his first-born son Eliezer and gave

Pirkei DeRabbi Eliezer 16

him to Avraham as a perpetual slave.

When Eliezer had thus dealt kindly with Yitzhak. Yitzhak set him free, and the Holy One, blessed be He, gave him his reward in this world, so that there should not be a reward for the wicked in the world to come; and He raised him to kingship, and he is **Og**, king of Bashan.

Rebbi Yosef said: From whom do we learn that there should be seven days of the wedding banquet? From our father Yaakov, who made a banquet with rejoicing for seven days, and he took Leah as his wife. Again, he kept another seven days of banquet and rejoicing, and took Rachel as his wife, as it is said, "And Lavan gathered together all the men of the place, and made a feast" [Genesis 29:22]. The Holy One, blessed be He, said to them: Ye have shown loving-kindness to Yaakov, My servant. I will give a reward to your children, so that there be no reward for the wicked in the world to come: "Because by him the Hashem had given victory unto Syria" [Kings-B 5:1]. From whom do we learn that there should be seven days of banquet? From Samson the Nazirite of God, for when he went down to the land of the Philistines, he took a wife and kept seven days of banquet and rejoicing, as it is said, "And it came to pass, when they saw him, that they brought thirty companions to be with him" [Judges 14:11]. What were they doing with him? They were eating and drinking and rejoicing, as it is said, "And Samson said unto them. Let me now put forth a riddle unto you" [Judges 14:12]; and another text says, "They could not declare

Pirkei DeRabbi Eliezer 16

the riddle in three days" [Judges 14:14].

The bridegroom is like a king. Just as a king is praised by everybody, so is the bridegroom praised by everybody during the seven days of the feast. Just as a king is dressed in garments of glory, so the bridegroom is dressed in garments of glory. Just as a king is rejoicing, with feasts in his presence, all his days, so the bridegroom is rejoicing and has feasts before him all the seven days of the banquet. Just as the king does not go into the market-place alone, likewise the bridegroom does not go into the market-place alone. Just as the face of a king is shining like the light of a sun, so the face of the bridegroom is shining like the light of a sun, as it is said, "And he is as a bridegroom coming out of his chamber, and rejoicing to run his course" [Psalms 19:5].

Chapter 17

Concerning the one who tenders the service of loving-kindness to mourners. Whence do we learn of the service of loving-kindness to mourners? From the Omnipresent, who alone showed loving-kindness to Moshe, His servant, and buried him with His own hand. If this story had not been written in the Torah, it would be impossible to say it, as it is said, "And he buried him in the valley in the land of Moav" [Deuteronomy 34:6].

Rabban Gamaliel, the son of Rebbi Yehuda, said: Not to Moshe alone did He show loving-kindness, but also to Aharon. For when they went up Mount Hor all the tribes of Israel were contending and saying, Moshe and Eleazar have left Aharon on Mount Hor and have gone down by themselves. They did not believe that he was dead. To show loving-kindness to him, what did the Holy One, blessed be He, do? He took Aharon's coffin and brought it above the camp of Israel, and all Israel saw Aharon's coffin flying and moving in the air. They then believed that he was dead, and they showed loving-kindness to him, as it is said: "And all the congregation saw that Aharon was dead" [Numbers 20:29]. Only the men showed loving-kindness to Moshe, as it is said, "And the sons of Israel wept for Moshe" [Deuteronomy 34:8]. The men and the women and the children showed loving-kindness to Aharon.

Pirkei DeRabbi Eliezer 17

Why was this? Because Aharon loved peace and pursued peace, and passed daily through the entire camp of Israel and promoted peace between a man and his wife, and between a man and his neighbour; therefore, all Israel showed loving-kindness to him, as it is said, "And when all the congregation saw that Aharon was dead, they wept for Aharon thirty days, even all the house of Israel" [Numbers 20:29].

Rebbi Yosef said: From whom do we learn of the seven days of mourning? From Yaakov, our father, for thus did his son Yosef unto him, as it is said, "And he made a mourning for his father seven days" [Genesis 50:10].

Whence do we learn the duty of showing loving-kindness to mourners? From Isabel, the daughter of Ithobaal. The palace of Isabel's daughter of Ithobaal, was near the market-place. When any corpse was carried through the market-place, she would go forth from her palace, and she clapped with the palms of her hands and praised with her mouth, and she followed the corpse ten steps. And every groom who would walk through the market would come out of her house and ring with her hands. Eliyahu, may he remembered for good, prophesied and said: "In the portion of Jezreel Valley shall the dogs eat the flesh of Isabel" [Kings-B 9:36]. But over the limbs which were employed in showing loving-kindness, the dogs had no power, as it is said, "And they went to bury her: but they found no more of her than the skull, and the feet, and the palms of her hands" [Kings-B 9:35].

Pirkei DeRabbi Eliezer 17

Whence do we learn the duty of showing loving-kindness to mourners? From the men of Yavesh-Gilead. For when Shaul and his sons were slain, the men of Yavesh Gilead said: Are we not bound to show loving-kindness to the man who delivered us from the disgrace of the sons of Ammon? All their mighty men arose and went all night to the walls of Beit She'an and they took the body of Shaul and the bodies of his sons from the walls of Beit She'an, as it is said, "All the valiant men arose, and took away the body of Shaul" [samuel-A 31:12].

The mourners are comforted with bread and wine, as it is said, "Give strong drink unto him that is ready to perish, and wine unto the bitter in soul" [Proverbs 31:6].

The men of Yavesh-Gilead showed loving-kindness to Shaul and his sons. God said, I will also give you and your sons your reward in the future; for when the Holy One, blessed be He, in the future will gather Israel from the four corners of the world, the first whom He will gather, will be the half-tribe of Menashe, as it is said, "Gilead is mine, and Menashe is mine" [Psalms 60:7]. Afterwards will He gather in Ephraim, as it is said, "Ephraim is the defence of mine head" [Psalms 60:7]. Afterwards Yehuda will be gathered in, as it is said, "Yehuda is my sceptre" [Psalms 60:7].

Gilead is mine, refers to Ahab, king of Israel, who died in Ramoth-Gilead; "and Menashe is mine," is to be taken literally; "Ephraim is the defence of mine

Pirkei DeRabbi Eliezer 17

head," refers to Jeroboam; "Yehuda is my sceptre," points to Ahithophel; "Moav is my washpot " [Psalms 60:8], means Gehazi; "upon Aram will I cast my shoe" [Psalms 60:8], refers to Doeg; "Philistia, shout thou because of me" [Psalms 60:8]. The Holy One, blessed be He, said: It is for Me to search for merit on their behalf, and to make them friendly towards one another.

Rebbi Pinchas said: Thirty years after Shaul and his sons had been killed, a famine lasting three years arose in the days of David, year after year, as it is said, "And there was a famine in the days of David three years, year after year" [Samuel-B 21:1]. Why was it year after year? In the first year all Israel went up to [celebrate the great] festivals. David said to them: Go and look if perchance there be among you some who worship idols, for because of the sin of idolatry rain is withheld, as it is said, "Take heed to yourselves, lest your heart be deceived, and ye turn aside, and serve other gods, and worship them" [Deuteronomy 11:16]. What is written after this? "And the anger of the Hashem will be kindled against you, and he will shut up the heaven, that there be no rain" [Deuteronomy 11:17]. They went forth and investigated, but did not find any idolatry.

In the second year all Israel went up to celebrate the festivals. David said to them: Go forth and see if there be among you people who lead immoral lives, because owing to the sin of immorality the heavens are closed, as it is said, "And thou hast polluted the land with thy whorArams" [Jeremiah 3:2]. What is

Pirkei DeRabbi Eliezer 17

written after this in this context? "Therefore, the showers have been withholden, and there hath been no latter rain" [Jeremiah 3:3]. They investigated, but they did not find any immoral people.

In the third year all Israel went up to celebrate the festivals. David said to them: Go forth and see if there be among you people who shed blood, because on account of the sin of those who murder the rain is withheld, as it is said, "So ye shall not pollute the land wherein ye are; for blood, it polluteth the land" [Numbers 35:33]. They went forth and investigated, but they did not find any murderer. David said to them: Henceforth the matter only depends upon me. David arose and prayed before the Holy One, blessed be He. And He answered him: It is for Shaul; was not Shaul one who was anointed with the oil of consecration? And was it not Shaul in whose days there was no idolatry in Israel? And was it not Shaul who secured his portion with Samuel the prophet? Yet ye are in the land of Israel and he is buried outside the land of Israel.

David forthwith arose and gathered together all the elders of Israel and the nobles, and they crossed the JorDaniel They came to Yavesh-Gilead and they found the bones of Shaul and Yehonaton his son. No worm had been able to touch them, as it is said, "He keepeth all his bones, not one of them is broken" [Psalms 34:20]. They took the bones of Shaul and Yehonaton his son, and placed them in a coffin, and they crossed the Jordan, as it is said, "And they buried the bones of Shaul and Yehonaton his son…

Pirkei DeRabbi Eliezer 17

and they performed all that the king commanded" [Samuel-B 21:14]. The king commanded that they should bring the coffin of Shaul in all the borders of each tribe. And it came to pass that the tribe wherein they brought the coffin of Shaul, the people there with their wives and their sons and their daughters came forth and displayed loving-kindness to Shaul and to his sons, so that all Israel should discharge their obligation of showing loving-kindness. And thus [did they do] until it came to the border of his possession to the border of Jerusalem, in the land of Binyamin in Jerusalem, as it is said, "And they buried the bones of Shaul and Yehonaton his son in the country of Binyamin" [Samuel-B 21:14], in the vicinity of Jerusalem. When the Holy One, blessed be He, saw that all Israel had displayed loving-kindness to him, He was forthwith full of compassion, and He sent rain upon the land, as it is said, "And after that God was intreated for the land" [Samuel-B 21:14].

Rebbi Natanel said: Three hundred years before the birth of Josiah, was his name mentioned, as it is said, "Behold, a child shall be born unto the house of David, Josiah by name" [Kings-A 13:2]; "And he was eight years old when he began to reign" [Kings-B 22:1]. What is the disposition of a lad of eight years of age? He despised the idols and broke in pieces the pillars, and smashed the images and cut down the groves. His merit was great before the Throne of Glory. Because of the evil which Israel did in secret the righteous one was gathered to his fathers, as it is said, "For the righteous is taken away because of the

Pirkei DeRabbi Eliezer 17

evil" [Isaiah 57:1]. All Yehuda gathered together also with Jeremiah the prophet to show loving-kindness to Josiah, as it is said, "And Jeremiah lamented for Josiah, and all the singing men and the singing women spake of Josiah" [Chronicles-B 35:25]. Rebbi Meir said: "The singing men" refer to the Levites, who stood upon the platform singing; "and the singing women" refer to their wives. Rebbi Shimon said: These terms do not refer merely to the Levites and their wives; but to the skilled women, as it is said, "Thus saith the Hashem of hosts, consider ye, and call for the mourning women, that they may come; and send for the cunning women, that they may come: and let them make haste, and take up a wailing for us" [Jeremiah 9:17, 18]. Hence the wise men instituted the rule that this should be done to all the wise men of Israel and to their great men, as it is said, "And they made them an ordinance in Israel" [Chronicles-B 35:25].

King Solomon saw that the observance of loving-kindness was great before the Holy One, blessed be He. When he built the Temple, he erected two gates, one for the bridegrooms, and the other for the mourners and the excommunicated. On Sabbaths the Israelites went and sat between those two gates; and they knew that anyone who entered through the gate of the bridegrooms was a bridegroom, and they said to him, May He who dwells in this house cause thee to rejoice with sons and daughters. If one entered through the gate of the mourners with his upper lip covered, then they knew that he was a mourner, and they would say to him. May He who dwells in this

Pirkei DeRabbi Eliezer 17

house comfort thee. If one entered through the gate of the mourners without having his upper lip covered, then they knew that he was excommunicated, and they would say to him, May He who dwells in this house put into thy heart the desire to listen to the words of thy associates, and may He put into the hearts of thy associates that they may draw thee near to themselves, so that all Israel may discharge their duty by rendering the service of loving-kindness.

When the Temple was destroyed, the sages instituted the rule that the bridegrooms and mourners should go to the synagogues and to the houses of study. The men of the place see the bridegroom and rejoice with him; and they see the mourner and sit with him upon the earth, so that all the Israelites may discharge their duty in the service of loving-kindness. With reference to them he says: Blessed art Thou, who giveth a good reward to those who show loving-kindness.

Chapter 18

The School of Shammai said: The heavens were created first, and the earth afterwards, as it is said, "In the beginning God created the heavens and the earth" [Genesis 1:1]. The School of Hillel said: The earth was created first, and the heavens afterwards, as it is said, "Of old hast thou laid the foundation of the earth; and the heavens are the work of thy hands" [Psalms 102:25]. The School of Shammai said: The heavens were created first, and the earth afterwards, as it is said, "These are the generations of the heavens and of the earth" [Genesis 2:4]. The School of Hillel said: The earth was created first, and the heavens afterwards, as it is said, "In the day that the Hashem God made earth and heaven" [Genesis 2:4]. The School of Shammai said: The heavens were created first, because it is said, "And the heavens and the earth were finished" [Genesis 2:1]. The School of Hillel said: The earth was created first, and the heavens afterwards, as it is said, "Yea, mine hand hath laid the foundation of the earth, and my right hand hath spread out the heavens" [Isaiah 48:18]. The School of Shammai said: The heavens were created first, and the earth afterwards, because it is said, "Thus saith the Hashem, the heaven is my throne, and the earth is my footstool" [Isaiah 66:1]. Contention arose between The Schools of Shammai and Hillel on this question, until the Holy Spirit rested between them, and they both agreed that both heavens and earth were created in one hour and at one moment.

Pirkei DeRabbi Eliezer 18

What did the Holy One, blessed be He, do? He put forth His right hand and stretched forth the heavens, and He put forth His left hand and founded the earth, as it is said, "Yea, mine hand hath laid the foundation of the earth, and my right hand hath spread out the heavens: when I called unto them, they stood up together " [Isaiah 48:13]. Both of them were created simultaneously, as it is said, "And the heavens and the earth were finished, and all their host" [Genesis 2:1]. And, indeed, were the heavens and the earth completed [so as not to require God's providence] for their continued existence and maintenance? Has it not been written concerning them, "Thus saith the Hashem The heaven is my throne, and the earth is my footstool" [Isaiah 66:1], But they were finished with reference to the original deed of creation and with reference to the work of being created and being called into existence. Therefore, it is said, "And the heavens and the earth were finished " [Genesis 2:1].

Yisrael spake before the Holy One, blessed be He: Sovereign of the worlds. Thou didst complete the heavens and the earth with reference to being made, created, and called into existence; let not Thy mercy and loving-kindness be withheld, for if Thou withholdest Thy mercy and loving-kindness we are unable to exist, because the world rests upon Thy mercy and loving-kindness, as it is said, "For the mountains shall depart, and the hills be removed; but my kindness shall not depart from thee… saith the Hashem that hath mercy on thee" [Isaiah 54:10]; and it says elsewhere, "Remember, O Hashem, thy tender

Pirkei DeRabbi Eliezer 18

mercies and thy loving-kindnesses; for they have been ever of old" [Psalms 25:6].

"**And** on the seventh day God finished his work" [Genesis 2:2]. The Holy One, blessed be He, created seven dedications, six of them He dedicated, and one is reserved for the future generations. He created the first day and finished all His work and dedicated it, as it is said, "And it was evening, and it was morning, one day" [Genesis 1:5]. He created the second day and finished all His work and dedicated it, as it is said, "And it was evening, and it was morning, a second day" [Genesis 1:8]; And so, through the six days of creation. He created the seventh day, but not for work, because it is not said in connection therewith, "And it was evening and it was morning." Why? For it is reserved for the generations to come, as it is said, "And there shall be one day which is known unto the Hashem; not day, and not night " [Zechariah 14:7].

A parable - To what is this matter to be compared? To a man who had precious utensils. And he did not desire to give them as an inheritance except to his son; likewise with the Holy One, blessed be He. The day of blessing and holiness which was before Him, He did not desire to give it as an inheritance except to Israel. Know that it is so. Come and see. for when the Israelites went forth from Egypt, whilst yet the Torah had not been given to them, He gave them the Sabbath as an inheritance. Israel kept two Sabbaths whilst as yet the Torah had not been given to them, as it is said, "And thou madest known unto them thy

Pirkei DeRabbi Eliezer 18

holy Sabbath" [Nehemiah 9:14]. And afterwards He gave them the Torah, as it is said, "And commandedst them commandments, and statutes, and Torah by the hand of Moshe, thy servant" [Nehemiah 9:14].

The Holy One, blessed be He, observed and sanctified the Sabbath, and Israel is obliged only to observe and sanctify the Sabbath. Know that it is so. Come and see. for when He gave them the Manna, He gave it to them in the wilderness during forty years on the six days of creation, but on the Sabbath, He did not give it to them. Wilt thou say that He did not have power enough to give it to them every day? But the fact was the Sabbath was before Him; therefore, He gave to them bread for two days on the Friday, as it is said, "See, for that the Hashem hath given you the Sabbath, therefore he giveth you on the sixth day the bread of two days" [Exodus 16:29]. When the people saw that Sabbath was observed before Him, they also rested, as it is said, "So the people rested on the seventh day" [Exodus 16:30].

"**And** God blessed the seventh day, and hallowed it" [Genesis 2:3]. The Holy One, blessed be He, blessed and hallowed the Sabbath day, and Israel is bound only to keep and to hallow the Sabbath day. Hence, they said: Whosoever says the benediction and sanctification over the wine on the eves of Sabbath, his days will be increased in this world, and in the world to come, For by me thy days shall be multiplied, in this world; "And the years of thy life

Pirkei DeRabbi Eliezer   18

shall be increased" [Proverbs 9:11] in the world to come.

"**Ye** shall keep the Sabbath, for it is holy unto you" [Exodus 31:14]. What is the keeping of the Sabbath? Neither to do any work thereon, nor to kindle fire thereon, neither to take forth nor to bring in beyond the **Techum** [A distance that a Jew can get out of the city] of the Sabbath even one foot, nor to fetch in his hand something which is not his food nor the food for his cattle. This is the keeping of the Sabbath, as it is said, "Wherefore the children of Israel shall keep the Sabbath" [Exodus 31:16].

"**It** is a sign between me and the children of Israel for ever" [Exodus 31:17]. The Holy One, blessed be He, said: This Sabbath have I given to Israel as a sign between Me and them; for in the six days of creation I fashioned all the world, and on the Sabbath I rested, therefore have I given to Israel the six days of work, and on the Sabbath, a day for blessing and sanctification, for Me and for them; therefore it is said, "Between me and the children of Israel it is a sign for ever" [Exodus 31:17].

The Holy One, blessed be He, created seven firmaments, and He selected from them all **ARavoth** only for the place of the throne of glory of His kingdom, as it is said, "Cast up a highway for him that rideth on the ARavoth, with B-Yh, his name" [Psalms 68:4]. The Holy One, blessed be He, created seven lands, and He chose from all of them the land of Israel only, as it is said, "A land… the eyes of the

Pirkei DeRabbi Eliezer 18

Hashem thy God are always upon it, from the beginning of the year even unto the end of the year" [Deuteronomy 11:12]. Another verse says, "I said, I shall not see the Hashem, even the Hashem in the land of the living" [Isaiah 38:11]. The Holy One, blessed be He, created seven deserts, and of them all He chose the desert of Sinai only to give therein the Torah, as it is said, "The mountain which God hath desired for his abode" [Psalms 68:16].

The Holy One, blessed be He, created seven seas, and of them all He chose the Sea of Kinnereth only, and gave it as an inheritance to the tribe of Naphtali, as it is said, "O Naphtali, satisfied with favour, and full with the blessing of the Hashem possess thou the sea and the south" [Deuteronomy 33:23].

The Holy One, blessed be He, created seven deserts, and of them all He chose the seventh on only; the six deserts are for the going in and coming out of God's creatures for war and peace.

Seven worlds were created by the Holy One, Blessed be He, and from all of them He chose only a seventh world. Six to go out and come and one that is all Sabbath and rest for **OLAM HABA** [World to come].

The Holy One, blessed be He, created seven days, and of them all He chose the seventh day only, as it is said, "And God blessed the seventh day, and

Pirkei DeRabbi Eliezer 18

hallowed it" [Genesis 2:3].

For seven years the Holy One, Blessed be He, created, and from them he chose nothing but the **Shmita** [a sabbatical year].

Everyone who keeps the Sabbath, happy is he in this world and happy will he be in the world to come, as it is said, "Happy is the man that doeth this, and the son of man that holdeth fast by it: who keepeth the Sabbath from profaning it" [Isaiah 56:2]. Do not read - He who keepeth the Sabbath] from profaning it, but read - He who keepeth the Sabbath is pardoned, concerning all his transgression.

Chapter 19

Ten things were created on the eve of the Sabbath, in the twilight [The time that is doubtful day doubtful night, from sunset to sunset until it gets really dark and the stars come out]: The mouth of the earth; The mouth of the well; The mouth of the She-Ass; The rainbow; The Manna [The food that the children of Israel ate during their wanderings in the desert, and according to the narrator in the Torah, would come down from heaven to them every day]; The Shamir; The shape of the alphabet; The writing and the tables of the law [the Ten Commandments]. Some sages say: the destroying spirits also, And the sepulchre of Moshe, and the ram of Yitzhak. And other sages say: the tongs also.

At the seventh hour on the day on first Friday, the first man entered the garden of Eden, and the ministering angels were praising before him, and dancing before him, and escorting him into the garden of Eden; and at twilight at the eve of Sabbath, he was driven forth, and he went out. The ministering angels were crying aloud concerning him, saying to him: "Man in glory tarrieth not overnight, when he is like the beasts that pass away" [Psalms 49:13].

The Sabbath day arrived and became an advocate for the first man, and it spake before Him: Sovereign of all worlds. No murderer has been slain in the world during the six days of creation, and wilt Thou

Pirkei DeRabbi Eliezer 19

commence to do this with me? Is this its sanctity, and is this its blessing? as it is said, "And God blessed the seventh day, and hallowed it" [Genesis 2:8]. By the merit of the Sabbath day Adam was saved from the judgment of Gehinnom. When Adam perceived the power of the Sabbath, he said: Not for nought did the Holy One, blessed be He, bless and hallow the Sabbath day. He began to observe [the Sabbath] and to utter a psalm for the Sabbath day, and he said: "A psalm, a song for the Sabbath day" [Psalms 92:1]. Rebbi Shimon said: The first man said this psalm, and it was forgotten throughout all the generations until Moshe came and renewed it according to his name, "A psalm, a song for the Sabbath day" [Psalms 92:1], for the day which is entirely Sabbath and rest in the life of eternity.

"**It** is good to confess to the Hashem" [Psalms 92:2]. The first man said: Let all the generations learn from me, that whosoever sings and utters psalms to the name of the Most-High, and confesses his transgressions in the court of justice and abandons them, will be delivered from the judgment of Gehinnom, as it is said, "It is good to confess to the Hashem" [Psalms 92:2].

"**To** declare thy loving-kindness in the morning" [Psalms 92:3]. Adam said: This refers to, all who enter this world which is like unto the night; and to all who come into the world to come, which is like unto the morning. They shall declare the faithfulness and love of the Holy One, blessed be He, which He has shown to me, for He has delivered me from the

Pirkei DeRabbi Eliezer 19

judgment of Gehinnom, as it is said, "To declare thy loving-kindness in the morning, and thy faithfulness every night" [Psalms 92:3].

"**Upon** a ten-stringed instrument and upon the psaltery" [Psalms 92:4]. All testimonies reliable to Israel are celebrated with ten males. The harp upon which David played had ten strings. The testimony for the dead is through ten males. The testimony for the public benediction of God's Name is through ten males. The testimony of the covenant of circumcision is through ten males. The testimony for Chalizah [under the Torah system of levirate marriage known as Yibbum, the process by which a childless widow and a brother of her deceased husband may avoid the duty to marry. The process involves the widow making a declaration, taking off a shoe of the brother, and spitting on the floor] Testimony of marriage blessing is through ten males, as it is said, "And he took ten men of the elders of the city" [Ruth 4:2].

The Holy One, blessed be He, said: I desire of Israel the meditation of their mouths like the psaltery and an instrument of ten strings, as it is said, "With the meditation of the harp" [Psalms 92:4].

"**For** thou, O Hashem, hast made me glad through thy work" [Psalms 92:5]. Adam said: The Holy One, blessed be He, had made me glad and brought me into the garden of Eden, and showed me the place of the abode of the righteous in the garden of Eden, and He showed me the four kingdoms, their rule and

Pirkei DeRabbi Eliezer 19

their destruction; and He showed me David, the son of Jesse, and his dominion in the future that is to come. I took from my years seventy years and added them to his days, as it is said, "Thou wilt add days to the days of the king; his years shall be as many generations" [Psalms 61:7]. I have given to God praise, and song lauding His works, as it is said, "I will sing of the works of thy hands" [Psalms 92:5].

"**How** great are thy works, O Hashem." [Psalms 92:6]. Adam began to glorify and to praise the Name of the Most-High, as it is said, "How great are thy works, O Hashem." [Psalms 92:6] but Thy thoughts are very deep, like the great deep exceedingly deep, as it is said, "Thy thoughts are very deep" [Psalms 92:6]. "A brutish man knoweth not" [Psalms 92:7]. Every man of Israel who is brutish in knowledge and has not learnt understanding, let the wise men of Israel teach him the ways of the Torah, as it is said, "Consider, ye brutish among the people" [Psalms 94:8]. But a man who is an expert among the nations of the world is still foolish. Why? For he knoweth not the words of the Torah, as it is said, "Neither doth a fool understand this " [Psalms 92:7].

"**When** the wicked spring up as the grass" [Psalms 92:8]. True it is that Thou, O Hashem, beholdest the wicked, that they are as numerous as the grass to cover the face of all the earth, and all the worshippers of idols flourish, thou knowest that they and their works are an evil iniquity for the days of the Mashiach. The Holy One, blessed be He, has only multiplied them in order to destroy them from this world and from the world to come, as it is said, "To have them destroyed for ever and ever [Psalms 92:8]. And thou, O Hashem, art on high for evermore" [Psalms 92:9]. King David saw that the wicked increased like grass, so as to cover the face of all the earth, and that all the worshippers of idols flourished, and that they and their works were iniquity, and he did not say **Hallelujah** [praise ye the Hashem] until he perceived that in the future they would be destroyed from this world and from the world to come; and he said **Hallelujah**, as it is said, "Sinners shall be consumed out of the earth, and the wicked shall be no more. Bless the Hashem, O my soul. Praise ye the Hashem " [Psalms 104:35]. Then will He be King exalted in the heights and in the depths, as it is said, "And thou, O Hashem, art on high for evermore" [Psalms 92:9].

"**For**, lo, thine enemies, O Hashem" [Psalms 92:10]; Israel said: Sovereign of all worlds. Thou hast placed all our enemies over us to afflict us with a heavy yoke on our backs, but we know that they are doomed to destruction, as it is said, "O Hashem, for, lo, thine enemies shall perish" [Psalms 92:10]. And all idolaters, for they and their works are iniquity, shall be scattered like chaff before the wind. That was said, "All evildoers are scattered" [Psalms 92:10].

"**But** my horn hast thou exalted like that of the reem" [Psalms 92:11]. Just as the horns of the reem are taller than those of all beasts and animals, and it gores to its right and to its left, likewise is it with Menachem, son of Ammiel, son of Yosef, his horns are taller

Pirkei DeRabbi Eliezer 19

than those of all kings, and he will gore in the future towards the four corners of the heavens, and concerning him Moshe said this verse, "His firstling bullock, majesty is his, and his horns are the horns of the reem: with them he shall gore the peoples all of them, even the ends of the earth" [Deuteronomy 33:17]. All the kings will rise up against him to slay him, as it is said, "The kings of the earth set themselves, and the rulers" [Psalms 2:2]. And Israel who will be in the Land of Palestine, will experience great trouble, but in their troubles, they will be like a green olive, as it is said, "I am anointed with fresh oil" [Psalms 92:11].

"**Mine** eyes have looked on mine enemies" [Psalms 92:12]. The Israelites in the Land of Israel behold the downfall of their enemies, as it is said, "Mine eyes have looked on mine enemies" [Psalms 92:12]. And such who in the future will come against them [Yisrael], their ears shall hear of their destruction, as it is said, "Mine ears have heard concerning the evil-doers that rise up against me" [Psalms 92:12].

"**The** righteous shall flourish like the palm tree" [Psalms 92:13]. Just as this palm tree is beautiful in all its appearance, and all its fruits are sweet and good, likewise the son of David [The Mashiach] is beautiful in his appearance and in his glory, and all his deeds are good and sweet before the Holy One, blessed be He, as it is said, "The righteous shall flourish like the palm tree he shall grow like a cedar in Lebanon" [Psalms 92:13]. Just as this cedar has very many roots beneath the earth, and even if the four

Pirkei DeRabbi Eliezer 19

winds of the world came against it, they could not move it from its place, as it is said, "He shall grow like a cedar in Lebanon. They that are planted in the house of the Hashem" [Psalms 92:13]. In the future when the Holy One, blessed be He, will gather Israel from the four corners of the world, just like this gardener who transplants his fir trees from one garden-bed to another garden-bed, likewise in the future will the Holy One, blessed be He, gather them from an impure land and plant them in a pure land, as it is said, "They that are planted in the house of the Hashem" [Psalms 92:14]. Like this grass, they shall blossom and sprout forth in the Temple, as it is said, "In the courts of our God they shall flourish" [Psalms 92:14].

"**They** shall still bring forth fruit in old age" [Psalms 92:15]. Just as this old age is glory and honour to old men, so shall they be in glory and honour before the Holy One, blessed be He, as it is said, "They shall be full of sap and green" [Psalms 92:15]. These are the mighty heroes by reason of their good deeds, as it is said, "They shall be full of sap and green, to declare that the Hashem is upright" [Psalms 92:15]. Why all these statements? To declare, and to proclaim clearly the works of the Holy One, blessed be He, for He is righteous and upright, and that there is no unrighteousness in Him, as it is said, "And there is no unrighteousness in him" [Psalms 92:16].

Chapter 20

"**So**, he drove out the man" [Genesis 3:24]. Driving out and he went forth outside the garden of Eden, and he abode on Mount Moriah [The Temple Mount], for the gate of the garden of Eden is nigh unto Mount Moriah. Thence He took him and thither He made him return to the place whence he was taken, as it is said, "To till the ground from whence he was taken" [Genesis 3:23].

Rebbi Yehuda said: The Holy One, blessed be He, kept the Sabbath first in the heavenly regions, and Adam kept the Sabbath first in the lower regions. The Sabbath day protected him from all evil, and comforted him on account of all the doubts of his heart, as it is said, "In the multitude of my doubts within me, thy comforts delight my soul" [Psalms 94:19].

Rebbi Yehoshua ben Karha said: From the tree under which they hid themselves, they took leaves and sewed them, as it is said, "And they sewed fig leaves together, and made themselves aprons" [Genesis 3:7]. Rebbi Eliezer said: From the skin which the serpent sloughed off, the Holy One, blessed be He, took and made coats of glory for Adam and his wife, as it is said, "And the Hashem God made for Adam and for his wife coats of skin, and clothed them" [Genesis 3:21].

At twilight on Saturday evening, Adam was

Pirkei DeRabbi Eliezer 20

meditating in his heart and saying: Perhaps the serpent, which deceived me, will come in the evening, and he will bruise me in the heel. A pillar of fire was sent to him to give illumination about him and to guard him from all evil. Adam saw the pillar of fire and rejoiced in his heart, and he put forth his hands to the light of the fire, and said: Blessed art Thou, O Hashem our God, King of the universe, who creates the flames of fire. And when he removed his hands from the light of the fire, he said: Now I know that the holy day has been separated from the work day here below [on earth], for fire may not be kindled on the Sabbath day; and in that hour he said: Blessed art Thou, O Hashem our God, King of the universe, who divides the holy from the profane, the light from the darkness.

Rebbi Mana said: How must a man say the Habdalah blessing? He does this over the cup of wine, with the light of fire, and he says: Blessed art Thou, O Hashem our God, King of the universe, who creates the various flames of fire; and when he removes his hand from the fire [flame] he says: Blessed art Thou, O Hashem, who divides the holy from the profane.

If he has no wine, he puts forth his hands towards the light of the lamp and looks at his nails, which are whiter than his body, and he says: Blessed art Thou, O Hashem our God, King of the universe, who creates various flames of fire; and when he has removed his hands from the fire, he says: Blessed art

Pirkei DeRabbi Eliezer 20

Thou, O Hashem, who divides the holy from the profane.

And if he has no fire, he puts forth his hand to the light of the stars, which are also fire, and says: Blessed art Thou, O Hashem our God, King of the universe, who creates the various flames of fire. If the heavens be darkened, he lifts up a stone outside, and says: Blessed art Thou, O Hashem our God, who creates the various flames of fire.

Rebbi Zadok said: Whosoever does not make Habdalah at the termination of Sabbaths, or does not listen to those who perform the ceremony of Habdalah, will never see a sign of blessing. Everyone who makes Habdalah at the termination of Sabbaths, or whosoever hears those who perform the Habdalah, the Holy One, blessed be He, calls him holy to be His holy treasure, and delivers him from the affliction of the peoples, as it is said, "And ye shall be holy unto me: for I the Hashem am holy" [Leviticus 20:26]. "You shall be My treasured possession among all the peoples" [Exodus 19:5].

On the first day of the week [Sunday], he went into the waters of the upper to the river of the **Gihon** until the waters reached up to his neck, and he fasted seven weeks of days, until his body became like a species of seaweed. Adam said before the Holy One, blessed be He: Sovereign of all worlds. Remove, I pray Thee, my sins from me and accept my repentance, and all the generations will learn that repentance is a reality. What did the Holy One,

Pirkei DeRabbi Eliezer 20

blessed be He, do? He put forth His right hand, and accepted his repentance, and took away from him his sin, as it is said, "I acknowledge my sin unto thee, and mine iniquity have I not hid: I said, I will confess my transgressions unto the Hashem; and thou forgavest the iniquity of my sin. Selah" [Psalms 32:5]. Selah in this world and Selah in the world to come. Adam returned and meditated in his heart, and said: I know that death will remove me to "the house appointed for all living" [Job 30:28]. Adam said: Whilst I am yet alive, I will build for myself a mausoleum to rest therein. He planned and built for himself a mausoleum to rest therein beyond Mount Moriah. Adam said: If in the case of the tables [of stone, just because in the future they will be written by the finger of God, the waters of the Jordan are destined to flee before them; how much more so will this be the case with my body which His two hands kneaded, and because He breathed into my nostrils the breath of the spirit of His mouth? After my death they will come and take my bones, and they will make them into an image for idolatry; but verily I will put my coffin deep down beneath the cave and within the cave. Therefore, it is called the Cave of Machpelah, which is a double cave. There Adam was put and his help-meet, Avraham and his help-meet, Yitzhak and his help-meet, Yaakov and his help-meet. Therefore, it is called **Kiryat Arba** [The city of four]; for four pairs were buried there, and concerning them the verse says, "He entereth into peace; they rest in their beds, each one that walketh in his up-rightness" [Isaiah 57:2].

Chapter 21

It is written - "But of the fruit of the tree which is in the midst of the garden" [Genesis 3:3]. It was taught in a Baraitha, Rebbi Ze'era said: "Of the fruit of the tree" - here "tree" only means man, who is compared to the tree, as it is said, "For man is the tree of the field" [Deuteronomy 20:19]. "Which is in the midst of the garden" - "in the midst of the garden" is here merely a euphemism. "Which is in the midst of the garden" - for "garden" means here merely woman, who is compared to a garden, as it is said, "A garden shut up is my sister, a bride" [Song of Songs 4:12]. Just as with this garden whatever is sown therein, it produces and brings forth, so with this woman, what seed she receives, she conceives and bears through sexual intercourse.

Sammae"l [The angel of death] riding on the serpent came to her, and she conceived; afterwards Adam came to her, and she conceived Abel, as it is said, "And Adam knew Eve his wife" [Genesis 4:1]. What is the meaning of "knew"? [He knew] that she had conceived. And she saw his likeness that it was not of the earthly beings, but of the heavenly beings, and she prophesied and said: "I have gotten a man with the Hashem" [Genesis 4:1].

Rebbi Yishmael says from there all the generations of the wicked, the rebels, and the criminals ascended to heaven, and says - we do not need a drop of your rains, which is said - [Job 21:14] and they will say to the Lord from him.

Rebbi Miasha said: Cain was born, and his wife, his twin-sister, with him. Rebbi Shimon said to him: Has it not already been said, "And if a man shall take his sister, his father's daughter, or his mother's daughter, and see her nakedness, and she see his nakedness; it is a shameful thing"? [Leviticus 20:17]. From these words know that there were no other women whom they could marry, and these were permitted to them, as it is said, "For I have said, The world shall be built up by love" [Psalms 89:2]. With love was the world built up before the Torah had been given. Rebbi Yosef said: Cain and Abel were twins, as it is said, "And she conceived, and bare with Cain" [Genesis 4:1]. At that hour she had an additional capacity for child-bearing as it is said, "And she continued to bear his brother Abel" [Genesis 4:2].

Now Cain was a man who loved the ground in order to sow seed; and Abel was a man who loved to tend the sheep; the one gave of his produce as food for the other, and the latter gave of his produce as food for his brother. The evening of the festival of Passover arrived. Adam called his sons and said to them: In this night in the future Israel will bring Paschal offerings, bring ye also offerings before your Creator.

Cain brought the remnants of his meal of roasted grain, and the seed of flax. And Abel brought of the firstlings of his sheep, and of their fat, he-lambs,

Pirkei DeRabbi Eliezer 21

which had not been shorn of their wool. The offering of Cain was precluded, and the offering of Abel was acceptable, as it is said, "And the Hashem had respect unto Abel and to his offering" [Genesis 4:4].

Rebbi Yehoshua ben Karha said: The Holy One, blessed be He, said: Heaven forbid. Never let the offerings of Cain and Abel be mixed up with one another, even in the weaving of a garment, as it is said, "Thou shalt not wear a mingled stuff, wool and linen together" [Deuteronomy 22:11]. And even if it be combined let it not come upon thee, as it is said, "Neither shall there come upon thee a garment of two kinds of stuff mingled together" [Leviticus 19:19].

Rebbi Zadok said: A great hatred entered Cain's heart against his brother Abel, because his offering had been accepted. Not only on this account, but also because Abel's twin-sister was the most beautiful of women, and he desired her in his heart. Moreover, he said: I will slay Abel my brother, and I will take his twin-sister from him, as it is said, "And it came to pass when they were in the field" [Genesis 4:8]. **In the field** means woman, who is compared to a field.

Cain took the stone and embedded it in the forehead of Abel, and slew him, as it is said, "And Cain rose up against Abel his brother, and slew him" [Genesis 4:8].

Rabban Yohanan ben Zakkai said: Cain did not know that the secrets are revealed before the Holy

Pirkei DeRabbi Eliezer 21

One, blessed be He. He took the corpse of his brother Abel and hid it in the field. The Holy One, blessed be He, said to him: "Where is Abel thy brother?" [Genesis 4:9]. He replied to Him: Sovereign of the world. A keeper of vineyard and field hast Thou made me. A keeper of my brother Thou hast not made me; as it is said, "Am I my brother's keeper?" [Genesis 4:9]. The Holy One, blessed be He, said to him: "Hast thou killed, and also taken possession?" [Kings-A 21:19]. "The voice of thy brother's blood crieth unto me from the ground" [Genesis 4:10]. When Cain heard this word, he was confused. And He cursed him, that he became a wanderer on the earth because of the shedding of the blood, and because of the evil death.

Cain spake before the Holy One, blessed be He: Sovereign of all the worlds. "My sin is too great to be borne" [Genesis 4:13], for it has no atonement. This utterance was reckoned to him as repentance, as it is said, "And Cain said unto the Hashem, My sin is too great to be borne" [Genesis 4:13]; further, Cain said before the Holy One, blessed be He: Now will a certain righteous one arise on the earth and mention Thy great Name against me and slay me. What did the Holy One, blessed be He, do? He took one letter from the twenty-two letters, and put [it] upon Cain's arm that he should not be killed, as it is said, "And the Hashem appointed a sign for Cain" [Genesis 4:15]. The dog which was guarding Abel's flock also guarded his corpse from all the beasts of the field and all the fowl of the heavens. Adam and his helpmate were sitting and weeping and mourning

Pirkei DeRabbi Eliezer 21

for him, and they did not know what to do with Abel, for they were unaccustomed to burial. A raven came, one of its fellow birds was dead at its side. The raven said: I will teach this man what to do. It took its fellow and dug in the earth, hid it and buried it before them. Adam said: Like this raven will I act. He took the corpse of Abel and dug in the earth and buried it. The Holy One, blessed be He, gave a good reward to the ravens in this world. What reward did He give them? When they bear their young and see that they are white they fly from them, thinking that they are the offspring of a serpent, and the Holy One, blessed be He, gives them their sustenance without lack, as it is said, "Who provideth for the raven his food, when his young ones cry unto God, and wander for lack of meat" [Job 38:41]. Moreover, that rain should be given upon the earth for their sakes, and the Holy One, blessed be He, answers them, as it is said, "He giveth to the beast his food, and to the young ravens which cry" [Psalms 147:9].

Chapter 22

It is said: "And Adam lived an hundred and thirty years, and he begat in his own likeness after his image" [Genesis 5:3]. Hence, thou mayest learn that Cain was not of Adam's seed, nor after his likeness, nor after his image. Adam did not beget in his own image, until **Seth** was born, who was after his father Adam's likeness and image, as it is said, "And he begat in his own likeness, after his image" [Genesis 5:3].

Rebbi Shimon said: From Seth arose and were descended all the generations of the righteous. From Cain arose and were descended all the generations of the wicked, who rebel and sin, who rebelled against their Rock, and they said: We do not need the drops of Thy rain, neither to walk in Thy ways, as it is said, "Yet they said unto God, Depart from us" [Job 21:14].

Rebbi Meir said: The generations of Cain went about stark naked, men and women, just like the beasts, and they defiled themselves with all kinds of immorality, a man with his mother or his daughter, or the wife of his brother, or the wife of his neighbour, in public and in the streets, with evil inclination which is in the thought of their heart, as it is said, "And the Hashem saw that the wickedness of man was great in the earth" [Genesis 6:5].

Rebbi said: The angels who fell from their holy

place in heaven saw the daughters of the generations of Cain walking about naked, with their eyes painted like harlots, and they went astray after them, and took wives from amongst them, as it is said, "And the sons of Elohim saw the daughters of men that they were fair; and they took them wives of all that they chose" [Genesis 6:2].

Rebbi Yehoshua said: The angels are flaming fire, as it is said, "His servants are a flaming fire" [Psalms 104:4], and fire came with the coition of flesh and blood, but did not burn the body; but when they fell from heaven, from their holy place, their strength and stature became like that of the sons of men, and their frame was made of clods of dust, as it is said, "My flesh is clothed with worms and clods of dust" [Job 7:5].

Rebbi Zadok said: From them were born the **Anakim** [giants], who walked with pride in their heart, and who stretched forth their hand to all kinds of robbery and violence, and shedding of blood, as it is said, "And there we saw the Nephilim, the sons of Anak" [Numbers 13:33]; and it says, "The Nephilim were on the earth in those days" [Genesis 6:4].

Rebbi Yehoshua said: The Israelites are called "Sons of God," as it is said, "Ye are the sons of the Hashem your God" [Deuteronomy 14:1]. The angels are called **Sons of God**, as it is said, "When the morning stars sang together, and all the sons of God shouted for joy" [Job 38:7]; and whilst they were still in their holy place in heaven, these were called "Sons of

God," as it is said, "And also after that, when the sons of God came in unto the daughters of men, and they bare children to them; the same became the mighty men, which were of old, men of renown" [Genesis 6:4].

Rebbi Levi said: They bare their sons and increased and multiplied like a great reptile, six children at each birth. In that very hour they stood on their feet, and spoke the holy language, and danced before them like sheep, as it is said, "They cast their young like sheep, and their children danced" [Job 21:11].

Noah said to them: Turn from your ways and evil deeds, so that He bring not upon you the waters of the Flood, and destroy all the seed of the children of men. They said to him: Behold, we will restrain ourselves from multiplying and increasing, so as not to produce the offspring of the children of men. What did they do? When they came to their wives, they spilled the issue of their seed upon the earth so as not to produce offspring of the children of men, as it is said, "And God saw the earth, and behold it was spilled" [Genesis 6:12]. They said: If He bring from heaven the waters of the Flood upon us, behold, we are of high stature, and the waters will not reach up to our necks; and if He bring the waters of the depths against us, behold, the soles of our feet can close up all the depths. What did they do? They put forth the soles of their feet, and closed up all the depths. What did the Holy One, blessed be He, do? He heated the waters of the deep, and they arose and burnt their flesh, and peeled off their skin from

Pirkei DeRabbi Eliezer 22

them, as it is said, "What time they wax warm, they vanish; when it is hot, they are consumed out of their place" [Job 6:17]. Do not read thus "When it is hot, בְּזֻמָּם" but read "in his hot waters" בְּחַמֵּיבָמָיו.

Chapter 23

It is said: "And this is how thou shalt make the ark" [Genesis 6:15]. Rebbi Shemiah taught: The Holy One, blessed be He, showed Noah with a finger and said to him, like this and that shalt thou do to the ark. One hundred and fifty rooms were along the length at the left side of the ark, thirty-three rooms across the width in the side within, and thirty-three rooms in the side across the width on the outside; and ten compartments in the centre, which were for the storerooms for the food. And there were five protected cisterns on the right side of the ark, and fifty protected cisterns on the left side of the ark, and the openings for the water pipes opened and closed, and so was it in the lowest division; and so, on the second floor, and so on the third floor.

The dwelling-place of all the cattle and animals was in the lowest compartment, the dwelling-place for all fowl was in the second compartment, and the dwelling-place for the reptiles and the human beings was in the third compartment. Hence, thou mayest learn that there were 365 kinds of cattle on the earth, and 365 kinds of fowl on the earth, and 365 kinds of reptiles on the earth, for thus was the number in the lowest compartment, so in the second compartment, and so in the third floor, as it is said, "With lower, second, and third stories shalt thou make it" [Genesis 6:16].

Rebbi Tachanah said: Noah made the ark during

Pirkei DeRabbi Eliezer 23

fifty-two years, so that they should repent of their ways. But they did not repent. Whilst yet the Flood had not come, the **Unclean animals** [Not Kosher] were more numerous than the **Clean animals** [Kosher]. But when the waters of the Flood came, and the Holy One, blessed be He, wished to increase the clean and to diminish the unclean animals, He called to Noah and said to him: Take to thee into the ark of all clean beasts seven and seven, the male and his female; and of the unclean beasts two and two, the male and his female, as it is said, "Of every clean beast thou shalt take to thee seven and seven, the male and his female; and of the beasts that are not clean two, the male and his female" [Genesis 7:2].

Noah said to the Holy One, blessed be He: Sovereign of all the world. Have I then the strength to collect them unto me to the ark? The angels appointed over each kind went down and gathered them, and with them all their food unto him to the ark. They came to him of their own accord, as it is said, "And they came unto Noah into the ark" [Genesis 7:9]; they came by themselves. "And they brought them to Noah" is not written here, but, "And they came unto Noah into the ark."

Rebbi Mana said: When all the creatures had entered to the ark, the Holy One, blessed be He, closed and sealed with His hand the gate of the ark, as it is said, "And the Hashem shut him in" [Genesis 7:16].

One pearl was suspended in the ark, and shed light

upon all the creatures in the ark, like a lamp which gives light inside the house, and like the sun yonder which shines in his might, as it is said, "A light shalt thou make to the ark" [Genesis 6:16].

Rebbi Zadok said: On the 10th of the month of Marcheshvan all the creatures entered the ark; on the 17th month of Marcheshvan the waters of the Flood descended from heaven upon the earth, for they were the waters endowed with the male principle. And there came up the waters of the depths, for they are the waters endowed with the female principle, and they were joined with one another, and they prevailed so as to destroy the world, as it is said, "And the waters prevailed exceedingly upon the earth" [Genesis 7:19].

And all living things which were upon the face of the earth decayed, as it is said, "And every living thing was destroyed which was upon the face of the ground" [Genesis 7:23], except Noah and those who were with him in the ark, as it is said, "And Noah only was left, and they that were with him in the ark" [Genesis 7:23], except **Og**, king of Bashan, who sat down on a piece of wood under the gutter of the ark. He swore to Noah and to his sons that he would be their servant for ever. What did Noah do? He bored an aperture in the ark, and he put through it his food daily for him, and he also was left, as it is said, "For only Og, king of Bashan, remained of the remnant of the giants" [Deuteronomy 3:11]. The Flood was universal except in the land of Israel, upon which the water of the Flood did not descend from heaven, but

Pirkei DeRabbi Eliezer 23

the waters were gathered together from all lands, and they entered therein, as it is said, "Son of man, say unto her, thou art a land that is not cleansed, nor rained upon, in the day of indignation" [Ezekiel 22:24].

He sent forth the raven to ascertain what was the state of the world. It went and found a carcase of a man cast upon the summit of a mountain, and it settled thereon for its food, and it did not return with its message to its sender, as it is said, "And he sent forth the raven" [Genesis 8:7]. He sent forth the dove to see what was the state of the world, and she brought back her message to her sender, as it is said, "And the dove came in to him at eventide, and, lo, in her mouth an olive leaf pluckt off" [Genesis 8:11]. And why in her mouth was an olive leaf pluckt off? The dove spake before the Holy One, blessed be He, saying: Sovereign of all worlds. Let my food be bitter like this olive, and let it be entrusted to Thy hand, and let it not be sweet even as honey, and given by the hand of flesh and blood. Hence, they said: He who sends a message by the hand of an unclean messenger is like sending by the hand of a fool, and he who sends a message by the hands of a clean messenger is like sending by the hand of a messenger faithful to his senders.

Rebbi Zadok said: For twelve months all the creatures were in the ark; and Noah stood and prayed before the Holy One, blessed be He, saying before Him: Sovereign of all worlds. Bring me forth from this prison, for my soul is faint, because of the stench of lions. Through me will all the righteous crown Thee with a crown of sovereignty, because Thou hast brought me forth from this prison, as it is said, "Bring my soul out of prison, that I may give thanks unto thy name: for the righteous shall crown me, when thou wilt have dealt bountifully with me" [Psalms 142:8].

Rebbi Levitas, a man of Jamnia, said: He separated the males from the females of all which came to the ark when they came into the ark, as it is said, "And Noah went in, and his sons, and his wife, and his sons' wives" [Genesis 7:7]. Verily the males were on one side. When they went forth from the ark, He caused the males to be joined with the females, as it is said, "Go forth of the ark, thou, and thy wife, and thy sons, and thy sons' wives with thee" [Genesis 8:16]. Verily a man with his wife went forth, "Thy sons, and thy sons' wives with thee" [Genesis 7:7] He blessed them, that they might increase and multiply on the earth, as it is said, "And God blessed Noah and his sons, and said unto them, Be fruitful, and multiply, and replenish the earth" [Genesis 9:1]. The sons of Noah were fruitful and multiplied, and they begat sons with their twins with them.

Noah found a vine which was lying there, which had come out of the garden of Eden. It had its clusters with it, and he took of its fruit and ate, and rejoiced in his heart, as it is said, "My wine, which cheereth God and man" [Judges 9:13]. He planted a vineyard with it. On the selfsame day it produced and became ripe with its fruits, as it is said, "In the day of thy planting thou dost make it grow, and in the morning

Pirkei DeRabbi Eliezer 23

thou makest thy seed to blossom" [Isaiah 17:11]. He drank wine thereof, and he became exposed in the midst of the tent, as it is said, "And he drank of the wine, and was drunken; and he was uncovered within his tent" [Genesis 9:21]. Canaan entered and saw the nakedness of Noah, and he bound a thread where the mark of the Covenant was, and emasculated him. He went forth and told his brethren. Ham entered and saw his nakedness. He did not take to heart the duty of honouring [one's father]. But he told his two brothers in the market, making sport of his father. His two brothers rebuked him. What did they do? They took the curtain of the east with them, and they went backwards and covered the nakedness of their father, as it is said, "And Shem and Japheth took a garment, and laid it upon both their shoulders, and went backward, and covered the nakedness of their father; and their faces were backward, and they saw not their father's nakedness" [Genesis 9:23].

Noah awoke from his wine, and he knew what the younger son of Ham had done unto him, and he cursed him, as it is said, "And he said, cursed be Canaan" [Genesis 9:24]. Noah sat and mused in his heart, saying: The Holy One, blessed be He, delivered me from the waters of the Flood, and brought me forth from that prison, and am I not obliged to bring before Thee a sacrifice and burnt offerings? What did Noah do? He took from the clean animals an ox and a sheep, and from all the clean birds, a turtle-dove and pigeons; and he built up the first altar upon which Cain and Abel had brought offerings, and he brought four burnt offerings, as it is said, "And Noah built an altar unto the Hashem; and took of every clean beast, and of every clean fowl, and he offered burnt offerings on the altar" [Genesis 8:20]. It is written here only, "and he offered burnt offerings on the altar," and the sweet savour ascended before the Holy One, blessed be He, and it was pleasing to Him, as it is said, "And the Hashem smelled the sweet savour" [Genesis 8:21]. What did the Holy One, blessed be He, do? He put forth His right hand, and swore to Noah that He would not bring the waters of the Flood upon the earth, as it is said, "For this is as the waters of Noah unto me; for as I have sworn that the waters of Noah should no-more go over the earth" [Isaiah 54:9]. And He gave a sign in the rainbow as a sign of the covenant of the oath between Himself and the people, as it is said, "I do set my bow in the cloud, and it shall be for a token of a covenant" [Genesis 9:13].

And thus, our sages instituted that they should mention the oath to Noah every day, as it is said, "That your days may be multiplied, and the days of your children, upon the land which the Hashem swore unto your fathers to give them, as the days of the heavens above the earth" [Deuteronomy 11:21].

Chapter 24

Noah brought his sons and his grandsons, and he blessed them with their several settlements, and he gave them as an inheritance all the earth. He especially blessed **Shem** and his sons, making them dark but comely, and he gave them the habitable earth. He blessed **Ham** and his sons, making them **Black** like the raven, and he gave them as an inheritance the coast of the sea. He blessed **Japheth** and his sons, making them entirely white, and he gave them for an inheritance the desert and its fields; these are the inheritances with which he endowed them.

Rebbi Eiezer said: They begat their sons and increased and multiplied like a great reptile, six at each birth, and they were all one people, and one heart, and one language, as it is said, "And the whole earth was of one language and of one speech" [Genesis 11:1]. They despised the pleasant land, as it is said, "And it came to pass, as they journeyed in the east" [Genesis 11:2]. They went to the land of Shinar, and found there a large stone, very extensive, and the whole plain, and they dwelt there, as it is said, "And they found a plain in the land of Shinar, and they dwelt there" [Genesis 11:2].

Rabbi Akiva said: They cast off the Kingdom of Heaven from themselves, and appointed Nimrod king over themselves; a slave son of a slave. Are not all the sons of Ham slaves? And woe to the land

Pirkei DeRabbi Eliezer 24

when a slave rules, as it is said, "For a servant, when he is king" [Proverbs 30:22].

Rebbi Chakhinai said: Nimrod was a mighty hero, as it is said, "And Cush begat Nimrod, who began to be a mighty one in the earth" [Genesis 10:8].

Rebbi Yehuda said: The coats which the Holy One, blessed be He, made for Adam and his wife, were with Noah in the ark, and when they went forth from the ark, Ham, the son of Noah, brought them forth with him, and gave them as an inheritance to Nimrod. When he put them on, all beasts, animals, and birds, when they saw the coats, came and prostrated themselves before him. The sons of men thought that this was due to the power of his might; therefore, they made him king over themselves, as it is said, "Wherefore it is said, Like Nimrod, a mighty hunter before the Hashem" [Genesis 10:9].

Nimrod said to his people: Come, let us build a great city for ourselves, and let us dwell therein, lest we be scattered upon the face of all the earth, as the first people were. Let us build a great tower in its midst, ascending to heaven, for the power of the Holy One, blessed be He, is only in the water, and let us make us a great name on the earth, as it is said, "And let us make us a name" [Genesis 11:4].

Rebbi Pinchas said: There were no stones there where-with to build the city and the tower. What did they do? They baked bricks and burnt them like a builder would do, until they built it seven mils high,

Pirkei DeRabbi Eliezer 24

and it had ascents on its east and west. The labourers who took up the bricks went up on the eastern ascent, and those who descended went down on the western descent. If a man fell and died, they paid no heed to him, but if a brick fell, they sat down and wept, and said: Woe is us. when will another one come in its stead?

Avraham, son of Terah, passed by, and saw them building the city and the tower, and he cursed them in the name of his God, as it is said, "Swallow up, O Hashem, divide their language" [Psalms 55:9]. But they rejected his words, like a stone cast upon the ground. Is it not a fact that every choice and good stone is only put at the corner of a building? and with reference to this, the text says, "The stone which the builders rejected is become the head of the corner" [Psalms 118:22].

Rebbi Shimon said: The Holy One, blessed be He, called to the seventy angels, who surround the throne of His glory, and He said to them: Come, let us descend and let us confuse the seventy nations and the seventy languages.

Whence do we know that the Holy One, blessed be He, spake to them? Because it is said, "Go to, let us go down" [Genesis 11:7]. "I will go down" is not written, but "Go to, let us go down." And they cast lots among them. Because it is said, "When the Most High gave to the nations their inheritance" [Deuteronomy 32:8]. The lot of the Holy One, blessed be He, fell upon Avraham and upon his seed, as it is

Pirkei DeRabbi Eliezer 24

said, "For the Hashem's portion is his people; Yaakov is the lot of his inheritance" [Deuteronomy 32:9].

The Holy One, blessed be He, said: The portion and lot which have fallen to Me. My soul liveth thereby, as it is said, "The lots have fallen unto me in pleasures; yea, I have a goodly heritage" [Psalms 16:6]. The Holy One, blessed be He, descended with the seventy angels, who surround the throne of His glory, and they confused their speech into seventy nations and seventy languages. Whence do we know that the Holy One, blessed be He, descended? Because it is said, "And the Hashem God came down to see the city and the tower" [Genesis 11:5]. This was the second descent.

And they wished to speak one to another in the language of his fellow-countryman, but one did not understand the language of his fellow. What did they do? Every one took his sword, and they fought one another to destroy each other, and half the world fell there by the sword, and thence the Hashem scattered them upon the face of all the earth, as it is said, "So the Hashem scattered them abroad on that account, upon the face of all the earth" [Genesis 11:8].

Rebbi said: **Esav**, the brother of Yaakov, saw the coats of Nimrod, and in his heart, he coveted them, and he slew him, and took them from him. Whence do we know that they were desirable in his sight? Because it is said, "And Rivkah took the precious raiment of Esav, her elder son" [Genesis 27:15]. When

Pirkei DeRabbi Eliezer 24

he put them on, he also became, by means of them, a mighty hero, as it is said, "And Esav was a cunning hunter" [Genesis 25:27]. And when Yaakov went forth from the presence of Yitzhak, his father, he said: Esav, the wicked one, is not worthy to wear these coats. What did he do? He dug in the earth and hid them there, as it is said, "A noose is hid for him in the earth" [Job 18:10].

Chapter 25

The third descent which He descended was at Sodom, as it is said, "I will go down now and see" [Genesis 18:21]. The Holy One, blessed be He, said: Shall I not tell My friend Avraham an important matter which I will do in My world in the future, as it is said, "And the Hashem said, Shall I hide from Avraham that which I do?" [Genesis 18:17].

Rebbi Chanina, son of Dosa, said: The Holy One, blessed be He, was revealed, and three angels [appeared] unto our father Avraham, as it is said, "And he lifted up his eyes and looked, and, lo, three men" [Genesis 18:2]. He began to inform him about the conception of the womb by Sarah his wife, as it is said, "I will certainly return unto thee when the season cometh round" [Genesis 18:10]. Afterwards He told [him] about the doom of Sodom, as it is said, "And the Hashem said, Because the cry of Sodom and Gomorrah is great" [Genesis 18:20].

Hence, thou mayest learn: Everyone, who wishes to tell his companion a matter which is a disgrace to him, begins with a good word and concludes with the evil matter which is unpleasant to him. Whence do we learn this? From the Holy One, blessed be He, for when He was revealed to our father Avraham, He began to announce to him the good news concerning the conception by Sarah his wife. Afterwards He told him about the fate of Sodom, as it is said, "And the Hashem said, Because the cry of

Pirkei DeRabbi Eliezer 25

Sodom and Gomorrah is great" [Genesis 18:20].

Avraham began to ask for compassion before Him on behalf of Lot, the son of his brother. He spake before Him: Sovereign of all worlds. Like the death of the wicked shall the death of the righteous be? As it is said, "Wilt thou consume the righteous with the wicked?" [Genesis 18:23]. The Holy One, blessed be He, answered him: Avraham. By the merit of the righteous [one] will I forgive Sodom. "If I find in Sodom fifty righteous" [Genesis 18:26], then will I forgive it all its sins.

Hence, they said: If there be fifty righteous in the world, the world exists through their righteousness. Avraham arose and began to beseech God, and made supplication before Him until he brought [the number down to ten. Hence the sages said: When there are ten people in a place, the place is delivered by their righteousness, as it is said, "And he said, I will not destroy it for the sake of the ten" [Genesis 18:32].

Rebbi Ze'era said: The men of Sodom were the wealthy men of prosperity, on account of the good and fruitful land whereon they dwelt. For every need which the world requires, they obtained therefrom. They procured gold therefrom, as it is said, "And it had dust of gold" [Job 28:6]. What is the meaning of the text, "And it had dust of gold"? At the hour when one of them wished to buy a vegetable, he would say to his servant, Go and purchase for me for the value of an assar. He went and bought [it], and found

Pirkei DeRabbi Eliezer 25

beneath it heaps of gold; thus it is written, "And it had dust of gold" [Job 28:6]. They obtained silver therefrom, as it is said, "Surely there is a mine for silver" [Job 28:1]. They procured precious stones and pearls thence, as it is said, "The stones thereof are the place of sapphires" [Job 28:6]. They obtained bread therefrom, as it is said, "As for the earth, out of it cometh bread" [Job 28:5]. But they did not trust in the shadow of their Creator, but [they trusted] in the multitude of their wealth, for wealth thrusts aside its owners from the fear of Heaven, as it is said, "They that trust in their wealth" [Psalms 49:6].

Rebbi Natanel said: The men of Sodom had no consideration for the honour of their Owner by [not] distributing food to the wayfarer and the stranger, but they [even] fenced in all the trees on top above their fruit so that they should not be seized; [not] even by the bird of heaven, as it is said, "That path no bird of prey knoweth" [Job 28:7].

Rebbi Yehoshua, son of Karha, said: They appointed over themselves judges who were lying judges, and they oppressed every wayfarer and stranger who entered Sodom by their perverse judgment, and they sent them forth naked, as it is said, "They have oppressed the stranger without judgment" [Ezekiel 22:29].

They were dwelling in security without care and at ease, without the fear of war from all their surroundings, as it is said, "Their houses are safe from fear" [Job 21:9]. They were sated with all the

Pirkei DeRabbi Eliezer 25

produce of the earth, but they did not strengthen with the loaf of bread either the hand of the needy or of the poor, as it is said, "Behold, this was the iniquity of thy sister Sodom; pride, fullness of bread, and prosperous ease was in her and in her daughters; neither did she strengthen the hand of the poor and needy" [Ezekiel 16:49].

Rebbi Yehuda said: They made a proclamation in Sodom saying: Everyone who strengthens the hand of the poor or the needy with a loaf of bread shall be burnt by fire. **Paltith**, daughter of Lot, was wedded to one of the magnates of Sodom. She saw a certain very poor man in the street of the city, and her soul was grieved on his account, as it is said, "Was not my soul grieved for the needy?" [Job 30:25]. What did she do? Every day when she went out to draw water she put in her bucket all sorts of provisions from her home, and she fed that poor man. The men of Sodom said: How does this poor man live? When they ascertained the facts, they brought her forth to be burnt with fire. She said: Sovereign of all worlds. Maintain my right and my cause at the hands of the men of Sodom. And her cry ascended before the Throne of Glory. In that hour the Holy One, blessed be He, said: "I will now descend, and I will see" [Genesis 18:21] whether the men of Sodom have done according to the cry of this young woman, I will turn her foundations upwards, and the surface thereof shall be turned downwards, as it is said, "I will now descend, and I will see whether they have done altogether according to her cry, which is come unto me" [Genesis 18:21]. "According to their cry" is not written here in the text, only "According to her cry."

And thus, the text says, "He who walketh with wise men shall be wise: but the companion of fools shall be broken" [Proverbs 13:20]. "He who walketh with wise men shall be wise." To what is this like? To one who enters a perfumer's shop, although he neither takes anything nor gives anything, nevertheless he absorbs a good scent, and goes away therewith. Likewise, everyone who walks with the righteous acquires some of their good ways and deeds. Therefore, it is said, "He who walketh with wise men shall be wise." "But the companion of fools shall be broken" [Proverbs 13:20]. To what is this comparable? To a man who enters a tannery, although he neither takes nor gives anything, nevertheless he has absorbed a foul odour. Likewise, he who walks with the wicked acquires some of their evil ways and deeds, that is according to what is written, "But the companion of fools shall be broken" [Proverbs 13:20].

Another explanation: "He who walketh with wise men shall be wise" [Proverbs 13:20]. This refers to Lot, who walked with our father Avraham, and learned of his good deeds and ways. They said: What did our father Avraham do? He made for himself a house opposite to Haran, and he received everyone who entered into or went out from Haran, and he gave him to eat and to drink. He said to them: Say Ye, The God of Avraham is the only one in the universe. When Lot came to Sodom he did likewise. When they made proclamation in Sodom: All who

Pirkei DeRabbi Eliezer 25

strengthen the hand of the poor or needy with a loaf of bread shall be burnt by fire, he was afraid of the men of the city, and did not venture to do so by day, but he did it by night, as it is said, "And the two angels came to Sodom at even; and Lot sat in the gate of Sodom" [Genesis 19:1]. Why did Lot sit in the gate of Sodom? Because he was afraid of the men of the city, and did not venture to act charitably by day, but he did so by night. He saw the two angels walking in the street of the city, and he thought that they were wayfarers in the land, and he ran to meet them. He said to them: Come and lodge ye overnight in my house, eat and drink, and ye shall go your way in peace. But the men would not accept this for themselves, and he took them by the hand against their will, and brought them inside his house, as it is said, "And he urged them greatly" [Genesis 19:3].

A certain young man of the people of that city saw them, and he ran and told all the men of that city, and they all gathered together at the door of the house to do according to their wont, even deeds of sodomy, as it is said, "And they called unto Lot, and said unto him, where are the men who came to thee to-night? Bring them forth unto us that we may know them" [Genesis 19:5]. What did Lot do? Just as Moshe gave his life for the people, so Lot gave up his two daughters instead of the two angels, as it is said, "Behold, now, I have two daughters" [Genesis 19:8]. But the men would not agree [and did not accept them]. What did the angels do to them? They smote them with blindness until the dawn of the next morning. All were treated with measure for

Pirkei DeRabbi Eliezer 25

measure. Just as he had taken them by the hand without their will and taken them into his house, so they took hold of his hand, and the hand of his wife, and the hand of his two daughters, and took them outside the city, as it is said, "But he lingered; and the men laid hold upon his hand" [Genesis 19:16]. And they said to them: Do not look behind you, for verily the **Shekhinah** [divine presence] of the Holy One, blessed be He, has descended in order to rain upon Sodom and upon Gomorrah brimstone and fire. The pity of 'Edith the wife of Lot was stirred for her daughters, who were married in Sodom, and she looked back behind her to see if they were coming after her or not. And she saw behind the Shekhinah [divine presence], and she became a pillar of salt, as it is said, "And his wife looked back from behind him, and she became a pillar of salt" [Genesis 19:26].

Chapter 26

Our father Avraham was tried with ten trials, and he stood firm in them all.

The first trial was when our father Avraham was born; all the magnates of the kingdom and the magicians sought to kill him, and he was hidden under the earth for thirteen years without seeing sun or moon. After thirteen years he went forth from beneath the earth, speaking the holy language; and he despised idols and held in abomination the graven images, and he trusted in the shadow of his Creator, and said: "Blessed is the man who trusts in thee" [Psalms 84:13].

The second trial was when he was put into prison for ten years - three years in Kuthi, seven years in Budri. After ten years they sent and brought him forth and cast him into the furnace of fire, and the King of Glory put forth His right hand and delivered him from the furnace of fire, as it is said, "And he said to him, I am the Hashem who brought thee out of the furnace of the Chaldees" [Genesis 15:7].

The third trial was his migration from his father's house and from the land of his birth; and He brought him to Haran, and there his father **Terach** died, and **Athrai** his mother. Migration is harder for man than for any other creature. Whence do we know of his migration? Because it is said, "Now the Hashem said unto Abram, Get thee out" [Genesis 12:1].

Pirkei DeRabbi Eliezer 26

The fourth trial was the famine. From the day when the heavens and the earth were created, the Holy One, blessed be He, had not brought into the world a famine but only in the days of Avraham, and not in any of the lands but only in the land of Canaan, in order to try him and to bring him down into Egypt, as it is said, "And there was a famine in the land, and Abram went down into Egypt" [Genesis 12:10].

The fifth trial was when Sarah his wife was taken to Pharaoh to be his wife. And is there any man, who seeing his wife taken away to another man, would not rend his garments? But he trusted in the Holy One, blessed be He, that he would not approach her. Whence do we know that Sarah was taken to Pharaoh to be his wife? Because it is said, "And the princes of Pharaoh saw her" [Genesis 12:15].

Rebbi Yehoshua, son of Karha, said: In that night when our mother Sarah was taken, it was Passover night, and the Holy One, blessed be He, brought upon Pharaoh and upon his house great plagues, to make known that thus in the future would He smite the people of his land, as it is said, "And the Hashem plagued Pharaoh and his house with great plagues" [Genesis 12:17]. Concerning the Egyptians, it is written, "Yet one plague more will I bring upon Pharaoh, and upon Egypt" [Exodus 11:1]. Was this a plague? Was it not [the slaying of] the first-born of the Egyptians? But the slaying is compared with the plagues, therefore it is said, "And the Hashem plagued Pharaoh" [Genesis 12:17].

Pirkei DeRabbi Eliezer 26

Rebbi Yehoshua ben Karha said: Because of his love for her, Pharaoh wrote in her marriage document, giving her all his wealth, whether in silver, or in gold, or in man-servants, or land, and he wrote giving her the land of Goshen for a possession. Therefore, the children of Israel dwelt in the land of Goshen, in the land of their mother Sarah. He also wrote giving her **Hagar**, his daughter from a concubine, as her handmaid. And whence do we know that Hagar was the daughter of Pharaoh? Because it is said, "Now Sarai Abram's wife bore him no children; and she had a handmaid, an Egyptian, whose name was Hagar" [Genesis 16:1].

Pharaoh rose up early in the morning confused because he had not approached her, and he sent and called Avraham, and said to him: Behold, Sarai thy wife is before thee, and all the deeds of her marriage contract are with her, take her and go, do not tarry in this land, as it is said, "Now therefore behold thy wife, take her, and go" [Genesis 12:19]. "And Pharaoh gave men charge concerning him, and they sent him forth" [Genesis 12:20]. And he had Avraham led so as to come to the land of Canaan. He sojourned in the land of the Philistines in order to be refreshed there. And he went away. And everything is foreseen by the Holy One, blessed be He, and Avimelech sent and took Sarah, thinking to raise up children from her, as it is said, "And **Avimelech**... sent, and took Sarah" [Genesis 20:2].

And Avimelech became impotent, and all the women of his house became barren, even to the smallest insect which also became barren, as it is said, "For the Hashem had fast closed up all the wombs of the house of Avimelech" [Genesis 20:18]. And the angel **Michael** descended and drew his sword against him. Avimelech said to him: Is this a true judgment and a true sentence to slay me as long as I had no knowledge? "Wilt thou slay even a righteous nation?" [Genesis 20:4]. He said unto him: "Restore the man's wife, for he is a prophet and he shall pray for thee, and thou shalt live". [Genesis 20:7].

Rebbi Yehoshua, son of Karha, rehearsed before Rebbi Ṭarphon saying: Whatever Pharaoh gave, he gave to Sarah; whatever Avimelech gave, he gave to Avraham; as it is said, "And Avimelech took sheep and oxen" [Genesis 20:14]. Avraham arose and prayed before the Holy One, blessed be He, and said before Him: Sovereign of all the worlds. Thou hast created the whole world to increase and multiply, and let Avimelech and all the females of his household increase and multiply. The Holy One, blessed be He, was entreated of him, as it is said, "And Avraham prayed unto God: and God healed Avimelech, and his wife, and his maidservants; and they bore children" [Genesis 20:17].

Chapter 27

The sixth trial was when all the kings came against him to slay him. They said: Let us first begin with the house of his brother, and afterwards let us begin with him. On account of Lot, they took all [the wealth of] Sodom and Gomorrah, as it is said, "And they took all the goods of Sodom and Gomorrah" [Genesis 14:11]. Afterwards they took Lot captive, and all his wealth, as it is said, "And they took Lot... and his goods" [Genesis 14:12].

The angel Michael came and told Avraham, as it is said, "And there came one who had escaped, and told Abram the Hebrew" [Genesis 14:13]. He is the prince of the world, he was the one who told, as it is said, "Curse not the king, no, not in thy thought; he who hath wings shall tell the matter" [Ecclesiastes 10:20]. Why his name was called "Paliṭ". "One who had escaped"? Because in the hour when the Holy One, blessed be He, caused Sammae"l [The angel of death] and his band to descend from heaven from their holy place, he caught hold of the wings of Michael to make him fall with himself, and the Holy One, blessed be He, saved him from his power; therefore was his name called "The one who had escaped." Concerning him Ezekiel said, "One who had escaped out of Jerusalem came to me, saying, the city is smitten" [Ezekiel 33:21].

Avraham rose up early in the morning, and he took his three disciples, Aner, Eshcol, and Mamre, with

Pirkei DeRabbi Eliezer 27

him, and Eliezer his servant with him also, and he pursued after them as far as Dan, which is Pameas, as it is said, "And he pursued as far as Dan" [Genesis 14:14]. And there the righteous man was hindered, for there it was told him: Avraham, know thou that in the future thy children's children will serve idols in this place; therefore, was he hindered there. Whence do we know that Israel served idols there? Because it is said, "And he made two calves of gold… and he set the one in Bethel, and the other put he in Dan" [Kings-A 12:28-29]. There he left his three disciples, and he took his servant Eliezer. The numerical value of the letters of his name equals 318. He pursued them as far as the left of Damascus, as it is said, "And he pursued them unto **Hobah**" [Genesis 14:15].

Samuel the Younger said: There the night was divided for him; the night when the children of Israel went forth out of Egypt, that was the night in which Avraham smote the kings and their camps with them, as it is said, "And he divided himself against them by night, he and his servants" [Genesis 14:15].

Hillel the Elder said: Avraham took all the wealth of Sodom and Gomorrah and all the wealth of Lot, the son of his brother, and he returned in peace, and not even one of his men failed him, as it is said, "And he brought back all the goods, and also his brother Lot" [Genesis 14:16].

Rebbi Meir said: Avraham was the first to begin to give a tithe. He took all the tithe of the kings and all the tithe of the wealth of Lot, the son of his brother,

Pirkei DeRabbi Eliezer 27

and gave [it] to Shem, the son of Noah, as it is said, "And he gave him a tenth of all" [Genesis 14:20].

Shem, the son of Noah, came forth to meet him, and when he saw all the deeds which he had done and all the wealth which he had brought back, he wondered in his heart. He began to praise, to glorify, and to laud the name of the Most-High, saying: "And blessed be God the Most-High, who hath delivered thine enemies into thy hand" [Genesis 14:20]. Avraham arose and prayed before the Holy One, blessed be He, saying: Sovereign of all worlds. Not by the power of my hand, nor by the power of my right hand have I done all these things, but by the power of Thy right hand with which Thou dost shield me in this world and in the world to come, as it is said, "But thou, O Hashem, art a shield about me" [Psalms 3:3] in this world; "my glory, and the lifter up of mine head" [Psalms 3:3] in the world to come. The angels answered and said: Blessed art Thou, O Hashem, the shield of Avraham.

Chapter 28

The seventh trial of Avraham was as follows: "After these things the word of the Hashem came unto Abram in a vision, saying" [Genesis 15:1]. To all the prophets He was revealed in a vision, but to Avraham He was revealed in a revelation and in a vision. Whence do we know of the revelation? Because it is said, "And the Hashem appeared unto him by the **Oaks of Mamre**" [Genesis 18:1]. Whence do we know of the vision? Because it is said, "After these things the word of the Hashem came unto Abram in a vision" [Genesis 15:1]. He said to him: Avraham. Do not fear, for My right hand is shielding thee in every place where thou goest; it is like a shield against misfortunes, and it gives thee a good reward, even to thee and to thy children, in this world and in the world to come, as it is said, "Thy exceeding great reward" [Genesis 15:1].

Rebbi said: The Holy One, blessed be He, brought Avraham outside his house on the night of Passover, and He said to him: Avraham. Hast thou the ability to count all the host of heaven? He said before Him: Sovereign of all worlds. Is there then a limit to Thy troops of angels? He said to him: Likewise, thy seed shall not be counted owing to their great number, as it is said, "And he said unto him, so shall thy seed be" [Genesis 15:5].

Rebbi Eliezer said: The Holy One, blessed be He, showed to our father Avraham at the covenant

Pirkei DeRabbi Eliezer 28

between the pieces the four kingdoms, their dominion and their downfall, as it is said, "And he said unto him, Take me an heifer of three years old, and a she-goat of three years old" [Genesis 15:9]. "An heifer of three years old" [Genesis 15:9]. refers to the kingdom of Aram, which is like the heifer of a sheep. "And a she-goat of three years old" [Genesis 15:9]. refers to the kingdom of Greece, as it is said, "And the he-goat magnified himself exceedingly" [Daniel 8:8]. "And a ram of three years old" [Genesis 15:9]; this is the kingdom of Media and Persia, as it is said, "And the ram which thou sawest that had the two horns, they are the kings of Media and Persia" [Daniel 8:23]. "And a turtle-dove" [Genesis 15:9]; this refers to the sons of Yishmael. This expression is not to be understood in the literal meaning of **Tor** turtle-dove, but in the Aramaic language, in which Tôr means Ox, for when the male ox is harnessed to the female, they will open and break all the valleys, even as it says about "the fourth beast" [Daniel 7:19]. "And a young pigeon" [Genesis 15:9]; this refers to the Israelites, who are compared to a young pigeon, as it is said, "O my dove, thou art in the clefts of the rock" [Song of Songs 2:14]. For thy voice is pleasant in prayer, and thy appearance is beautiful in good deeds. "And a young pigeon" [Genesis 15:9]; this refers to the Israelites, who are compared to a young pigeon: "My dove, my perfect one, is but one" [Song of Songs 6:9].

Rebbi Acha ben Yaakov said: This expression, "three years old" [Genesis 15:9], is said only with reference to the mighty in power, as it is said, "And a threefold cord is not quickly broken" [Ecclesiastes 4:12].

Rebbi Mesharshyah said: Three years old, refers to a threefold dominion which they would exercise three times in the future in the land of Israel. At the first time each one would rule by himself; at the second time two together would rule; on the third occasion all altogether to fight against the house of David, as it is said, "The kings of the earth set themselves, and the rulers take counsel together, against the Hashem, and against his anointed" [Psalms 2:2].

Rebbi Yehoshua said: Avraham took his sword and divided them, each one into two parts, as it is said, "And he took him all these, and he divided them in the midst" [Genesis 15:10]. Were it not for the fact that he divided them, the world would not have been able to exist, but because he divided them, he weakened their strength, and he brought each part against its corresponding part, as it is said, "And he laid each half over against the other" [Genesis 15:10]. And the young pigeon he left alive, as it is said, "But the bird he divided not" [Genesis 15:10]. Hence, thou mayest learn that there was not any other bird there except a young pigeon. The bird of prey came down upon them to scatter them and to destroy them. "The bird of prey" is nought else but David, the son of Jesse, who is compared to a "speckled bird of prey," as it is said, " Is mine heritage unto me as a speckled bird of prey?" [Jeremiah 12:9].

Pirkei DeRabbi Eliezer 28

When the sun was about to rise in the east, Avraham sat down and waved his scarf over them, so that the bird of prey should not prevail over them until the raven came.

Rebbi Elazar ben Azariah said: From this incident thou mayest learn that the rule of these four kingdoms will only last one day according to the day of the Holy One, blessed be He. Rebbi Elazar ben 'Arakh said unto him: Verily it is so, according to thy word, as it is said, "He hath made me desolate and faint all the day" [Lamentations 1:13], except for two-thirds of an hour of God. Know that it is so. Come and see, for when the sun turns to set in the west, during two hours its power is weakened, and it has no light, likewise whilst the evening has not yet come, the light of Israel shall arise, as it is said, "And it shall come to pass, that at evening time there shall be light" [Zechariah 14:7].

Avraham arose and prayed before the Holy One, blessed be He, that his children should not be enslaved by these four kingdoms. A deep sleep fell upon him, and he slept, as it is said, "A deep sleep fell upon Abram" [Genesis 15:12]. Does then a man lie down and sleep, and yet be able to pray? But this teaches thee that Avraham was lying down and sleeping because of the intensity of his prayer that his children might enslave these four kingdoms, as it is said, "And, lo, an horror of great darkness fell upon him" [Genesis 15:12]. "Horror" refers to the kingdom of Aram, as it is written, "And behold a fourth beast, terrible and powerful, and strong

Pirkei DeRabbi Eliezer 28

exceedingly" [Daniel 7:7]. "Darkness" is the kingdom of those who darken the eyes of Israel [by preventing the observance of] all the precepts which are in the Torah. "Great" [Genesis 15:12] refers to the kingdom of Media and Persia, which was great [enough to be able to afford] to sell Israel for nought. "Fell" [ibid.] refers to the kingdom of Babylon, because in their hand fell the crown of Israel, as it is said, "Babylon is fallen, is fallen" [Isaiah 21:9]. "Upon him" [Genesis 15:12] refers to the Yishmaelites, upon whom the Son of David will flourish, as it is said, "His enemies will I clothe with shame: but upon him shall his crown flourish" [Psalms 132:18].

Rebbi Ze'era said: These kingdoms were created only as fuel for Gehinnom, as it is said, "Behold, a smoking furnace, and a flaming torch that passed" [Genesis 15:17]. Here the word "furnace" signifies only Gehinnom, which is compared to a furnace, as it is said, "Saith the Hashem, whose fire is in Zion, and his furnace in Jerusalem" [Isaiah 31:9].

Chapter 29

The eighth trial of Abram was as follows: "And when Abram was ninety-nine years old" [Genesis 17:1], the Holy One, blessed be He, said to him: Until now thou hast not been perfect before me; but circumcise the flesh of thy foreskin, and "walk before me, and be thou perfect" [Genesis 17:1]. Moreover, the foreskin is a reproach, as it is said, "For that is a reproach unto us" [Genesis 34:14], because the foreskin is more unclean than all unclean things, as it is said, "For henceforth there shall no-more come into thee the uncircumcised and the unclean" [Isaiah 52:1]. For the foreskin is a blemish above all blemishes. Circumcise the flesh of thy foreskin and be perfect.

Rabban Gamaliel said: Avraham sent and called for Shem, the son of Noah, and he circumcised the flesh of the foreskin of our father Avraham, and the flesh of the foreskin of Yishmael his son, as it is said, "In the selfsame day was Avraham circumcised, and Yishmael his son" [Genesis 17:26]. "In the self-same day", means in the might of the sun at midday. Not only that, but it indicates the tenth day of the month, the Day of Atonement. It is written in connection with the Day of Atonement, "Ye shall do no manner of work on that self-same day, for it is a day of atonement" [Leviticus 23:28]; and in the present instance the text says, "In the self-same day was Avraham circumcised" [Genesis 17:26]. Know then that on the Day of Atonement Avraham our

Pirkei DeRabbi Eliezer 29

father was circumcised. Every year the Holy One, blessed be He, sees the blood of our father Avraham's circumcision, and He forgives all the sins of Israel, as it is said, "For on this day shall atonement be made for you, to cleanse you" [Leviticus 16:30]. In that place where Avraham was circumcised and his blood remained, there the altar was built, and therefore, "And all the blood thereof shall he pour out at the base of the altar" [Leviticus 4:30]. It says also, "I said unto thee, in thy blood, live; yea, I said unto thee, in thy blood, live" [Ezekiel 16:6].

Rebbi Chanina ben Dosa said: All who are circumcised have excessive pain on the third day, as it is said, "And it came to pass on the third day, when they were sore" [Genesis 34:25]. They may wash the child on the third day, when it happens to fall on the Sabbath, and all things necessary for a circumcision are permitted to be done on the Sabbath.

Every uncircumcised man shall not eat of the Qorban Pesach [Exodus 12:48], and shall not touch the sanctuary. He who separates himself from circumcision is like one separated from the Holy One, blessed be He.

Rabban Gamaliel, the son of Rebbi Yehuda the Prince, said: When our father Avraham was circumcised, on the third day he was very sore, in order to test him. What did the Holy One, blessed be He, do? He pierced one hole in the midst of Gehinnom, and He made the day hot, like the day of

Pirkei DeRabbi Eliezer 29

the wicked. He went forth, and sat down at the entrance of the tent in the cool of the day, as it is said, "And he sat at the tent door in the heat of the day" [Genesis 18:1]. The Holy One, blessed be He, said to the ministering angels: Come ye, let us descend and visit the sick, for the virtue of visiting the sick is great before me. The Holy One, blessed be He, and the angels descended to visit our father Avraham, as it is said, "And the Hashem appeared unto him" [Genesis 18:1]. The Holy One, blessed be He, said to the ministering angels: Come ye and see ye the power of circumcision. Before Avraham was circumcised, he fell on his face before me, and afterwards I spake with him, as it is said, "And Avraham fell upon his face" [Genesis 17:17]. Now that he is circumcised, he sits and I stand. Whence do we know that the Holy One, blessed be He, was standing? Because it is said, "And he looked, and, lo, three men stood over against him" [Genesis 18:2].

Rebbi Ze'era said: There are five kinds of Orlah [things uncircumcised] in the world: four with reference to man, and one concerning trees. Whence do we know this concerning the four terms applying to man? Namely, the uncircumcision of the **Ear**, the uncircumcision of the lips, the uncircumcision of the heart, and the uncircumcision of the flesh. Whence do we know of the uncircumcision of the ear? Because it is said, "Behold, their **Ear** is uncircumcised" [Jeremiah 6:10]. Whence do we know of the uncircumcision of the **Lips**? Because it is said, "For I am of uncircumcised **Lips**" [Exodus 6:12]. Whence do we know of the uncircumcision of the

Pirkei DeRabbi Eliezer 29

Heart? Because it is said, "Circumcise the foreskin of your **Heart**" [Deuteronomy 10:16]; and the text says, "For all the nations are uncircumcised, and all the house of Israel are uncircumcised in **Heart**" [Jeremiah 9:26]. Whence do we know of the uncircumcision of the **Flesh**? Because it is said, "And the uncircumcised male who is not circumcised in the **Flesh** of his foreskin" [Genesis 17:14]. And "all the nations are uncircumcised" in all the four cases, and "all the house of Israel are uncircumcised in heart." The uncircumcision of the heart does not suffer Israel to do the will of their Creator. And in the future the Holy One, blessed be He, will take away from Israel the uncircumcision of the heart, and they will not harden their stubborn heart any more before their Creator, as it is said, "And I will take away the stony heart out of your **Flesh**, and I will give you an heart of flesh" [Ezekiel 36:26]; and it is said, "And ye shall be circumcised in the **Flesh** of your foreskin" [Genesis 17:11]. Whence do we know concerning the one **Orlah** for trees? Because it is said, "And when ye shall come into the land, and shall have planted all manner of trees for food, then ye shall count the fruit thereof as their uncircumcision: three years shall they be as uncircumcised unto you" [Leviticus 19:23].

Rebbi Ze'era taught: The tree which is mentioned here is none other than the vine tree. If they do not cut off from the tree the fruit of the first three years, all the fruit which it yields will be gleanings fit to be pluckt off, and not good; and its wine will be disqualified for the altar; but if they cut off from the

Pirkei DeRabbi Eliezer 29

tree the fruit of the first three years, all the fruit which it yields will be good for the sight, and their wine will be selected to be brought upon the altar. So, with our father Avraham; before he was circumcised, the fruit which he produced was not good [in its effects, and was disqualified from the altar; but when he had been circumcised, the fruit which he produced was good in its effects, and his wine] was chosen to be put upon the altar like wine for a libation, as it is said, "And wine for the drink offering" [Numbers 15:5].

Rebbi Yishmael said: Avraham did not delay aught with reference to all [things] which He commanded him, as it is said, "And he that is eight days old shall be circumcised" [Genesis 17:12]; and when Yitzhak was born, and when he was eight days old Avraham brought him to be circumcised, as it is said, "And Avraham circumcised his son Yitzhak when he was eight days old" [Genesis 21:4]. Hence, thou mayest learn that everyone who brings his son for circumcision is as though he were a high Ha-Kohen bringing his meal offering and his drink offering upon the top of the altar. Hence the sages said: A man is bound to make festivities and a banquet on that day when he has the merit of having his son circumcised, like Avraham our father, who circumcised his son, as it is said, "And Avraham circumcised his son Yitzhak" [Genesis 21:4].

Rebbi Yohanan: All heathens who come to Israel are circumcised by their own freewill and with their consent, and in the fear of Heaven are they

Pirkei DeRabbi Eliezer 29

circumcised. We do not believe a proselyte until seven generations have passed, so that the waters should not return to their source. But slaves are circumcised both by their freewill and with their consent as well as without their consent, and no confidence is placed in slaves. Likewise with all the slaves who were circumcised with our father Avraham, they did not remain true converts in Israel, neither they nor their seed, because it is said, "All the men of his house, those born in the house, and those bought with money of the stranger, were circumcised with him" [Genesis 17:27]. Why did he circumcise them? Because of purity, so that they should not defile their masters with their food and with their drink, for whosoever aetat with an uncircumcised person is as though he were eating flesh of abomination. All who bathe with the uncircumcised are as though they bathed with carrion, and all who touch an uncircumcised person are as though they touched the dead, for in their lifetime they are like the dead; and in their death they are like the carrion of the beast, and their prayer does not come before the Holy One, blessed be He, as it is said, "The dead praise not the Hashem" [Psalms 115:17]. But Israel who are circumcised, their prayer comes before the Holy One, blessed be He, like a sweet savour, as it is said, "But we will bless the Hashem from this time forth and for evermore. Praise Ye the Hashem" [Psalms 115:18].

Rebbi said: Yitzhak circumcised Yaakov, and Esav; and Esav despised the covenant of circumcision just as he despised the birthright, as it is said, "So Esav

Pirkei DeRabbi Eliezer 29

despised his birthright" [Genesis 25:34]. Yaakov clung to the covenant of circumcision, and circumcised his sons and his grandsons. Whence do we know that the sons of Yaakov were circumcised? Because it is said, "Only on this condition will the men consent unto us to dwell with us… if every male among us be circumcised, as they are circumcised." [Genesis 34:22]. Hence, thou canst learn that the sons of Yaakov were circumcised. The sons of Yaakov circumcised their sons and their grandsons. They gave it to them as an inheritance for an everlasting statute, until Pharaoh the Wicked arose and decreed harsh laws concerning them, and withheld from them the covenant of circumcision. And on the day when the children of Israel went forth from Egypt all the people were circumcised, both young and old, as it is said, "For all the people that came out were circumcised" [Yehoshua 5:5].

The Israelites took the blood of the covenant of circumcision, and they put it upon the lintel of their houses, and when the Holy One, blessed be He, passed over to plague the Egyptians, He saw the blood of the covenant of circumcision upon the lintel of their houses and the blood of the Korban Pesach, He was filled with compassion on Israel, as it is said, "And when I passed by thee, and saw thee weltering in thy twofold blood, I said unto thee, In thy twofold blood, live; yea, I said unto thee, In thy twofold blood, live" [Ezekiel 16:6]. "In thy blood" is not written here, but in "thy twofold blood," with twofold blood, the blood of the covenant of circumcision and the blood of the Korban Pesach; therefore, it is said, "I

Pirkei DeRabbi Eliezer 29

said unto thee, In thy twofold blood, live; yea, I said unto thee, In thy twofold blood, live" [Ezekiel 16:6].

Rebbi Eliezer said: Why did the text say twice, "I said unto thee, in thy blood, live; yea, I said unto thee, in thy blood, live"? But the Holy One, blessed be He, said: By the merit of the blood of the covenant of circumcision and the blood of the Korban Pesach ye shall be redeemed from Egypt, and by the merit of the covenant of circumcision and by the merit of the covenant of the Passover in the future ye shall be redeemed at the end of the fourth kingdom; therefore, it is said, "I said unto thee, In thy blood, live; yea, I said unto thee, In thy blood, live" [Ezekiel 16:6].

There are three afflictions, namely, the affliction of the fast, the affliction of the prison, and the affliction of the road. Whence do we know of the affliction of the fast? Because it is said, "I afflicted my soul with fasting" [Psalms 35:13]. Whence do we know of the affliction of the prison? Because it is said, "They hurt his feet with fetters" [Psalms 105:18]. Whence do we know of the affliction of the road? Because it is said, "He weakened my strength in the way" [Psalms 102:23]. On account of the affliction of the road, [the children of Israel] did not circumcise, and when they went forth from Egypt all the people were circumcised, both young and old, as it is said, "For all the people that came out were circumcised" [Yehoshua 5:5].

Rebbi Yishmael said: Did the uncircumcised hear

Pirkei DeRabbi Eliezer 29

the voice of the Holy One, blessed be He, on Mount Sinai, saying, "I am the Hashem thy God" [Exodus 20:2]? They were circumcised, but not according to its regulation. They had cut off the foreskin, but they had not uncovered the corona. Everyone who has been circumcised, but has not had the corona uncovered, is as though he had not been circumcised, therefore the text says, "Yisrael was not circumcised of old."

When they came to the land of Isreal, the Holy One, blessed be He, said to Yehoshua: Yehoshua. Dost thou not know that the Israelites are not circumcised according to the proper regulation? He again circumcised them a second time, as it is said, "The Hashem said unto Yehoshua. Make thee knives of flint, and circumcise again the children of Israel a second time" [Yehoshua 5:2]. "And Yehoshua made him knives of flint" [Yehoshua 5:3], and he gathered all the foreskins until he made them as high as a hill, as it is said, "And he circumcised the children of Israel at the hill of the foreskins" [Yehoshua 5:3]. The Israelites took the foreskin and the blood and covered them with the dust of the wilderness. When Balaam came, he saw all the wilderness filled with the foreskins of the Israelites, he said: Who will be able to arise by the merit of the blood of the covenant of this circumcision, which is covered by the dust? As it is said, "Who can count the dust of Yaakov?" [Numbers 23:10].

Hence the sages instituted that they should cover the foreskin and the blood with the dust of the earth,

Pirkei DeRabbi Eliezer 29

because they are compared to the dust of the earth, as it is said, "And thy seed shall be as the dust of the earth" [Genesis 28:14]. Thus, the Israelites were wont to circumcise until they were divided into two kingdoms. The kingdom of Ephraim cast off from themselves the covenant of circumcision. Eliyahu, may he be remembered for good, arose and was zealous with a mighty passion, and he adjured the heavens to send down neither dew nor rain upon the earth. Isabel heard thereof, and sought to slay him. Eliyahu arose and prayed before the Holy One, blessed be He.

The Holy One, blessed be He, said to him: "Art thou better than thy fathers?" Esav sought to slay Yaakov [Genesis 27:41]. but he fled before him, as it is said, "And Yaakov fled into the field of Aram" [Hosea 12:12]. Pharaoh sought to slay Moshe, who fled before him and he was saved, as it is said, "Now when Pharaoh heard this thing, he sought to slay Moshe. And Moshe fled from the face of Pharaoh" [Exodus 2:15]. Shaul sought to slay David, who fled before him and was saved, as it is said, "If thou save not thy life to-night, to-morrow thou shalt be slain" [Samuel-A 19:11]. Learn that everyone, who flees, is saved. Eliyahu, may he be remembered for good, arose and fled from the land of Israel, and he betook himself to Mount Horeb, as it is said, "And he arose, and did eat and drink" [Kings-A 19:8]. There the Holy One, blessed be He, was revealed unto him, and He said to him: "What doest thou here, Eliyahu?" [Kings-A 19:9]. He answered Him, saying: "I have been very zealous" [Kings-A 19:10]. The Holy One, blessed be

Pirkei DeRabbi Eliezer 29

He, said to him: Thou art always zealous. Thou wast zealous in Shittim on account of the immorality. Because it is said, "Pinchas, the son of Eleazar, the son of Aharon the Ha-Kohen, turned my wrath away from the children of Israel, in that he was zealous with my zeal among them" [Numbers 25:11]. Here also art thou zealous. By thy life. They shall not observe the covenant of circumcision until thou seest it done with thine eyes.

Hence the sages instituted the custom that people should have a seat of honour for the Messenger of the Covenant; for Eliyahu, may he be remembered for good, is called the Messenger of the Covenant, as it is said, "And the messenger of the covenant, whom ye delight in, behold, he cometh" [Malachi 3:1].

Chapter 30

The ninth trial of Avraham was as follows: Yishmael was born with the prophecy of the bow, and he grew up with the bow, as it is said, "And God was with the lad, and he grew ... and he became an archer" [Genesis 21:20]. He took bow and arrows and began to shoot at the birds. He saw Yitzhak sitting by himself, and he shot an arrow at him to slay him. Sarah saw this, and told Avraham. She said to him: Thus, and thus has Yishmael done to Yitzhak, but now arise and write a will in favour of Yitzhak, [giving him] all that the Holy One has sworn to give to thee and to thy seed. The son of this handmaid shall not inherit with my son, with Yitzhak, as it is said, "And she said unto Avraham, Cast out this bondwoman and her son" [Genesis 21:10].

Yehuda Ben Tema said: Sarah said to Avraham, write a bill of divorce, and send away this handmaid and her son from me and from Yitzhak my son, in this world and from the world to come. More than all the misfortunes which overtook Avraham, this matter was exceedingly evil in his eyes, as it is said, "And the thing was very grievous in Avraham's sight on account of his son" [Genesis 21:11].

Rebbi Yehuda said: In that night the Holy One, blessed be He, was revealed unto him. He said to him: Avraham. Dost thou not know that Sarah was appointed to thee for a wife from her mother's womb? She is thy companion, and the wife of thy

Pirkei DeRabbi Eliezer 30

covenant; Sarah is not called thy handmaid, but thy wife; neither is Hagar called thy wife, but thy handmaid; and all that Sarah has spoken she has uttered truthfully. Let it not be grievous in thine eyes, as it is said, "And God said unto Avraham, let it not be grievous in thy sight" [Genesis 21:12].

Avraham rose up early, and wrote a bill of divorce, and gave it to Hagar, and he sent her and her son away from himself, and from Yitzhak his son, from this world and from the world to come, as it is said, "And Avraham rose up early in the morning, and took bread and a bottle of water" [Genesis 21:14]. He sent her away with a bill of divorcement, and he took the veil, and he bound it around her waist, so that it should drag behind her to disclose [the fact] that she was a bondwoman. Not only this, but also because Avraham desired to see Yishmael, his son, and to see the way whereon they went.

By the merit of our father Avraham the water did not fail in the bottle, but when she reached the entrance to the wilderness, she began to go astray after the idolatry of her father's house; and forthwith the water in the bottle was spent, as it is said, "And she departed and wandered" [Genesis 21:14], Yishmael was seventeen years old when he went forth from the house of Avraham, and Yitzhak was forty years old. By the merit of our father Avraham the water did not fail in the bottle, but when she reached the entrance to the wilderness, she began to go astray after the idolatry of her father's house; the water in the bottle was spent, and the soul of Yishmael was faint with

Pirkei DeRabbi Eliezer 30

thirst.

"**And** she departed and wandered" [Genesis 21:14]. The meaning of "and she wandered" is merely idolatry, because it is written, concerning this root, "They are vanity, a work of delusion" [Jeremiah 10:15]. He went and cast himself beneath the thorns of the wilderness, so that the moisture might be upon him, and he said: O God of my father Avraham. Thine are the issues of death; take away from me my soul, for I would not die of thirst. And He was entreated of him, as it is said, "For God hath heard the voice of the lad where he is" [Genesis 21:17]. The well which was created at twilight was opened for them there, and they went and drank and filled the bottle with water, as it is said, "And God opened her eyes, and she saw a well of water" [Genesis 21:19]. And there they left the well, and thence they started on their way, and went through all the wilderness until they came to the wilderness of Paran, and they found there streams of water, and they dwelt there, as it is said, "And he dwelt in the wilderness of Paran" [Genesis 21:21]. Yishmael sent for a wife from among the daughters of Moav, and **Ayeshah** was her name.

After three years Avraham went to see Yishmael his son, having sworn to Sarah that he would not descend from the camel in the place where Yishmael dwelt. He arrived there at midday and found there the wife of Yishmael. He said to her: Where is Yishmael? She said to him: He has gone with his mother to fetch the fruit of the palms from the wilderness. He said to her: Give me a little bread and

Pirkei DeRabbi Eliezer 30

a little water, for my soul is faint after the journey in the desert. She said to him: I have neither bread nor water. He said to her: When Yishmael comes [home] tell him this story, and say to him: A certain old man came from the land of Canaan to see thee, and he said, Exchange the threshold of thy house, for it is not good for thee. When Yishmael came [home] his wife told him the story. A son of a wise man is like half a wise man. Yishmael understood. His mother sent and took for him a wife from her father's house, and her name was Fatimah.

Again, after three years Avraham went to see his son Yishmael, having sworn to Sarah as on the first occasion that he would not descend from the camel in the place where Yishmael dwelt. He came there at midday, and found there Yishmael's wife. He said to her: Where is Yishmael? She replied to him: He has gone with his mother to feed the camels in the desert. He said to her: Give me a little bread and water, for my soul is faint after the journey of the desert. She fetched it and gave it to him. Avraham arose and prayed before the Holy One, blessed be He, for his son, and thereupon Yishmael's house was filled with all good things of the various blessings. When Yishmael came home his wife told him what had happened, and Yishmael knew that his father's love was still extended to him, as it is said, "Like as a father pitieth his sons" [Psalms 103:13]. After the death of Sarah, Avraham again took Hagar his divorced wife, as it is said, "And Avraham again took a wife, and her name was Keturah" [Genesis 25:1]. Why does it say "And he again"? Because on the

Pirkei DeRabbi Eliezer 30

first occasion she was his wife, and he again betook himself to her. Her name was Keturah, because she was perfumed with all kinds of scents.

Another explanation of Keturah is: because her actions were beautiful like incense, and she bare him six sons, and they were all called according to the name of Yishmael, as it is said, "And she bore him **Zimran** [Genesis 25:2].

Like a woman sent away from her husband, so likewise Avraham arose and sent them away from Yitzhak his son, from this world and from the world to come, as it is said, "But unto the sons of the concubines, which Avraham had, Avraham gave gifts, and he sent them away from Yitzhak his son" [Genesis 25:6], by a deed of divorcement.

Corresponding to the name of Yishmael's son **Kedar**, the sons of Kedar were so called, as it is said, "Of Kedar, and of the kingdoms of Hazor" [Jeremiah 49:28]. Corresponding to the name of Yishmael's son "Kedemah" Kedemah is east [Genesis 25:15], the "sons of Kedem" were so called. Because they dwelt in the territory belonging to Cain, his children were called "sons of Cain," as it is said, "Now **Heber** [Father-in-law of Moshe Rabbeinu] the Kenite had separated himself from Cain" [Judges 4:11]. Were not all the sons of Cain cut off by the waters of the Flood? But because they dwelt in the territory of the children of Cain, his children were called "sons of Cain," as it is said, "Nevertheless Cain shall be wasted, as long as Asshur shall dwell in thy place" [Numbers 24:22].

Pirkei DeRabbi Eliezer 30

"Nevertheless, Cain shall be wasted away" by fire, through the seed of Yishmael, the latter shall cause the kingdom of Assyria to cease.

Balaam said: Of the seventy nations that the Holy One, blessed be He, created in His world, He did not put His name on any one of them except on Israel; and since the Holy One, blessed be He, made the name of Ishmael similar to the name of Israel, woe to him who shall live in his days, as it is said, "Alas, who shall live when God establisheth him?" [Numbers 24:23].

Rebbi Yishmael said: In the future the children of Yishmael will do fifteen things in the land [of Israel] in the latter days, and they are: They will measure the land with ropes; they will change a cemetery into a resting-place for sheep and a dunghill; they will measure with them and from them upon the tops of the mountains; falsehood will multiply and truth will be hidden; the statutes will be removed far from Israel; sins will be multiplied in Israel; worm-crimson will be in the wool, and he will cover with insects paper and pen; he will hew down the rock of the kingdom, and they will rebuild the desolated cities and sweep the ways; and they will plant gardens and parks, and fence in the broken walls of the Temple; and they will build a building in the Holy Place; and two brothers will arise over them, princes at the end; and in their days the Branch, the Son of David, will arise, as it is said, "And in the days of those kings shall the God of heaven set up a kingdom, which shall never be destroyed" [Daniel 2:44].

Pirkei DeRabbi Eliezer 30

Rebbi Yishmael also said: Three wars of trouble will the sons of Yishmael in the future wage on the earth in the latter days, as it is said, "For they fled away from the swords" [Isaiah 21:15]. "Swords" signify only wars, one in the forest of ARavia, as it is said, "From the drawn sword" [Isaiah 21:15]; another on the sea, as it is said, "From the bent bow" [Isaiah 21:15]; and one in the great city which is in Rome, which will be more grievous than the other two, as it is said, "And from the grievousness of the war" [ibid]. From there the Son of David shall flourish and see the destruction of these and these, and thence will He come to the land of Israel, as it is said, "Who is this that cometh from Aram, with crimsoned garments from Bozrah? This that is glorious in his apparel, marching in the greatness of his strength? I that speak in righteousness, mighty to save" [Isaiah 63:1].

Chapter 31

The tenth trial was of Avraham as follows: "And it came to pass after these things, that God did prove Avraham" [Genesis 22:1]. He tried Avraham each time in order to know his heart, whether he would be able to persevere and keep all the commandments of the Torah or not, and whilst as yet the Torah had not been given, Avraham kept all the precepts of the Torah, as it is said, "Because that Avraham obeyed my voice, and kept my charge, my commandments, my statutes, and my Torah" [Genesis 26:5]. And Yishmael went repeatedly from the wilderness to see his father Avraham.

Rebbi Yehuda said: In that night was the Holy One, blessed be He, revealed unto him, and He said unto him: Avraham. "Take now thy son, thine only son, whom thou lovest, even Yitzhak" [Genesis 22:2]. And Avraham, having pity upon Yitzhak, said before Him: Sovereign of all worlds. Concerning which son dost Thou decree upon me? Is it concerning the son lacking circumcision, or the son born for circumcision? He answered him: "Thine only son." He rejoined: This one is the only son of his mother, and the other son is the only son of his mother. He said to him: "The one, whom thou lovest." He said to Him: Both of them do I love. He said to him: "Even Yitzhak."

"**And** offer him there for a burnt offering" [Genesis 22:2]. He spake to Him: Sovereign of all worlds. On

Pirkei DeRabbi Eliezer 31

which mountain hast Thou told me to offer him? God answered him: In every place where thou dost see My glory abiding and waiting for thee there, and saying, this is Mount Moriah; as it is said, "Upon one of the mountains which I will tell thee of" [Genesis 22:2].

Avraham rose up early in the morning, and he took with him Yishmael, and Eliezer, and Yitzhak his son, and he saddled the ass. Upon this ass did Avraham ride? This was the ass, the offspring of that ass which was created during the twilight, as it is said, "And Avraham rose early in the morning, and saddled his ass" [Genesis 22:8]. The same ass was also ridden upon by Moshe when he came to Egypt, as it is said, "And Moshe took his wife and his sons, and set them upon the ass" [Exodus 4:20]. This same ass will be ridden upon in the future by the Son of David, as it is said, "Rejoice greatly, O daughter of Zion; shout, O daughter of Jerusalem: behold, thy king cometh unto thee: he is just, and saved; lowly, and riding upon an ass, even upon a colt, the foal of an ass" [Zechariah 9:9].

Yitzhak was thirty-seven years old when he went to Mount Moriah, and Yishmael was fifty years old. Contention arose between Eliezer and Yishmael. Yishmael said to Eliezer: Now that Avraham will offer Yitzhak his son for a burnt offering, kindled upon the altar, and I am his first-born son, I will inherit the possessions of Avraham. Eliezer replied to him, saying: He has already driven thee out like a woman divorced from her husband, and he has sent

Pirkei DeRabbi Eliezer 31

thee away to the wilderness, but I am his servant, serving him by day and by night, and I shall be the heir of Avraham. The Holy Spirit answered them, saying to them: Neither this one nor that one shall inherit.

On the third day they reached **Zophim** [A place on the way to the Mountain], and when they reached Zophim they saw the glory of the Shekhinah [divine presence] resting upon the top of the mountain, as it is said, "On the third day Avraham lifted up his eyes, and saw the place afar off" [Genesis 22:4]. What did he see? He saw a pillar of fire standing from the earth to the heavens. Avraham understood that the lad had been accepted for the perfect burnt offering. He said to Yishmael and Eliezer: Do ye see anything upon one of those mountains? They said to him: **No**. He considered them as dull as an ass. He told them: Since ye do not see anything, "Abide ye here with the ass" [Genesis 22:5], with such who are similar to the ass.

He took the wood and placed it upon the back of his son Yitzhak, and he took the fire and the knife in his hand, and they went both of them together. Yitzhak said to his father: O my father. Behold the fire and the wood, where is the lamb for the burnt offering? He replied to him: My son. Thou art the lamb for the burnt offering, as it is said, "And Avraham said, God will provide for himself the lamb" [Genesis 22:8].

Rebbi Shimon said: The Holy One, blessed be He, pointed out the altar with a finger to Avraham our

Pirkei DeRabbi Eliezer 31

father, and said to him: This is the altar. That was the altar whereon Cain and Abel sacrificed; it was the same altar whereon Noah and his sons sacrificed, as it is said, "And Avraham built the altar there" [Genesis 22:9]. "And Avraham built an altar there" is not written here, but "And Avraham built the altar there." That was the altar whereon the first ones, of old had sacrificed.

Yitzhak said to his father Avraham: O my father. Bind for me my two hands, and my two feet, so that I do not curse thee; for instance, a word may issue from the mouth because of the violence and dread of death, and I shall be found to have slighted the precept, "Honour thy father" [Exodus 20:12]. He bound his two hands and his two feet, and bound him upon the top of the altar, and he strengthened his two arms and his two knees upon him, and put the fire and wood in order, and he stretched forth his hand and took the knife. Like a high Ha-Kohen he brought near his meal offering, and his drink offering; and the Holy One, blessed be He, was sitting and beholding the father binding with all his heart and the son bound with all his heart. And the ministering angels cried aloud and wept, as it is said, "Behold, the **Erelim** [Type of angels] cry without; the angels of peace weep bitterly" [Isaiah 33:7]. The ministering angels said before the Holy One, blessed be He: Sovereign of all the worlds. Thou art called merciful and compassionate, whose mercy is upon all His works; have mercy upon Yitzhak, for he is a human being, and the son of a human being, and is bound before tree like

Pirkei DeRabbi Eliezer 31

an animal, "O Hashem, thou preservest man and beast"; as it is said, "Thy righteousness is like the mighty mountains; thy judgments are like a great deep: O Hashem, thou preservest man and beast" [Psalms 36:7].

Rebbi Yehuda said: When the blade touched his neck, the soul of Yitzhak fled and departed, but when he heard His voice from between the two **Cherubim** [Type of angels], saying to Avraham, "Lay not thine hand upon the lad" [Genesis 22:12], his soul returned to his body, and Avraham set him free, and Yitzhak stood upon his feet. And Yitzhak knew that in this manner the dead in the future will be quickened. He opened [his mouth], and said: Blessed art thou, O Hashem, who quickeneth the dead.

Rebbi Zechariah said: That ram, which was created at the twilight, ran and came to be offered up instead of Yitzhak, but Sammae"l [The angel of death] was standing by, and distracting it, in order to annul the offering of our father Avraham. And it was caught by its two horns in the trees, as it is said, "And Avraham lifted up his eyes, and looked, and behold, behind him a ram caught in the thicket by its horns" [Genesis 22:13]. What did that ram do? It put forth its leg and took hold of the coat of our father Avraham, and Avraham looked, saw the ram, and he went and set it free. He offered it up instead of Yitzhak his son, as it is said, "And Avraham went and took the ram, and offered it up for a burnt offering in the stead of his son" [Genesis 22:13].

Pirkei DeRabbi Eliezer 31

Rebbi Berachiah said: The sweet savour of the ram ascended before the Holy One, blessed be He, as though it were the sweet savour of Yitzhak, and He swore that He would bless him in this world and in the world to come, as it is said, "By myself have I sworn, saith the Hashem, because thou hast done this thing"; and it says, "That in blessing I will bless thee, and in multiplying I will multiply thy seed, as the stars of the heaven" [Genesis 22:16, 17]. "That in blessing" refers to this world; "I will bless thee," in the world to come; and "I will greatly multiply thy seed," [Genesis 22:17]. in the future that is to come.

Rebbi Chanina ben Dosa said: From that ram, which was created at the twilight, nothing came forth which was useless. The ashes of the ram were the base which was upon the top of the inner altar. The sinews of the ram were the strings of the harp whereon David played. The ram's skin was the girdle around the loins of Eliyahu, may he be remembered for good, as it is said, "And they answered him, He was a hairy man, and girt with a girdle of leather about his loins" [Kings-B 1:8]. The horn of the ram of the left side was the one wherein He blew upon Mount Sinai, as it is said, "And it shall come to pass, that when the ram's horn soundeth long" [Yehoshua 6:5]. The horn of the right side, which is larger than that of the left, is destined in the future to be sounded in the world that is to come, as it is said, "And it shall come to pass in that day, that a great trumpet shall be blown" [Isaiah 27:13]; and it is said, "And the Hashem shall be king over all the earth" [Zechariah 14:9].

Pirkei DeRabbi Eliezer 31

Rebbi Yitzhak said: Nothing has been created except by the merit of worship. Avraham returned from Mount Moriah only through the merit of worship, as it is said, "We will worship, and come again to you" [Genesis 22:5]. The Temple was fashioned only through the merit of worship, as it is said, "Exalt ye the Hashem our God, and worship" [Psalms 99:5].

Chapter 32

Six people were called by their names before they were created, and they are: Yitzhak, Yishmael, Moshe, Solomon, Josiah, and the name of King Mashiach.

How do we know this with reference to Yitzhak? Because it is said, "And God said, Sarah thy wife shall bear thee a son indeed; and thou shalt call his name Yitzhak" [Genesis 17:19]. Why his name was called Yitzhak? Because Yad י the first Hebrew letter of Yitzhak indicates, the ten trials wherewith our father Avraham was tried; and he withstood them all. Zaddi צ the second letter indicates the ninety years, for his mother was ninety years at the birth of Yitzhak, as it is said, "And shall Sarah, that is ninety years old, bear?" [Genesis 17:17]. Cheth ח the third letter points to the eighth day, for he was circumcised on the eighth day, as it is said, "And Avraham circumcised his son Yitzhak, being eight days old" [Genesis 21:4]. Ḳuf ק the fourth letter of the name marks] the hundred years, for his father Avraham was a hundred years old at Yitzhak's birth, as it is said, "And Avraham was a hundred years old" [Genesis 21:5].

Whence do we know about Yishmael? Because it is said, "And the angel of the Hashem said unto her, Behold, thou art with child… and thou shalt call his name Yishmael" [Genesis 16:11]. Why was his name called Yishmael? Because in the future the Holy

Pirkei DeRabbi Eliezer 32

One, blessed be He, will hearken to the cry of the people arising from the oppression which the children of Yishmael will bring about in the land in the last days; therefore, was his name called Yishmael. As it said: "God who has reigned from the first, who will have no successor" [Psalms 55:20].

Whence do we know about Moshe? Because it is said, "And the Hashem said, my spirit shall not abide בְּשַׁגָּם in man for ever in their going astray" [Genesis 6:3]. What is the implication of the expression, "In their going astray"? Retrospectively his name was called Moshe. For the life of Moshe was one hundred and twenty years, as it is said, "His days shall be a hundred and twenty years" [Genesis 6:3].

Whence do we know concerning Solomon? Because it is said, "Behold, a son shall be born to thee, who shall be a man of rest… for his name shall be Solomon" [Chronicles-A 22:9]. Why was his name called Solomon? Because his name was called Solomon in the Aramaic language, as it is said, "I will give peace Shalom and quietness unto Israel in his days" [Chronicles-A 22:9].

Whence do we know about Josiah? Because it is said, "Behold, a child shall be born unto the house of David, Josiah by name" [Kings-A 13:2]. Why was his name called Josiah? Because he was as acceptable as an offering upon the altar; she said: A worthy offering let him be before Thee יאי שׁי הו. Therefore, was his name called Josiah, as it is said,

Pirkei DeRabbi Eliezer 32

"And he cried against the altar," etc. [Kings-A 13:2].

Whence do we know concerning King Mashiach? Because it is said, "His name shall endure for ever. Before the sun his name shall be continued **Yinnon**" [Psalms 72:17]. Why was his name called Yinnon? For he will awaken those who sleep at Hebron out of the dust of the earth, therefore is his name called Yinnon, as it is said, "Before the sun his name is Yinnon" [Psalms 72:17].

When Avraham returned from Mount Moriah in peace, the anger of Sammae"l [The angel of death] was kindled, for he saw that the desire of his heart to frustrate the offering of our father Avraham had not been realized. What did he do? He went and said to Sarah: Hast thou not heard what has happened in the world? She said to him: No. He said to her: Thy husband, Avraham, has taken thy son Yitzhak and slain him and offered him up as a burnt offering upon the altar. She began to weep and to cry aloud three times, corresponding to the three sustained notes of the Shofar, and she gave forth three howlings corresponding to the three disconnected short notes of the Shofar, and her soul fled, and she died.

Avraham came and found that she was dead. Whence did he come? From Mount Moriah, as it is said, "And Avraham came to mourn for Sarah" [Genesis 23:2].

Rebbi Yossi said: Yitzhak observed mourning

Pirkei DeRabbi Eliezer 32

during three years for his mother. After three years he married Rivkah, and forgot the mourning for his mother. Hence, thou mayest learn that until a man marries a wife his love centres in his parents. When he marries a wife, his love is bestowed upon his wife, as it is said, "Therefore shall a man leave his father and his mother, and he shall cleave unto his wife" [Genesis 2:24]. Does a man then leave his father and mother with reference to the precept, "Honour"? But the love of his soul cleaves unto his wife, as it is said, "And his soul clave unto Dinah" [Genesis 34:3]; and it says, "And he shall cleave unto his wife" [Genesis 2:24].

Rebbi Yehuda said: Rivkah was barren for twenty years. After twenty years Yitzhak took Rivkah and went with her to Mount Moriah, to the place where he had been bound, and he prayed on her behalf concerning the conception of the womb; and the Holy One, blessed be He, was entreated of him, as it is said, "And Yitzhak beseeched Hashem" [Genesis 25:21]. The children were contending with one another within her womb like mighty warriors, as it is said, "And the children struggled together within her" [Genesis 25:22]. The time of her confinement came round, and her soul was nigh unto death owing to her pains. And she went to pray in the place whither she and Yitzhak had gone, as it is said, "And she went to inquire of the Hashem" [Genesis 25:22]. What did the Holy One, blessed be He, do? Yaakov took hold of the heels of Esav to make him fall, as it is said, "And after that came forth his brother, and his hand had hold on Esav's heel" [Genesis 25:26].

Pirkei DeRabbi Eliezer 32

Hence thou mayest learn that the descendants of Esav will not fall until a remnant from Yaakov will come and cut off the feet of the children of Esav from the mountain of Seir, as it is said, "Forasmuch as thou sawest that a stone was cut out of the mountain without hands" [Daniel 2:45]. Another Scripture text says, "Vengeance is mine, and a recompense, at the time when their foot shall slide" [Deuteronomy 32:35].

Rebbi Acha said: The two lads grew up; the one went by the way of life, and the other went by the way of death, as it is said, "And the boys grew, and Esav was a cunning hunter" [Genesis 25:27]. Yaakov went on the way of life, for he was dwelling in tents, and he studied the Torah all his days. Esav went on the way of death, because he slew Nimrod and his son Chavir, and he almost sought to kill Yaakov his brother, as it is said, "The days of mourning for my father are at hand, and I will slay my brother Yaakov" [Genesis 27:41].

Rebbi Shimon said: In the hour when Yitzhak was bound, he lifted up his eyes heavenwards and saw the glory of the Shekhinah [divine presence], as it is written, "For man shall not see me and live" [Exodus 33:20]. Instead of death his eyes grew dim in his old age, as it is said, "And it came to pass, that when Yitzhak was old, that his eyes were dim, so that he could not see" [Genesis 27:1]. Hence, thou mayest learn that the blind man is as though he were dead.

The night-fall of the festival day of Passover came,

Pirkei DeRabbi Eliezer 32

and Yitzhak called unto Esav his elder son, and said: O my son. To-night the heavenly ones utter songs, on this night the treasuries of dew are opened; on this day the blessing of the dews is bestowed. Make me savoury meat whilst I am still alive, and I will bless thee. The Holy Spirit rejoined, saying to him: "Eat thou not the bread of him that hath an evil eye, neither desire thou his dainties" [Proverbs 23:6]. He went to fetch it, and was delayed there. Rivkah said to Yaakov his other son: On this night the treasuries of dew will be opened, and on this night the angels utter a song. Make savoury meat for thy father that he may eat and whilst he still lives, he may bless thee.

Now Yaakov was skilled in the Torah, and his heart dreaded the curse of his father. His mother said to him: My son. If it be a blessing, may it be upon thee and upon thy seed; if it be a curse, let it be upon me and upon my soul, as it is said, "And his mother said to him, upon me be thy curse, my son" [Genesis 27:13]. He went and brought two kids of the goats. Were two kids of the goats the food for Yitzhak? But he brought one as a Korban offering, and with the other he prepared the savoury meat to eat; and he brought it to his father, and he said to him: "Arise, I pray thee, sit and eat of my venison" [Genesis 27:19]. Yitzhak said: "The voice is the voice of Yaakov" [Genesis 27:22]. Yaakov declares the unity of God. "The voice is the voice of Yaakov" [Genesis 27:22] in the meditation of the Torah. "And the hands are the hands of Esav" [Genesis 27:22], in all shedding of blood and in every evil death. Not only this, but also when

Pirkei DeRabbi Eliezer 32

they proclaim in heaven, "The voice is the voice of Yaakov," the heavens tremble. And when they proclaim on earth, "The voice is the voice of Yaakov" [Genesis 27:22], everyone who hears will make his portion with "The voice which is the voice of Yaakov." And every one who does not hear and does not act obediently, his portion is with "The hands, which are the hands of Esav."

Rebbi Yehuda said: Yitzhak blessed Yaakov with ten blessings concerning the dews of heaven and the corn of the earth, corresponding to the ten words whereby the world was created, as it is said, "And God give thee of the dew of the heaven" [Genesis 27:28]; "Let peoples serve thee, ..." [Genesis 27:29]. When Yaakov went forth from the presence of his father Yitzhak, he went forth crowned like a bridegroom, and like a bride in her adornment, and the quickening dew from heaven descended upon him, and refreshed his bones, and he also became a mighty hero; therefore, it is said, "By the hands of the mighty Yaakov, from thence is the shepherd, the stone of Israel" [Genesis 49:24].

Chapter 33

And Yitzhak sowed in that land" [Genesis 26 12]. Rebbi Eliezer said: Did Yitzhak sow the seed of corn? Heaven forbids. But he took all his wealth, and sowed it in charity to the needy, as it is said, "Sow to yourselves in righteousness, reap according to love" [Hosea 10:12]. Everything which he tithed, the Holy One, blessed be He, sent him in return one hundred times the value in different kinds of blessings, as it is said, "And he found in the same year a hundredfold: and the Hashem blessed him" [Genesis 26:12].

Rebbi Shimon said: Owing to the power of charity the dead will be quickened in the future. Whence do we learn this? From Eliyahu the Tishbite. For he betook himself to Zarephath, and a woman who was a widow, received him with great honour. She was the mother of **Yonah**, and they were eating and drinking his bread and oil; he, she, and her son, as it is said, "And she did eat, and he also" [Kings-A 17:15].

Rebbi Levi said: "He and she", indicate that it was by the merit of Eliyahu that they had to eat. After a period of days, the son of the woman fell sick and died, as it is said, "And it came to pass after these things that the son of the woman fell sick" [Kings-A 17:17]. The woman said to him Eliyahu: Thou didst come unto me for coition, and thou wilt bring my sin to remembrance against me, and my son is dead.

Pirkei DeRabbi Eliezer 33

Now take away all that which thou hast brought to me, and give me my son. Eliyahu, may he be remembered for good, arose and prayed before the Holy One, blessed be He, and said before Him: Sovereign of all the worlds. Is it not enough to endure all the evils which have befallen me, but also this woman; for I know that out of sorrow for her son has she spoken of a matter which has not occurred, which she has brought against me to vex me. Now let all the generations learn that there is a resurrection of the dead, and restore the soul of this lad within him; and He was entreated of him, as it is said, "And the Hashem hearkened unto the voice of Eliyahu" [Kings-A 17:22]. Another Scripture text says, "And Eliyahu took the child… See, thy son liveth" [Kings-A 17:23].

Rebbi Yehoshua ben Karha said: Art thou astonished at this? Do not be astonished, come and see, learn from **Elisha**, the son of Shaphat, for no woman was able to gaze at his face without dying; and he went from mount to mount, and from cave to cave, and he went to Shunem, and a great woman received him with great honour. She was a sister of Abishag, the **Shunammite**, the mother of Oded, the prophet, as it is said, "And it fell on a day, that Elisha passed to Shunem" [Kings-B 4:8], and the woman said to her husband: This man of God is holy, no woman is able to gaze at his face without dying; but, "Let us make, I pray thee, a little chamber on the wall; and let us set for him there a bed, and a table, and a stool, and a lampstand" [Kings-B 4:10]. And every time that he passes, he can turn thither into the chamber, as it

Pirkei DeRabbi Eliezer 33

is said, "And it fell on a day, that he came thither, and he turned into the chamber" [Kings-B 4:11]. And he called for the Shunammite, as it is said, "And he said, Call her. And when he had called her, she stood at the door" [Kings-B 4:15]. Why did she stand at the door? Because she was unable to gaze at his face, so that she should not die. He said to her:

"**At** this season, when the time cometh round, thou shalt embrace a son" [Kings-B 4:16], the fruit of thy womb. She said to him: My Hashem is very old, and the way of women has departed from me, and it is impossible to do this thing. "Nay, my Hashem, thou man of God, do not lie unto thine handmaid" [Kings-B 4:16].

Rebbi Zechariah said: "He will fulfill the desire of them that fear him" [Psalms 145:19]. The Holy One, blessed be He, fulfilled the desire of the prophet. She conceived and bore a child, and the child grew. He went forth to refresh himself, and to look at the reapers. A mishap overtook him, and he died, as it is said, "It fell on a day, that he went out to his father to the reapers" [Kings-B 4:18]; this restrained them [from work] until he came among them, and he died, as it is said, "And he sat on her knees till noon, and then died" [Kings-B 4:20].

The woman went to Mount Carmel, and fell on her face to the ground before Elisha, saying to him: Would that my vessel had remained empty. But it was filled, and now its contents are spilt. The prophet answered: Everything which the Holy One,

Pirkei DeRabbi Eliezer 33

blessed be He, doeth, He telleth to me, but He has hidden this matter, as it is said, "And when she came to the man of God… and Gehazi came near to thrust her away" [Kings-B 4:25]. What is the meaning of "to thrust her away"? To teach us that he put his hand upon her pride, which was upon her breasts, as it is said, "And the man of God said, Let her alone… and the Hashem hath hid it from me, and hath not told me" [Kings-B 4:27]. He took the staff which was in his hand, and gave it to Gehazi, saying to him: Do not speak with thy mouth any word at all; know that thou goest and placest the staff upon the face of the lad, that he may live.

Now as for Gehazi, the matter was laughable in his eyes, and to every man whom he met he said: Dost thou believe that this staff will bring the dead to life? Therefore, he did not succeed until **Elisha** went on foot and put his face upon the face of the child, and his eyes upon his eyes, and his hands upon his hands, and he began to pray before the Holy one, blessed be He: Sovereign of all the worlds. Just as Thou didst perform miracles by the hand of Eliyahu, my master, and brought the dead to life, likewise let this child live; and He was entreated of him, as it is said, "Then he returned, and walked in the house once to and fro; and went up, and stretched himself upon him" [Kings-B 4:35]; "and the child sneezed seven times" [Kings-B 4:35].

Rebbi Azariah said: Know thou the efficacy of charity. Come and see from the instance of Shallum, son of Tikvah, who was one of the important men of

Pirkei DeRabbi Eliezer 33

his generation, giving charity every day. What did he do? He filled the bottle with water, and sat at the entrance of the city, and he would give water to every person who came on the way, restoring his soul to him. On account of the charity which he did, the Holy Spirit rested upon his wife, as it is said, "So Hilkiah the Ha-Kohen… went unto Huldah the prophetess, the wife of Shallum, the son of Tikvah" [Kings-B 22:14]. Originally his name was "the son of Sachrah"; just as thou dost say, "Merchandise is better than the circulation of money" [Proverbs 3:14]. One Scripture text says, "The son of Sachrah." When her husband died, the charitable deeds of her husband ceased, and all Israel went forth to show loving-kindness to Shallum, son of Tikvah. But they spied the band, and they cast the man into the sepulchre of Elisha, and he came to life, as it is said, "And as soon as the man touched the bones of Elisha, he revived" [Kings-B 13:21]; and afterwards he begat Chanameel, as it is said, "Behold, Chanameel the son of Shallum thine uncle shall come unto thee" [Jeremiah 32:7].

Rebbi Eliezer said: Know thou the power of charity. Come and see from the instance of Shaul, the son of Kish, who removed the witches and the necromancers from off the earth, and once again he loved that which he had hated. He went to **En Dor** [A city in the Land of Israel], to the wife of Zephaniah, the mother of Abner, and he inquired of her for himself by the familiar spirit, and she brought for him Samuel the prophet, and the dead saw Samuel ascending, and they ascended with him, thinking that the resurrection of the dead had come, and the woman beheld, and she became very much confused, as it is said, "And the king said unto her, Be not afraid: for what seest thou?" [Samuel-A 28:13]. Some say: Many righteous men like Samuel came up with him in that hour.

Rebbi Eliezer said: All the dead will arise at the resurrection of the dead, dressed in their shrouds. Know thou that this is the case. Come and see from the analogy of the one who plants seed in the earth. He plants naked seeds and they arise covered with many coverings; and the people who descend into the earth dressed with their garments, will they not rise up dressed with their garments? Not only this, but come and see from Chananiah, Mishael, and Azariah, who went down into the fiery furnace dressed in their garments, as it is said, "And the satraps… being gathered together, saw these men, that the fire had no power upon their bodies… neither were their hosen changed" [Daniel 3:27]. Learn from Samuel, the prophet, who came up clothed with his robe, as it is said, "And she said, an old man cometh up; and he is covered with a robe" [Samuel-A 28:14].

Rebbi Yohanan said: All the prophets prophesied in their lifetime, and Samuel prophesied in his lifetime, and after his death, because Samuel said to Shaul: If thou wilt hearken to my advice to fall by the sword, then shall thy death be an atonement for thee, and thy lot shall be with me in the place where I abide. Shaul harkened to his advice, and fell by the sword,

Pirkei DeRabbi Eliezer 33

he and all his sons, as it is said, "So Shaul died, and his three sons" [Samuel-A 31:6]. Why? So that his portion might be with Samuel the prophet in the future life, as it is said, "And tomorrow shalt thou and thy sons be with me" [Samuel-A 28:19]. What is the meaning of "with me"? Rebbi Yohanan said: With me in my division in heaven.

Hillel the Elder, said: Samuel spake to Shaul, saying, was it not enough for thee that thou didst not hearken unto His voice, neither didst thou execute His fierce anger upon Amalek, but thou dost also inquire through one possessed of a familiar spirit, nor thou seekest to know the future. Woe is the shepherd, and woe is his flock. For on thy account has the Holy One, blessed be He, given Israel thy people into the hands of the Philistines, as it is said, "Moreover, the Hashem will deliver Israel also with thee into the hand of the Philistines" [Samuel-A 28:19].

Rebbi Tachanah said: Israel was exiled to Babylon, and did not forsake their evil deeds. Ahab, son of Kolaiah, and Zedekiah, son of Maaseiah, became lying healers, and they healed the wives of the Chaldeans, and came unto them for coition. The king heard thereof, and commanded that they should be burnt. They both said: Let us say that Yehoshua, the son of Yehozadak, was with us, and he will save us from the burning with fire. They said to him: O our Hashem, O king, this man was with us in every matter. The king commanded that the three should be burnt by fire. And the angel Michael descended and saved Yehoshua from the fiery flames, and

Pirkei DeRabbi Eliezer 33

brought him up before the throne of glory, as it is said, "And he shewed me Yehoshua, the high Ha-Kohen" [Zechariah 3:1]; and the other two were burnt by fire, as it is said, "And of them shall be taken up a curse…. The Hashem make thee like Zedekiah and like Ahab, whom the king of Babylon roasted in the fire" [Jeremiah 29:22]. It is not written here "whom the king of Babylon burnt with fire," but "whom he roasted," hence we learn that his hairs were singed on account of their sins, as it is said, "In the pride of the wicked the poor is hotly pursued" [Psalms 10:2]. Whence do we know that he was delivered? Because it is said, "And the Hashem said unto Satan, The Hashem rebuke thee, O Satan…. Is not this a brand plucked out of the fire?" [Zechariah 3:2].

Rebbi Yehuda said: When Nebuchadnezzar brought a false accusation against Israel to slay them, he set up an idol in the plain of Dura, and caused a herald to proclaim: Anyone who does not bow down to this idol shall be burnt by fire. Israel did not trust in the shadow of their Creator, and came with their wives and sons and bowed down to the idolatrous image - except Daniel, whom they called by the name of their God, and it would have been a disgrace to them to burn him in fire, as it is said, "But at the last Daniel came in before me" [Daniel 4:8]. And they took Chananiah, Mishael, and Azariah, and put them into the fiery furnace, and the angel Gabriel descended and saved them from the fiery furnace. The king said to them: Ye knew that ye had a God who saves and delivers; why have ye forsaken your God and worshipped idols which have no power to deliver?

Pirkei DeRabbi Eliezer 33

But just as ye did in your own land and destroyed it, so do ye attempt to do in this land, namely to destroy it. The king commanded, and they slew all of them. Whence do we know that they were all slain by the sword? Because it is said, "Then said he unto me, Prophesy... O breath, and breathe upon these slain, that they may live" [Ezekiel 37:9].

Rebbi Pinchas said: After twenty years, when all of them had been slain in Babylon, the Holy Spirit rested upon Ezekiel, and brought him forth into the plain of Dura, and called unto him very dry bones, and said to him: Son of Man. What dost thou see? He answered: I see here dry bones. The Spirit said to him: Have I power to revive them? The prophet did not say: Sovereign of all the worlds. Thou hast power to do even more than this here; but he said: "O Hashem God, thou knowest" [Ezekiel 37:3], as though he did not believe; therefore, his own bones were not buried in a pure land, but in an unclean land, as it is said, "And thou shalt die in a land that is unclean" [Amos 7:17]. "Prophesy over these bones" [Ezekiel 37:4]. He said before Him: Sovereign of all the worlds. What. Will the prophecy bring upon them flesh and sinews and bones? Or will the prophecy bring upon them all the flesh and bones which cattle, beast, and bird have eaten, and they also have died in the land? Immediately the Holy One, blessed be He, caused His voice to be heard, and the earth shook, as it is said, "And as I prophesied there was a thundering, and behold an earthquake" [Ezekiel 37:7], and every animal, beast, and bird which had eaten thereof and died in another land the earth brought

Pirkei DeRabbi Eliezer 33

together, "bone to his bone" [Ezekiel 37:7].

Rebbi Yehoshua ben Karha said: There came down upon them the quickening dew from heaven, which was like a fountain, which was bubbling and bringing forth water; so likewise, the bones were moving and bringing forth upon themselves flesh, other bones and sinews, as it is said, "And I beheld, and lo, there were sinews upon them, and flesh came up, and skin covered them above" [Ezekiel 37:8]. He said to him: Prophesy unto the wind, as it is said, "Then said he unto me, Prophesy unto the wind.… Come from the four winds, O breath, and breathe upon these slain, that they may live" [Ezekiel 37:9]. In that hour the four winds of the heaven went forth, and opened the treasure-house of the souls, and each spirit returned to the body of flesh of man, as it is said, "So I prophesied as he commanded me, and the breath came into them, and they lived… an exceeding great army" [Ezekiel 37:10]; and it is written about Egypt, "And the children of Israel were fruitful… and waxed exceeding mighty" [Exodus 1:7]. What is the meaning of "exceeding"? Just as in the latter case there were 600,000 men, so in the former case there were 600,000 men, and they all stood upon their feet except one man. The prophet said: Sovereign of all the worlds. What is the nature of this man? He answered him: He gave out money for usury, and he took with interest. As I live, he shall not live. In that hour the Israelites were sitting and weeping, and saying: We hoped for light, and darkness came. We hoped to stand up with all Israel at the resurrection of the dead, and now "our hope is

Pirkei DeRabbi Eliezer 33

lost" [Ezekiel 37:11]. We hoped to arise so as to be gathered with all Israel, and now "we are clean cut off" [Ezekiel 37:11]. In that hour the Holy One, blessed be He, said to the prophet: Therefore, say to them, As I live, I will cause you to stand at the resurrection of the dead in the future that is to come, and I will gather you with all Israel to the land, as it is said, "Behold, I will open your graves, and cause you to come up out of your graves... and I will bring you into the land of Israel.... And I will put my spirit in you, and ye shall live" [Ezekiel 37:12-14].

Chapter 34

"**See** now that I, even I, am he, and there is no God with me" [Deuteronomy 32:89]. Only the Holy One, blessed be He, said: " I am " in this world, and " I am " in the world to come; I am the one who redeemed Israel from Egypt, and I am the one who, in the future, will redeem them at the end of the fourth kingdom; therefore, it is said, "I, even I, am he, and there is no God with me" [Deuteronomy 32:89]. Every nation who says that there is a second God, I will slay them as with a second death which has no resurrection; and every nation who say that there is no second God, I will quicken them for the eternal life. And in the future, I will slay those first mentioned and quicken these, therefore it is said, "I kill, and I make alive" [Deuteronomy 32:89]. I have wounded Jerusalem and her people on the day of my anger, and in great mercy I will heal them, therefore it is said, "I have wounded, and I will heal" [Deuteronomy 32:89]. Neither any angel nor any seraph will deliver the wicked from the judgment of Gehinnom, as it is said, "And there is none that can deliver out of my hand" [Deuteronomy 32:89].

Rebbi Yehonaton said: All the dead will arise at the resurrection of the dead, except the generation of the Flood, as it is said, "The dead shall not live, the deceased Rephaim shall not rise" [Isaiah 26:14]. "The dead who shall not live" refer to the heathens, who are like the carcase of cattle; they shall arise for the day of judgment, yet they shall not live; but the men

Pirkei DeRabbi Eliezer 34

of the generation of the Flood, even for the day of judgment they shall not arise, as it is said, "The Rephaim shall not rise" [Isaiah 26:14]. All their souls become winds, accursed, injuring the sons of men, and in the future world the Holy One, blessed be He, will destroy them out of the world, so that they should not do harm to a single Israelite, as it is said, "Therefore hast thou visited and destroyed them, and made all their memory to perish" [Isaiah 26:14].

Rebbi Zechariah said: The sleep at night is like this world, and the awakening of the morning is like the world to come. And just as in the sleep of the night a man lies down and sleeps, and his spirit wanders over all the earth, and tells him in a dream whatever happens, as it is said, "In a dream, in a vision of the night… then he openeth the ears of men" [Job 33:15-16], likewise with the dead, their spirit wanders over all the earth, and tells them all things that happen in the world, but they are silent and yet they give song and praise to God, who will quicken them in the future, as it is said, "Let the saints exult in glory" [Psalms 149:5]. The awakening in the morning is like the future world. A parable - unto what is the matter to be likened? To a man who awakens out of his sleep, in like manner will the dead awaken in the future world, as it is said, "O satisfy us in the morning with thy loving-kindness" [Psalms 90:14].

The voices of five objects of creation go from one end of the world to the other, and their voices are inaudible. When people cut down the wood of the tree which yields fruit, its cry goes from one end of

Pirkei DeRabbi Eliezer 34

the world to the other, and the voice is inaudible. When the serpent sloughs off its skin, its cry goes from one end of the world to the other and its voice is not heard. When a woman is divorced from her husband, her voice goeth forth from one end of the world to the other, but the voice is inaudible. When the infant comes forth from its mother's womb. When the soul departs from the body, the cry goes forth from one end of the world to the other, and the voice is not heard. The soul does not go out of the body until it beholds the **Shekhinah** [divine presence], as it is said, "For man shall not see me and live" [Exodus 33:20].

Rebbi Ze'era said: All the souls go forth and are gathered, each man's soul to the generation of his fathers and to his people. The righteous with the righteous, and the wicked with the wicked, for thus spake the Holy One, blessed be He, to Avraham: "But thou shalt go to thy fathers in peace" [Genesis 15:15]. And when the soul goes forth from the body, then the righteous come to meet them, and say to them: Yet he shall come to peace" [Isaiah 57:2]. One verse says, "Therefore, behold, I will gather thee to thy fathers, and thou shalt be gathered to thy grave in peace" [Kings-B 22:20].

Rebbi Huna said: All Israel who die outside the land of Israel, their souls are gathered into the land of Israel, as it is said, "Yet the soul of my Hashem shall be bound in the bundle of the living" [Samuel-A 25:29]. All the heathens who die in the land of Israel have their souls cast outside the

Pirkei DeRabbi Eliezer 34

land [of Israel], as it is said, "And the souls of thine enemies, them shall he sling out, as from the hollow of a sling" [Samuel-A 25:29], even beyond the land of Israel.

In the future world the Holy One, blessed be He, will take hold of the corners of the land of Israel, and shake it free from all unclean things, as it is said, "That it might take hold of the ends of the earth, and the wicked be shaken out of it" [Job 38:13].

A man has three friends in his lifetime, and they are: his sons and his household, his money, and his good deeds. At the hour of a man's departure from the world he gathers his sons and his household, and he says to them: I beg of you to come and save me from the judgment of this evil death. They answer him, saying to him: Hast thou not heard that there is no one who can prevail over the day of death? And is it not written thus, "None of them can by any means redeem his brother" [Psalms 49:7], "For the redemption of their soul is costly" [Psalms 49:8]. And he has his money fetched, and says to it: I beseech thee, save me from the judgment of this evil death. It answers him, saying: Hast thou not heard, "Riches profit not in the day of wrath" [Proverbs 11:4], He then has his good deeds fetched, and he says to them: I beseech you, come and deliver me from the judgment of this evil death. And they answer him and say to him: Before thou goest, verily, we will go in advance of thee, as it is said, "And charity delivereth from death" [Proverbs 11:4]. Does then charity deliver from death? This refers to an evil death only. Another

Pirkei DeRabbi Eliezer 34

Scripture says, "And thy righteousness shall go before thee, the glory of the Hashem shall be thy rearward" [Isaiah 58:8].

All the seven days of mourning the soul goeth forth and returneth from its former home to its sepulchral abode, and from its sepulchral abode to its former home. After the seven days of mourning the body begins to breed worms, and it decays and returns to the dust, as it originally was, as it is said, "And the dust returns to the earth as it was" [Ecclesiastes 12:7]. The soul goes forth and returns to the place whence it was given, from heaven, as it is said, "And the soul returns unto God who gave it" [Ecclesiastes 12:7]. And whence do we learn that the soul has been given from heaven? Come and see. When the Holy One, blessed be He, formed man, he did not have in him the spirit. What did the Holy One, blessed be He, do? He breathed with the spirit of the breath of His mouth, and cast a soul into him, as it is said, "And he breathed into his nostrils the breath of life" [Genesis 2:7].

Rebbi Yishmael said: All the bodies crumble into the dust of the earth, until nothing remains of the body except a spoonful of earthy matter. In the future life, when the Holy One, blessed be He, calls to the earth to return all the bodies deposited with it, that which had become mixed with the dust of the earth, like the yeast which is mixed with the dough, improves and increases, and it raises up all the body. When the Holy One, blessed be He, calls to the earth to return all the bodies deposited with it, that which

Pirkei DeRabbi Eliezer 34

has become mixed with the dust of the earth, improves and increases and raises up all the body without water. Forthwith the earth quakes and the mountains tremble, and the graves are opened, and the stones of the graves are scattered about one from the other, as it is said, "And the Hashem God shall save them in that day as the flock of his people: for they shall be as the stones of a crown, lifted on high over his land" [Zechariah 9:16].

Rebbi Azariah said: All the souls are in the hands of the Holy One, blessed be He, as it is said, "In whose hand is the soul of every living thing" [Job 12:10]. A parable - to what is the matter like? To a person who was going in the market with the key of his house in his hand. As long as the key is in his hand, all his money is in his hand. Likewise, the Holy One, blessed be He, has the key of the graves, and the key of the treasure-houses of the souls; and He will restore every spirit to the body of flesh of man, as it is said, "Thou sendest forth thy spirit, they are created; and thou renewest the face of the ground" [Psalms 104:30].

The soul is like its Creator. Just as the Holy One, blessed be He, sees and is not visible, so the soul sees and is not visible. Just as the Holy One, blessed be He, has no sleep in His presence, so the soul does not sleep. Just as the Holy One, blessed be He, bears His world, so the soul bears all the body. All souls are His, as it is said, "Behold, all souls are mine" [Ezekiel 18:4].

Pirkei DeRabbi Eliezer 34

Rebbi Yehuda said: From the day when the Temple was destroyed, the land of Israel is broken down on account of the wickedness of those who dwell therein; like a man who is sick and has no power to stand, so is the land broken down and is without power to yield her fruits, as it is said, "The earth also is polluted under the inhabitants thereof" [Isaiah 24:5].

In the future life the Holy One, blessed be He, will cause the reviving dew to descend, and He will quicken the dead and renew all things, as it is said," Thy dead shall live" [Isaiah 26:19]. They are the Israelites, who died trusting in His name. "My dead bodies shall arise" [Isaiah 26:19]. They are the heathens, who are like the carcase of the beast; they shall arise for the Day of Judgment, but they shall not live. "Awake and sing, ye that dwell in the dust" [Isaiah 26:19]. They are the righteous, for they dwell in the dust. "For thy dew is as the dew of light" [Isaiah 26:19]. The dew of the righteous is not the dew of darkness, but it is the dew of light, as it is said, "For thy dew is as the dew of light" [Isaiah 26:19]; and it gives healing to the earth, as it is said, "And the earth shall cast forth the dead" [Isaiah 26:19]. And what is the meaning of "And the earth shall cast forth the dead"?

Rebbi Tanchum said: On account of the seed of the earth, when it is commanded, it discharges the dew for the resurrection of the dead. From what place does it descend? From the head of the Holy One, blessed be He; for the head of the Holy One, blessed be He, is full of the reviving dew. In the future life

Pirkei DeRabbi Eliezer 34

the Holy One, blessed be He, will shake His head and cause the quickening dew to descend, as it is said, "I was asleep, but my heart waked… for my head is filled with dew, my locks with the drops of the night" [Song of Songs 5:2].

Chapter 35

"**Better** is the end of a thing than the beginning thereof" [Ecclesiastes 7:8]. The first blessings wherewith Yitzhak blessed Yaakov were concerning the dews of heaven, and concerning the corn of the earth, as it is said, "And God give thee of the dew of heaven, and of the fatness of the earth" [Genesis 27:28]. The final blessings were the blessings of the foundation of the world, and in them there is no interruption, either in this world or in the world to come, as it is said, "And God Almighty bless thee" [Genesis 28:3]. And he further added unto him the blessing of Avraham, as it is said, "And may he give thee the blessing of Avraham, to thee and to thy seed with thee" [Genesis 28:4]. Therefore say: "Better is the end of a thing than the beginning thereof" [Ecclesiastes 7:8]. "Better is the patient in spirit than the proud in spirit" [Ecclesiastes 7:8]. "Better is the patient in spirit" - this saying is applicable to our father Yaakov, for every day he was patient in spirit, and he spake all kinds of words of entreaty. The words "Than the proud in spirit" [Ecclesiastes 7:8] refer to the wicked Esav, because every day he was eating the flesh of that which he had hunted. Owing to his pride he did not give any of his food to Yaakov. Once he went out to hunt but he did not meet with any success. He saw Yaakov eating lentil food, and he desired this in his heart, and he said to him: "Let me gulp down, I pray thee, some of that red pottage" [Genesis 25:30]. Yaakov said to him: Thou camest forth red at thy birth from thy mother; now thou dost desire to eat

Pirkei DeRabbi Eliezer 35

this red food; therefore, he called his name "Aram" red, as it is said, "And Esav said to Yaakov" [Genesis 25:30].

Rebbi Eliezer said: Lentils are the food of mourning and sorrow. Know thou that this is so, for when Abel had been killed, his parents were eating lentil food as a sign of their mourning for him in mourning and sorrow. And Yaakov was eating lentil food in mourning and sorrow because the kingdom, the dominion, and the birthright belonged to Esav. Moreover, on that day Avraham, his grandfather, died. The Israelites eat lentil food in mourning and sorrow on account of the mourning and sorrow for the Temple, and on account of the exile of Israel. Hence, thou mayest learn that the children of Esav will not fall until a remnant from Israel shall come and give to the children of Esav lentil food in mourning and sorrow, and will take away from them the dominion of the kingdom and the birthright, which Yaakov acquired from Esav by oath, as it is said, "And Yaakov said, swear to me this day; and he swore unto him" [Genesis 25:33].

Rebbi Akiva said: Every place where our forefathers went, the well went in front of them, and they dug three times and found it before them. Avraham dug three times and found it before him, as it is said, "And Yitzhak dug again the wells of water, which they had dug in the days of Avraham" [Genesis 26:18]. And Yitzhak dug in the land of Canaan four times, and found it before him, as it is said, "And Yitzhak's servants dug in the valley" [Genesis

Pirkei DeRabbi Eliezer 35

26:19]. And it is written about Yerushalayim, "And it shall come to pass in that day, that living waters shall go out from Yerushalayim" [Zechariah 14:8]. This refers to the well which will arise in Yerushalayim in the future, and will water all its surroundings. Because they found the well seven times, he called it **Shib'ah** [seven]. As it said, He named it Shibah; therefore, the name of the city is Beer-sheba to this day.

Yaakov was seventy-seven years old when he went forth from his father's house, and the well went before him. From Beer-Sheba as far as Mount Moriah is a journey of two days, and he arrived there at midday, and the Holy One, blessed be He, met him, as it is said, "And he met in the place, and tarried there all night, because the sun was set" [Genesis 28:11]. Why is the name of the Holy One, blessed be He, called **Maḳom** [place] Because in every place where the righteous are He is found with them there, as it is said, "In every **Maḳom** where I record my name, I will come unto thee, and bless thee" [Exodus 20:21]. The Holy One, blessed be He, said to him: Yaakov. The bread is in thy bag, and the well is before thee, so that thou mayest eat and drink and sleep in this place. He said before Him: Sovereign of all the worlds. Till now the sun has still fifty degrees to set, and I am lying down in this place. And thereupon the sun set in the west, although not in its proper time. Yaakov looked and saw the sun setting in the west, and he tarried there, as it is said, "And he tarried there all night, because the sun was set" [Genesis 28:11].

Pirkei DeRabbi Eliezer 35

Yaakov took twelve stones of the stones of the altar, whereon his father Yitzhak had been bound, and he set them for his pillow in that place, to indicate to himself that twelve tribes were destined to arise from him. And they all became one stone, to indicate to him that all the tribes were destined to become one people on the earth, as it is said, "And who is like thy people Israel, a nation that is alone on the earth" [Chronicles-A 17:21].

Rebbi Levi said: In that night the Holy One, blessed be He, showed him all the signs. He showed him a ladder standing from the earth to the heaven, as it is said, "And he dreamed, and behold a ladder set up on the earth, and the top of it reached to heaven" [Genesis 28:12]. And the ministering angels were ascending and descending thereon, and they beheld the face of Yaakov, and they said: This is the face like the face of the Chayyah, which is on the Throne of Glory. Such angels who were on earth below were ascending to see the face of Yaakov among the faces of the Chayyah, for it was like the face of the Chayyah, which is on the Throne of Glory. Some [angels] ascended and some descended, as it is said, "And behold the angels of God were ascending and descending on it" [Genesis 28:12]. The Holy One, blessed be He, showed him the four kingdoms, their rule and their destruction, and He showed him the prince of the kingdom of Babylon ascending seventy rungs, and descending; and He showed him the prince of the kingdom of Media ascending fifty-two rungs and descending; and He showed him the prince of the kingdom of Greece ascending 180

Pirkei DeRabbi Eliezer 35

ascents and descending; and He showed him the prince of the kingdom of Aram ascending, and he was not descending, but was saying, "I will ascend above the heights of the clouds; I will be like the Most High" [Isaiah 14:14]. Yaakov replied to him: "Yet thou shalt be brought down to Sheol, to the uttermost parts of the pit" [Isaiah 14:15]. The Holy One, blessed be He, said to him: Even "though thou shouldest make thy nest as high as the eagle" [Jeremiah 49:16].

Yaakov rose up early in the morning in great fear, and said: The house of the Holy One, blessed be He, is in this place, as it is said, "And he was afraid, and said, how dreadful is this place. This is none other but the house of God" [Genesis 28:17]. Hence, thou canst learn that everyone who prays in Yerushalayim is reckoned as though he had prayed before the Throne of Glory, for the gate of heaven is there, and it is open to hear the prayers of Israel, as it is said, "And this is the gate of heaven" [Genesis 28:17].

And Yaakov returned to gather the stones, and he found them all turned into one stone, and he set it up for a pillar in the midst of the place, and oil descended for him from heaven, and he poured it thereon, as it is said, "And he poured oil upon the top of it" [Genesis 28:18]. What did the Holy One, blessed be He, do? He placed thereon His right foot, and sank the stone to the bottom of the depths, and He made it the keystone of the earth, just like a man who sets a keystone in an arch; therefore it is called

Pirkei DeRabbi Eliezer 35

the foundation stone, for there is the navel of the earth, and therefrom was all the earth evolved, and upon it the Sanctuary of God stands, as it is said, "And this stone, which I have set up for a pillar, shall be God's house" [Genesis 28:22].

And Yaakov fell upon his face to the ground before the foundation stone, and he prayed before the Holy One, blessed be He, saying: Sovereign of all worlds. If Thou wilt bring me back to this place in peace, I will sacrifice before Thee offerings of thanksgiving and burnt offerings, as it is said, "And Yaakov vowed a vow, saying" [Genesis 28:20]. There he left the well, and thence he lifted up his feet, and in the twinkle of the eye he came to Haran, as it is said, "And Yaakov went on his journey, and came to the land of the children of the east" [Genesis 29:1]; and the [text] says, "And Yaakov went from Beer-Sheba, and went to Haran" [Genesis 28:10]. "And the Holy God is sanctified in righteousness" [Isaiah 5:16]. The angels answered and said: Blessed art Thou, O Hashem, the Holy God.

Chapter 36

"**When** thou goest, thy steps shall not be straightened; and if thou runnest, thou shalt not stumble" [Proverbs 4:12].

Yaakov steps were not straitened, and his strength did not fail, and like a strong hero he rolled away the stone from the mouth of the well, and the well came up, and spread forth water outside itself, and the shepherds saw and they all wondered, for all of them were unable to roll away the stone from the mouth of the well; but Yaakov alone rolled the stone from off the mouth of the well, as it is said, "And Yaakov went near, and rolled the stone from the well's mouth" [Genesis 29:10].

Rebbi Akiva said: Anyone who enters a city, and finds maidens coming forth before him, his way will be prosperous before him. Whence dost thou know this? Know that it is so. Come and see from **Eliezer**, the servant of our father Avraham, who, whilst he had not yet entered the city, found maidens coming out before him, as it is said, "Behold, I stand by the fountain of water," etc. [Genesis 24:43]. And He prospered his way. As it is said, "Now that the LORD has made my errand successful" [Genesis 24:56].

Whence again dost thou learn this? Know that it is so. Come and see from **Moshe**, for, although he had not yet entered the city, he found maidens coming

Pirkei DeRabbi Eliezer 36

out before him, as it is said, "Now the Ha-Kohen of Midian had seven daughters; and they came" [Exodus 2:16]. And He prospered his way, and he redeemed Israel from Egypt.

Whence dost thou know this? Know that it is so. Come and see from **Shaul**, for whilst he had not yet entered the city, he found maidens coming forth before him, as it is said, "As they went up the ascent to the city, they found young maidens going out" [Samuel-A 9:11]. And He prospered his way and he acquired the sovereignty.

And whence do we know this? Know thou that it is so. Come and learn from Yaakov, for whilst he had not yet entered the city, he found maidens coming forth before him, as it is said, "And, behold, Rachel his daughter cometh" [Genesis 29:6].

Rav Huna said: Everything is revealed and foreseen before the Holy One, blessed be He. Before Yaakov came to Haran, what did the Holy One, blessed be He, do? He sent a plague among the sheep of Lavan, and few were left out of many, and Rachel was tending these, as it is said, "Rachel came with her father's sheep; for she kept them" [Genesis 29:9]. Whence do we know that few remained of the many? Because it is said, "And Yaakov fed the rest of Lavan's flocks" [Genesis 30:36], "the rest" which remained after the plague, in order to increase and multiply Lavan's flocks at the feet of Yaakov. Hence the sages said: Sometimes the foot of man destroys the house, and sometimes the foot of man blesses the

Pirkei DeRabbi Eliezer 36

house, as it is said, "And the Hashem hath blessed thee at my foot" [Genesis 30:30]. Likewise, Lavan said to Yaakov: "I have divined that the Hashem hath blessed me for thy sake" [Genesis 30:27].

When Lavan heard the tidings of Yaakov, the son of his sister, and the power of his might which he had displayed at the well, he ran to meet him, to kiss him, and to embrace him, as it is said, "And it came to pass, when Lavan heard the tidings of Yaakov, his sister's son" [Genesis 29:13]. "And Lavan said unto Yaakov, because thou art my brother" [Genesis 29:15]. Was he then his brother? Was he not the son of his sister? This teaches thee that the son of a man's sister is like his son, and the son of a man's brother is like his brother. Whence do we learn this? From Avraham, our father, because it is said, "And Abram said to Lot, let there not be strife… for we are brethren" [Genesis 13:8]. Another verse says, "And when Abram heard that his brother was taken captive" [Genesis 14:14]. Was he, his brother? Was he not the son of his brother? But it teaches thee that the sons of a man's brother are like his own brothers.

The sons of a man's sons are like his own sons. Whence do we learn this? From Yaakov, because it is said, "**Ephraim** and **Menashe**, even as Reuven and Shimon, shall be mine" [Genesis 48:5]. Were they, his sons? Were they not the sons of his son? But it teaches thee that the sons of a man's sons are as his own sons. And the sons of one's daughters are as one's own sons. Whence do we learn this? From Lavan, because it is said, "And Lavan answered and

Pirkei DeRabbi Eliezer 36

said unto Yaakov, the daughters are my daughters, and the sons are my sons" [Genesis 31:43]. Were they then his sons? Were they not the sons of his daughters? But it teaches thee that the sons of a man's daughters are like his own sons.

Yaakov began to serve for a wife for seven years. He made a banquet and rejoicing for seven days, and married **Rachel**, as it is said, "Fulfill the week of this one" [Genesis 29:27]. "And Yaakov did so, and fulfilled the week of this one" [Genesis 29:28]. All the men of the place were gathered together to show loving-kindness to our father Yaakov, as it is said, "And Lavan gathered together all the men of the place, and made a feast" [Genesis 29:22].

The Holy One, blessed be He, said: Ye have shown loving-kindness to Yaakov, My servant, I also will give you and your sons your reward in this world, so that there be no reward for the wicked in the future world, as it is said, "Now Naaman, captain of the host of the king of Aram… because by him the Hashem had given victory unto Aram" [Kings-B 5:1].

Lavan took his two handmaids, and gave them to his two daughters. Were they, his handmaids? Were they not his daughters? But according to the law of the land the daughters of a man by his concubines are called handmaids, as it is said, "And Lavan gave to Rachel his daughter Bilhah his handmaid to be her handmaid" [Genesis 29:29].

Rebbi Levi said: The Holy One, blessed be He, saw

Pirkei DeRabbi Eliezer 36

the sorrow of Leah, and He gave her power to conceive, [bringing] consolation to her soul; and she bore a male child, goodly in appearance, and wise; and she said: See ye a son which the Holy One, blessed be He, has given me, as it is said, "And Leah conceived, and bare a son, and she called his name Reuven; for she said, Because the Hashem hath looked upon my affliction" [Genesis 29:32]. Therefore, he called his name Reuven.

Rebbi Eliezer said: Leah bore her sons after seven months, and in seven years there were born unto Yaakov eleven sons and one daughter. And all of them were born, each with his partner with him, except Yosef, whose partner was not born with him, for **Asenath**, the daughter of Dinah, was destined to be his wife, and also except Dinah, whose partner was not born with her. She said: This child is [according to] justice and judgment, therefore she called her name Dinah.

Rebbi Eliezer also said: Yaakov fled in order to come to Lavan, and he fled to get away from Lavan. Whence do we know that he fled in order to come to Lavan? Because it is said, "And Yaakov fled into the field of Aram" [Hosea 12:13]. Whence do we know that he fled in order to get away from Lavan? Because it is said, "And it was told Lavan on the third day that Yaakov was fled" [Genesis 31:22]. Why did he flee? Because the Holy One, blessed be He, said to him: Yaakov. I cannot suffer My **Shekhinah** [divine presence] to dwell with thee outside the land, but "return unto the land of thy fathers, and to thy

Pirkei DeRabbi Eliezer 36

kindred; and I will be with thee" [Genesis 31:3]. Therefore, he fled. And Lavan took all the men of his city, mighty men, and he pursued after him, seeking to slay him. The angel Michael descended, and drew his sword behind him, seeking to slay him. He said to him: Do not speak to Yaakov, either good or bad, as it is said, "And God came to Lavan the Aramæan in a dream of the night, and said unto him, Take heed to thyself that thou speak not to Yaakov either good or bad" [Genesis 31:24]. Lavan rose up early in the morning, and saw all that Yaakov had, and he said to him: All these are mine, and since thou hast taken all these, yet wherefore hast thou stolen my Teraphim, which I worshipped?

What are the **Teraphim**? They slay a man, a firstborn, and he is red in colour. All that a man requires to know is not written here. This is impossible, since the men who dispute about the knowledge of making the Teraphim have increased. Everyone who follows that knowledge will ultimately go down to Gehinnom. And they pinch off his head, and salt it with salt, and they write upon a golden plate the name of an unclean [spirit], and place it under his tongue, and they put it in the wall, and they kindle lamps before it, and bow down to it, and it speaks unto them. Whence do we know that the Teraphim speak? Because it is said, "For the Teraphim have spoken vanity" [Zechariah 10:2]. On that account had Rachel stolen them, so that they should not tell Lavan that Yaakov had fled, and not only that, but also to remove idolatrous worship from her father's house.

Pirkei DeRabbi Eliezer 36

Now Yaakov knew nothing of all this, and he said: Anyone who has stolen thy Teraphim shall die before his proper time; and the utterance of a righteous person is like the speech from the mouth of an angel, and **Rachel** gave birth and died, as it is said, "And it came to pass, as her soul was in departing, for she died" [Genesis 35:18].

Rebbi Yehuda said: Three forefathers made covenants with the people of the land. With reference to Avraham the circumstances were as follows. When the angels were revealed unto him, he thought that they were travellers from among the people of the land, and he ran to meet them, and he wished to prepare for them a great banquet, and he told Sarah to prepare cakes for them. When Sarah was kneading, she perceived that the manner of women was upon her, therefore he did not hand them any of the cakes. He ran to fetch a calf. But the calf fled from before him, and went into the Cave of Machpelah, and he went in there after it, and he found Adam and his help-meet lying there upon their beds, and they slept, and lights were kindled above them, and a sweet scent was upon them like a sweet savour, therefore he desired to have the Cave of Machpelah as a burial possession. He spoke to the sons of **Jebus** [they lived in Yerushalayim], in order to purchase from them the Cave of Machpelah by a purchase with gold, and by a perpetual deed for a possession of a burying-place. Were they Jebusites? Were they not Hittites? But they were called Jebusites according to the name of the city of Jebus. The men did not accept [this request]. He began to

Pirkei DeRabbi Eliezer 36

bow down and prostrate himself unto them, as it is said, "And Avraham bowed himself down before the people of the land" [Genesis 23:12].

They said to him: We know that the Holy One, blessed be He, will give to thee and to thy seed in the future all these lands; make a covenant with us by an oath that thy seed shall not take possession of the cities of Jebus, and we will sell unto thee the Cave of Machpelah by a purchase with gold and by a perpetual deed and for a perpetual possession. He made with them a covenant with an oath that the Israelites would not take possession of the city of Jebus save by the consent of the sons of Jebus, and afterwards he bought the Cave of Machpelah by a purchase with gold, and a perpetual deed, for a perpetual possession, as it is said, "And Avraham hearkened unto Ephron; and Avraham weighed to Ephron the silver, which he had named in the hearing of the children of Heth, four hundred shekels of silver, current money with the merchant" [Genesis 23:16].

What did the men of Jebus do? They made images of copper, and set them up in the street of the city, and wrote upon them the covenant of the oath of Avraham. When the Israelites came to the land of Canaan, they wished to enter the city of the Jebusites, but they were not able to enter, because of the sign of the covenant of Avraham's oath, as it is said, "And the children of Binyamin did not drive out the Jebusites that inhabited Yerushalayim" [Judges 1:21]. When David reigned, he desired to enter the city of the Jebusites, but they did not allow him, as it is said, "And the king and his men went to Yerushalayim against the Jebusites, the inhabitants of the land; which spake unto David, saying, thou shalt not come in hither" [Samuel-B 5:6].

Although the Israelites were like the sand of the sea, yet it was owing to the force of the sign of the covenant of Avraham's oath. David saw this and turned backwards, as it is said, "And David dwelt in the stronghold" [Samuel-B 5:9]. They said to him: Thou wilt not be able to enter the city of the Jebusites until thou hast removed all those images upon which the sign of the covenant of Avraham's oath is written, as it is said, "Except thou take away the blind and the lame" [Samuel-B 5:6]. "The lame" refers to the images, as it is said, "Wherefore they say, the blind and the lame shall not come into the house" [Samuel-B 5:8]. Lest thou shouldst say, the blind and the lame did not enter the Sanctuary, Heaven forbid [that we should say this], but these "blind and lame" refer to the images which have eyes and see not, feet and they walk not, as it is said, "That are hated of David's soul" [Samuel-B 5:8]. Because David hated to hear of and to see idolatry, as it is said, "Wherefore they say, the blind and the lame shall not come into the house" [Samuel-B 5:8].

David said to his men: Whoever will go up first, and remove those images upon which the sign of the covenant of Avraham's oath is written, he shall be the chief. And Joab, the son of Zeruiah, went up, and he became the chief, as it is said, "And Joab the son

Pirkei DeRabbi Eliezer 36

of Zeruiah went up first, and was made chief" [Chronicles-A 11:6]. Afterwards he bought the city of the Jebusites for Israel by a purchase with gold and with a perpetual deed for a perpetual possession. What did David do? He took from each tribe fifty shekels; verily all of them amounted to six hundred shekels, as it is said, "So David gave to Ornan for the place six hundred shekels of gold by weight" [Chronicles-A 21:25].

Yitzhak made a covenant with the people of the land, when he sojourned in the land of the Philistines. He noticed that they turned their faces away from him. He went away from them in peace, and **Avimelech** and all his magnates came after him. He said to them: Ye turned aside your faces from me, and now ye come unto me, as it is said, "And Yitzhak said unto them, wherefore are ye come unto me, seeing ye hate me?" [Genesis 26:27]. "And they said, we saw plainly that the Hashem was with thee" [Genesis 26:28]. They said: We know that the Holy One, blessed be He, will give to thy seed in the future all these lands; make a covenant of an oath with us, that thy seed will not take possession of the land of the Philistines. He made a covenant of an oath with them. What did Yitzhak do? He cut off one cubit of the bridle of the ass upon which he was riding, and he gave it to them that it might be in their hands for a sign of the covenant of the oath.

When David reigned, he desired to enter the land of the Philistines, but he was unable [to do so] because of the power of the sign of the covenant oath of

Pirkei DeRabbi Eliezer 36

Yitzhak, until he had taken from them the sign of the covenant of Yitzhak's oath, as it is said, "And David took the bridle of the cubit out of the hand of the Philistines" [Samuel-B 8:1], as it is written, "So the Philistines were subdued, and they came no more within the border of Israel" [Samuel-A 7:13].

Yaakov made a covenant with the people of the land, because Lavan said to him: I know that the Holy One, blessed be He, will give to thy seed in the future all these lands; make a covenant of an oath with me, that the Israelites will not take possession of the land of Aram. He made with him a covenant with an oath, as it is said, "And Yaakov said unto his brethren, Gather ye stones" [Genesis 31:46]. Were they, his brethren? Were they not his sons? But this teaches thee that a man's sons are like his brethren. Lavan said to him: If the Israelites obtain possession of the land of Canaan, then they must not come into the land of Paddan Aram for an evil purpose, and if Aram obtain possession they must not come into the land of Israel for evil, as it is said, "That I will not pass over this heap to thee, and that thou shalt not pass over this heap and this pillar unto me, for harm" [Genesis 31:52].

When David reigned, he wished to come into the land of Aram, but he was unable on account of the power of the covenant of Yaakov's oath until he had broken that pillar. Concerning this, Solomon said: "And break in pieces their pillars" [Exodus 23:24]. Afterwards he conquered the land of Aram, as it is said, "David smote also Hadadezer the son of

Pirkei DeRabbi Eliezer 36

Rehov, king of Zorah, as he went to recover his dominion at the river" [Samuel-B 8:3].

Chapter 37

"**As** if a man did flee from a lion and a bear met him" [Amos 5:19]. The **lion** means Lavan, who pursued Yaakov, like a lion to destroy his life. The **bear** refers to Esav, who stood by the way like a bear bereaved by man, to slay the mother with the children. The lion is shamefaced, the bear is not shamefaced. Yaakov arose and prayed before the Holy One, blessed be He, saying: Sovereign of all the Universe. Hast Thou not spoken thus unto me, "Return unto the land of thy fathers, and to thy kindred, and I will be with thee" [Genesis 31:3].

And behold, Esav, the evil one, has now come to slay me; but I fear him and he does not fear Thee. Hence the sages say: Do not fear an executive officer or a ruler, but fear a man who has no fear of Heaven. Esav stood by the way like a bear bereaved by man, to slay mother and child.

What did the Holy One, blessed be He, do? He sent an angel to him to deliver him, and to save him from the hand of Esav; and he appeared unto him like a man, as it is said, "And there wrestled a man with him until the breaking of the day" [Genesis 32:25]. As soon as the dawn appeared, the angel said to him: Let me go, for the time has arrived when I must stand to sing and to chant praises before the Holy One, blessed be He. But Yaakov did not wish to let him go. What did the angel do? He began to sing and to chant praises from the earth, and when the angels

Pirkei DeRabbi Eliezer 37

[on high] heard the voice of the angel who was singing and praising from the earth, they said: Because of the honour of the righteous one do we hear the voice of the angel who is singing and praising from the earth; and concerning him the verse says, "From the uttermost part of the earth have we heard songs, glory to the righteous" [Isaiah 24:16].

Again, the angel said to him: "Let me go" [Genesis 32:27]. Yaakov answered him: I will not let thee go until thou hast blessed me; and he blessed him, as it is said, "And he blessed him there" [Genesis 32:30]. Again, he said to him: "Let me go" [Genesis 32:27]. He answered him: I will not let thee go until thou tallest me what thy name is. And the angel called his name Israel like his own name, for his own name was called Israel. Yaakov wished to prevail over the angel, and to throw him down upon the earth. What did the angel do? He took hold of the sinew of the hip, which was upon the hollow of Yaakov's thigh, and he lifted the sinew of his hip out of its place, and it became like the fat of the dead. Therefore, the children of Israel are forbidden to eat of the sinew of the hip which is upon the hollow of the animal's thigh, as it is said, "Therefore the children of Israel eat not the sinew of the hip which is upon the hollow of the thigh" [Genesis 32:33].

Yaakov wished to cross the ford of the Jabbok יַבֹּק and he was detained there. The angel said to him: Didst thou not speak thus - "Of all that thou shalt give me I will surely give a tenth unto thee" [Genesis

Pirkei DeRabbi Eliezer 37

28:22], What did our father Yaakov do? He took all the cattle in his possession which he had brought from Paddan-Aram, and he gave a tithe of them amounting to 550 animals. Hence, thou mayest learn that all the cattle in the possession of our father Yaakov, which he had brought from Paddan-Aram, amounted to 5500 animals. Again, Yaakov wished to cross the ford of the Jabbok, but he was hindered here. The angel said: Didst thou not speak thus "Of all that thou shalt give me I will surely give a tenth unto thee" [Genesis 28:22], Behold, thou hast sons. Thou hast not given a tithe of them. What did Yaakov do? He put apart the four firstborn children of the four mothers, and eight children remained. He began to count from Shimon, and finished with Binyamin, who was still in his mother's womb. Again, he began to count from Shimon, and he included Binyamin, and Levi was reckoned as the tithe, holy to God, as it is said, "The tenth shall be holy unto the Hashem" [Leviticus 27:82].

Rebbi Yishmael said: All firstborns are required to have a tithe taken only when they fall under the observation of the eye. Only Yaakov observed the law of tithe in advance; he began with Binyamin, who was in his mother's womb, and Levi was reckoned as holy to the Hashem, and concerning him the Scripture says, "The tenth shall be holy unto the Hashem" [Leviticus 27:82].

Michael the angel, descended and took Levi, and brought him up before the Throne of Glory, and he spake before Him: Sovereign of all the universe.

Pirkei DeRabbi Eliezer 37

This is Thy lot, and the portion of Thy works. And He put forth His right hand and blessed him that the sons of Levi should minister on earth before Him, like the ministering angels in heaven. Michael the angel spake before the Holy One, blessed be He: Sovereign of all worlds. Do not such who serve the king have provision of their food given to them, Therefore, He gave to the sons of Levi all holy things which accrue to His Name, as it is said, "They shall eat the offerings of the Hashem made by fire, and his inheritance" [Deuteronomy 18:1].

When Yaakov passed to come into the land of **Canaan** [The Holy Land], Esav came to him from Mount Seir in violent anger, contriving to slay him, as it is said, "The wicked plotteth against the just, and gnasheth upon him with his teeth" [Psalms 37:12]. Esav said: I will not slay Yaakov with bow and arrows, but with my mouth and with my teeth will I slay him, and suck his blood, as it is said, "And Esav ran to meet him, and embraced him, and fell on his neck, and kissed him; and they wept" [Genesis 33:4]. Do not read **Vayishakehu** [and he kissed him], but read **Vayishkehu** [and he bit him]. But Yaakov's neck became like ivory, and concerning him the Scripture says, "Thy neck is like the tower of ivory" [Song of Songs 7:5]. The wicked Esav's teeth became blunt, and when the wicked one saw that the desire of his heart was not realized he began to be angry, and to gnash with his teeth, as it is said, "The wicked shall see it, and be grieved; he shall gnash with his teeth, and melt away" [Psalms 112:10].

Yaakov took all the tithe of his possessions and sent it by the hand of his servants, and gave it to Esav, saying to them: Say ye to him, "Thus saith thy servant Yaakov" [Genesis 32:5]. The Holy One, blessed be He, said to him: Yaakov. That which was holy hast thou made profane? He replied to Him: Sovereign of all worlds. I flatter the wicked, so that he should not slay me. Hence the [wise men] say, we may flatter the wicked in this world for the sake of the ways of peace. Esav said to him: O my brother, I have enough; as it is said, "And Esav said, I have enough" [Genesis 33:9]. And because he gave honour to Yaakov, therefore the sons of Yaakov paid honour to the sons of Esav with the same expression; as it is said, "Ye have compassed this mountain long enough" [Deuteronomy 2:8]. The Holy One, blessed be He, said to him: Yaakov. Is it not enough for thee that thou hast made profane that which is holy? Nay, but I have said, "And the elder shall serve the younger" [Genesis 25:23]; and yet thou hast said, "Thy servant Yaakov" [Genesis 32:4]. By thy life. It shall be according to thy words; he shall rule over thee in this world, and thou shalt rule over him in the world to come. Therefore, Yaakov said to him to Esav: "Let my Hashem, I pray thee, pass over before his servant" [Genesis 33:14]. Hence, thou mayest learn that the sons of Esav will not fall until a remnant from Yaakov shall come, and cut off the feet of the children of Esav from Mount Seir, and the Holy One, blessed be He, will descend. "And there shall not be any remaining to the house of Esav; for the Hashem hath spoken it" [Obadiah 1:18].

Chapter 38

"**Or** went into the house and leaned his hand on the wall, and the serpent bit him" [Amos 5:19]. When Yaakov went into his house in the land of Canaan the serpent bit him. And who was the serpent? This was **Shechem**, the son of **Hamor**. Because the daughter of Yaakov was abiding in the tents, and she did not go into the street; what did Shechem, the son of Hamor, do? He brought dancing girls who were also playing on pipes in the streets. **Dinah** went forth to see those girls who were making merry; and he seized her, and he slept with her, and she conceived and bore **Asenath**. The sons of Israel said that she should be killed, for they said that now people would say in all the land that there was an immoral daughter in the tents of Yaakov.

What did Yaakov do, He wrote the Holy Name upon a golden plate, and suspended it about her neck and sent her away. She went her way. Everything is revealed before the Holy One, blessed be He, and Michael the angel descended and took her, and brought her down to Egypt to the house of **Potiphera**; because **Asenath** was destined to become the wife of Yosef. Now the wife of Potiphera was barren, and Asenath grew up with her as a daughter. When Yosef came down to Egypt he married her, as it is said, "And he gave him to wife Asenath the daughter of Potiphera Ha-Kohen of on" [Genesis 41:45].

Pirkei DeRabbi Eliezer 38

Shimon and Levi were moved by a great zeal on account of the immorality, as it is said, "And they said, should he deal with our sister as with a harlot?" [Genesis 34:31]. And each man took his sword and slew all the men of Shechem. When Yaakov heard thereof, he became sorely afraid. For he said: Now all the people of the land will hear, and they will gather together against me and smite me. He began to curse the wrath of his sons, as it is said, "Cursed be their anger, for it is fierce" [Genesis 49:7]; and he also cursed their sword in the Greek language, for he said: "Weapons of violence are their swords" [Genesis 49:5]. All the kings of the earth heard, thereof, and feared very much, saying: If two sons of Yaakov have done all these great things, if they all band themselves together, they will be able to destroy the world. And the dread of the Holy One, blessed be He, fell upon them, as it is said, "And the terror of God was upon the cities... and they did not pursue after the sons of Yaakov" [Genesis 35:5].

Yaakov took his sons and his grandsons, and his wives, and he went to **Kiryat Arba** [A city near Hebron, where Abraham and Yitzhak lived] so as to be near Yitzhak his father. And he found there Esav and his sons and his wives dwelling in the tents of Yitzhak. And he spread his tent apart from him; and Yitzhak saw Yaakov, his wives, his daughters, and all that belonged to him, and he rejoiced in his heart exceedingly. Concerning him the Scripture saith, "Yea, thou shalt see thy children's children, peace be upon Israel" [Psalms 128:6].

Pirkei DeRabbi Eliezer 38

Rebbi Levi said: In the hour of the ingathering of Yitzhak, he left his cattle and his possessions, and all that he had, to his two sons; therefore, they both rendered loving-kindness to him, as it is said, "And Esav and Yaakov his sons buried him" [Genesis 35:29].

Esav said to Yaakov: Divide all that my father has left into two portions, and I will choose first, because I am the elder. Yaakov said: This wicked man has not satisfied his eye with wealth, as it is said, "Neither are his eyes satisfied with riches" [Ecclesiastes 4:8]. What did Yaakov do? He divided all that his father had left as the one part, and the other part was to be the land of Israel and the Cave of Machpelah. What did Esav do? He went to Yishmael in the wilderness in order to consult him, as it is said, "And Esav went unto Yishmael" [Genesis 28:9]. Yishmael said to Esav: The Amorite and the Canaanite are in the land, and Yaakov trusts [in God] that he will inherit the land, therefore take all that thy father has left, and Yaakov will have nothing.

And Esav took all that his father had left, and he gave to Yaakov the land of Israel, and the Cave of Machpelah, and they wrote a perpetual deed between them. Yaakov said to Esav: Go from the land of my possession, from the land of Canaan. Esav took his wives, and his sons, and his daughters, and all that he had, as it is said, "And Esav took his wives… and all his possessions which he had gathered in the land of Canaan, and went into a land away from his brother Yaakov" [Genesis 36:6]. And as

Pirkei DeRabbi Eliezer 38

a reward because he removed all his belongings on account of Yaakov his brother, He gave him one hundred provinces from Seir unto Magdiel, and Magdiel is Rome, as it is said, "Duke Magdiel, Duke Iram" [Genesis 36:43].

Then Yaakov dwelt safely and in peace in the land of his possession, and in the land of his birth, and in the land of the sojournings of his father.

Rebbi Yishmael said: Every son of the old age is beloved of his father, as it is said, "Now Yisroel loved Yosef more than all his children, because he was the son of his old age" [Genesis 37:4]. Was he then the son of his old age? Was not Binyamin the son of his old age? But owing to the fact that Yaakov saw by his prophetic power that Yosef would rule in the future, therefore he loved him more than all his sons. And they envied him with a great envy, as it is said, "And his brethren saw that their father loved him more than all his brethren; and they hated him" [Genesis 37:4]. Further, because he saw in his dream that in the future he would rule, and he told his father, and they envied him yet more and more, as it is said, "And they hated him yet the more" [Genesis 37:5]. Moreover, he saw the sons of his father's concubines eating the flesh of the roes and the flesh of the sheep whilst they were alive, and he brought a reproach against them before Yaakov their father, so that they could not see his face any more in peace, as it is said, "And they could not speak peaceably unto him" [Genesis 37:4]. Yaakov said to Yosef: Yosef, my son. Verily I have waited many days without

Pirkei DeRabbi Eliezer 38

hearing of the welfare of thy brethren, and of the welfare of the flock, as it is said, "Go now, see whether it be well with thy brethren, and well with the flock" [Genesis 37:14]. And the lad was wandering in the field, and the angel Gabriel met him, as it is said, "And a certain man found him, and, behold, he was wandering in the field" [Genesis 37:15]. The word **Man** here in this context is **Gabriel** angel, as it is said, "The man Gabriel, whom I had seen in the vision" [Daniel 9:21].

And the angel Gabriel said to him: What seekest thou? He said to him: I seek my brethren, as it is said, "And he said, I seek my brethren" [Genesis 37:16]. And he led him to his brethren, and they saw him and sought to slay him, as it is said, "And they saw him afar off" [Genesis 37:18]. Reuven said to them: Do not shed his blood, as it is said, "And Reuven said unto them, shed no blood; cast him into this pit that is in the wilderness" [Genesis 37:22]. And his brethren listened to him, and they took Yosef and cast him into the pit, as it is said, "And they took him, and cast him into the pit" [Genesis 37:24]. What did Reuven do? He went and stayed on one of the mountains, so as to go down by night to bring up Yosef out of the pit. And his nine brethren were sitting down in one place, all of them like one man, with one heart and one plan. Yishmaelites passed by them, and the brethren said: Come, let us sell him to the Yishmaelites, and they will lead him to the end of the wilderness, and Yaakov will not hear any further report concerning him.

Pirkei DeRabbi Eliezer 38

The brethren sold him to the Yishmaelites for twenty pieces of silver, and each one of them took two pieces of silver [apiece] to purchase shoes for their feet, as it is said, "Thus saith the Hashem… Because they have sold the righteous for silver, and the needy for a pair of shoes" [Amos 2:6]. They said: Let us swear among ourselves that no one of us shall declare the matter to our father Yaakov. Yehuda said to them: Reuven is not here, and the ban cannot be valid through nine adults. What did they do? They associated the Omnipresent with them and proclaimed the ban.

And Reuven went down by night to bring up Yosef out of the pit, but he did not find him there. He said to them: Ye have slain Yosef; "and I, whither shall I go?" [Genesis 37:30]. And they told him what they had done, and the ban which they had proclaimed; and Reuven heard of the ban, and was silent; the Holy One, blessed be He, because of the ban, did not tell the matter to Yaakov, and [though] concerning Him it is written, "He sheweth his word unto Yaakov" [Psalms 147:19]; but this word He did not shew unto Yaakov, therefore Yaakov did not know what had been done to Yosef, and he said: "Yosef is without doubt torn in pieces" [Genesis 37:33].

Rebbi Yannai said: The sale of Yosef was not atoned by the tribes until they died, as it is said, "And the Hashem of hosts revealed Himself in mine ears, surely this iniquity shall not be purged from you till ye die" [Isaiah 22:14]. Owing to the sale of Yosef a famine came into the land of Israel for seven

Pirkei DeRabbi Eliezer 38

years, and the brethren of Yosef "went down to buy corn" [Genesis 42:3] in Egypt. And they found Yosef [still] living, and they absolved themselves of the ban; and Yaakov heard about Yosef that he was living, and his soul and his spirit revived. Did their father Yaakov's spirit die, so that it had to be revived? But, owing to the ban, the Holy Spirit had departed from him, and when they had removed the ban, the Holy Spirit rested on him as at first; that is what is written, "The spirit of Yaakov their father revived" [Genesis 45:27].

Rabbi Akiva said: The ban is as much as the oath, and an oath is as much as the ban; and everyone who violates the ban is as though he had violated the oath, and everyone who violates the oath is as though he had violated the ban. Everyone who knows the matter and does not declare it, the ban falls upon him and destroys his timber and his stones, as it is said, "I will cause it to go forth, saith the Hashem… and it shall enter into the house of him that sweareth falsely by my name… and shall consume it with the timber thereof and the stones thereof" [Zechariah 5:4].

Know the power of the ban. Come and see from Yehoshua, the son of Nun, who put Jericho under the ban; it was to be burnt with all things therein by fire. **Achan**, son of Carmi, son of Zerach, saw the Teraphim, and the silver which they brought [as offerings] before it, and the mantle which was spread before it, and one tongue of gold in its mouth. And in his heart, he coveted them, and went and buried them in the midst of his tent. On account of

Pirkei DeRabbi Eliezer 38

his trespass which he had committed, thirty-six righteous men died on his account, as it is said, "And the men of Ai smote of them about thirty and six men" [Yehoshua 7:5].

Yehoshua went and rent his garments, and fell upon his face to the ground before the Ark of the Covenant of God, and he sought to effect repentance, and the Holy One, blessed be He, was appeased by him, and He said to him: Yehoshua. Israel has trespassed the sin of trespass in the matter of the devoted things, as it is said, "Yisrael hath sinned" [Yehoshua 7:11]. Yehoshua gazed at the twelve stones which were upon the High Ha-Kohen, which correspond to the twelve tribes. Every tribe that had done some transgression, the light [of its stone] became dim, and he saw the stone of the tribe of Yehuda, the light of which became dim. And he knew that the tribe of Yehuda had transgressed in the matter of the devoted thing. He cast lots, and Achan was taken, as it is said, "And he brought near his household man by man; and **Achan**, the son of Carmi, was taken" [Yehoshua 7:18]. Yehoshua took Achan, the son of Zerach, with the silver and the mantle and the tongue of gold, and his sons and his daughters, and all that he had, and he brought them up into the valley of Achor. And it is written, "The fathers shall not be put to death for the children, neither shall the children be put to death for the fathers" [Deuteronomy 24:16]. But because they were cognizant of the matter, and did not report it, he stoned them and burnt them. If there was a burning, why [was there] a stoning, and if a stoning, why a

Pirkei DeRabbi Eliezer 38

burning? But the stoning was because they knew of the matter and did not report it; burning was inflicted because thirty-six righteous men died through him, as it is said, "And the men of Ai smote of them about thirty and six men" [Yehoshua 7:5].

Because Achan confessed before the Name of the Holy One, blessed be He, he has a portion in the world to come, as it is said, "And Yehoshua said, why thou hast troubled us? The Hashem shall trouble thee this day" [Yehoshua 7:25]. "This day" thou art troubled, but thou shalt not be troubled in the future world.

Know thou the power of the ban. Come and see from the [story of] the tribes, who were zealous because of immorality against the tribe of Binyamin. The Holy One, blessed be He, said to them: Ye are zealous because of the immorality, and ye are not zealous because of the image of Micah. Therefore, the **Binyamin tribe** slew some of them a first and a second and a third time, until they went before the Ark of the Covenant of the Hashem seeking repentance, and they were forgiven. They decreed that all Israel should make peace with them, and they repented both old and young, as it is said, "For they made a great oath concerning him that came not up unto the Hashem to Mizpah" [Judges 21:5]. Did all Israel take an oath? But the ban is the same as the oath.

The men of Yavesh-Gilead neither went up nor did they go with them in the assembly, and they incurred

Pirkei DeRabbi Eliezer 38

[the penalty of] death, as it is said, "Concerning him that came not up unto the Hashem to Mizpah, saying, He shall surely be put to death" [Judges 21:5].

Know thou the power of the ban. Come and see from the story of **Shaul**, the son of Kish, who decreed that all people, both young and old, should fast, as it is said, "Cursed be the man that eateth any food until it be evening" [Samuel-A 14:25]. Yehonaton did not hear of this, and ate a little honey, and his eyes were enlightened, as it is said, "And his eyes were enlightened" [Samuel-A 14:27]. Shaul saw the Philistines returning against Israel, and he knew that Israel had trespassed in the matter of the ban. He looked at the twelve stones; for each tribe which performed one of the precepts had its stone on the High **Ha-Kohen's breast-plate** shining with its light, and each tribe which transgressed, the light of its stone was dim. He knew that the tribe of Binyamin had trespassed in the matter of the ban. He cast lots concerning Binyamin, and Shaul and Yehonaton were taken, as it is said, "And Yehonaton and Shaul were taken" [Samuel-A 14:42]. Shaul took his sword to slay his son, as it is said, "God do so, and more also: for thou shalt surely die, Yehonaton" [Samuel-A 14:44]. The people said to him: Our Hashem king. It is an error. They brought on his behalf a sacrifice of a burnt offering for his error, and He was entreated of him, and they saved him from an evil death, as it is said, "So the people rescued Yehonaton, that he died not" [Samuel-A 14:45].

The Cutheans [The sects are the name of the group

Pirkei DeRabbi Eliezer 38

of Gentiles outwardly who converted, and there are laws in halakhah that are trusted, and there are those that are not trusted] are not considered as a nation of the seventy languages, but they were the remnant of the five nations precious to the king, as it is said, "And the king of Assyria brought men from Babylon, and from Cuthah, and from Avva, and from Hamath and Sepharvaim, and placed them in the cities of Samaria instead of the children of Israel" [Kings-B 17:24].

Rebbi Yosef said: He added four more nations to them, and they were in all nine nations, as it is said, "The Dinaites, and the Apharsathchites, the Tarpelites, the Apharsites, the Archevites, the Babylonians, the Shushanchites, the Dehaites, the Elamites, and the rest of the nations... set in the city of Samaria" [Ezra 4:9, 10].

And when the Israelites were exiled from Samaria to Babylon, the king sent his servants, and he caused them to dwell in Samaria, to raise tribute for his kingdom. What did the Holy One, blessed be He, do? He sent lions among them, which killed some of them, as it is said, "And so it was, at the beginning of their dwelling there, that they feared not the Hashem: therefore, the Hashem sent lions among them, which killed some of them" [Kings-B 17:25]. They sent to the king, saying: Our Hashem, the king. The land whither thou hast sent us will not receive us, for we are left but a few out of many. The king sent and called for all the elders of Israel, and said to them: All those years during which ye were in your land, the beasts of the field did not bereave you, and now it will not receive my servants. They gave him a word of advice, thinking perhaps he would restore them to their land. They said to him: Our Hashem, O king. That land does not receive a nation who do not study the Torah; behold, that land does not receive a nation who are not circumcised. The king said to them: Give me two of you, who shall go and circumcise them and teach them the book of the Torah; and there is no refusal to the word of the king. They sent Rebbi Dosethai of the Court-House, and Rebbi Yannai, and they circumcised them, and they taught them the book of the Torah in the Noṭarikon script, and they wept. Those nations followed the statutes of the Torah, and they served also their own gods.

When Ezra came up to Israel, with Zerubbabel, son of Shealtiel, and Yehoshua, son of Yehozadak, they began to build the Temple of the Hashem, as it is said, "Then rose up Zerubbabel, the son of Shealtiel, and Yehoshua, the son of Jozadak, and began to build the house of God" [Ezra 5:2]. And the Samaritans came against them to fight [with] 180,000 men. Were they Samaritans? Were they not Cutheans? But they were called Samaritans because of the city of Samaria. And further, they sought to kill Nehemiah, as it is said, "Come, let us meet together in one of the villages… but they thought to do me mischief" [Nehemiah 6:2]. Moreover, they made the work of the Hashem to cease for two years "Then ceased the work of the house of God, which is at Yerushalayim; and it ceased unto the second year of

Pirkei DeRabbi Eliezer 38

the reign of Darius, king of Persia" [Ezra 4:24].

What did Ezra, Zerubbabel son of Shealtiel, and Yehoshua son of Yehozadak, do? They gathered all the congregation to the Temple of the Hashem, and they brought 300 Ha-Kohens, 300 children, and 300 scrolls of the Torah in their hands, and they blew the trumpets, and the Levites sang songs and praises, and they excommunicated the Cutheans with the mystery of the Ineffable Name, and with the script such as was written upon the tables of the Law, and by the ban of the heavenly Court of Justice, and by the ban of the earthly Court of Justice [decreeing] that no one of Israel should eat the bread of the Cutheans. Hence the sages said: Everyone who eats the bread of the Cutheans is as though he had eaten of the flesh of swine. Let no man make a proselyte in Israel from among the Cutheans. They have no portion in the resurrection of the dead, as it is said, "Ye have nothing to do with us to build a house unto our God" [Ezra 4:3], neither in this world, nor in the world to come. So that they should have neither portion nor inheritance in Israel, as it is said, "But ye have no portion, nor right, nor memorial, in Yerushalayim" [Nehemiah 2:20].

They sent the ban letter to the Israelites who were in Babylon. Moreover, they added an additional ban upon them, and King Koresh ordained it as a perpetual ban upon them, as it is said, "And the God that hath caused his name to dwell there overthrow all kings and peoples that shall put forth their hand to alter the same, to destroy this house of God which

Pirkei DeRabbi Eliezer 38

is at Yerushalayim. I, Darius, have made a decree; let it be done with all diligence" [Ezra 6:12].

Chapter 39

The fourth descent was when He descended into Egypt, as it is said, "I will go down with thee into Egypt" [Genesis 46:4]. Yaakov heard concerning Yosef that he was living, and he was thinking in his heart, saying: Can I forsake the land of my fathers, the land of my birth, the land of the sojourning's of my fathers, the land where the **Shekhinah** [divine presence] of the Holy One, blessed be He, is in its midst, and shall I go to an unclean land in their midst, for there is no fear of Heaven therein? The Holy One, blessed be He, said to him: Yaakov, do not fear; "I will go down with thee into Egypt, and I will also surely bring thee up again" [Genesis 46:4].

Yaakov heard this word, and he took his wives, and his sons, and his daughters, and the daughters of his sons. Another Scripture says, "With his daughter Dinah" [Genesis 46:15]. And all that he had, and he brought them to Egypt, as it is said, "His sons, and his sons, sons with him," etc. Another Scripture says, "With his daughter, Dinah" [Genesis 46:15]. Whereas another text says, "His daughters" [Genesis 46:5], to teach thee that the daughters of Yaakov were the wives of his sons. And all the seed of Yaakov married their sisters and their blood-relations, so that they should not intermarry with the people of the lands, therefore they were called a true seed, as it is said, "Yet I had planted thee a noble vine, wholly a true seed" [Jeremiah 2:21].

Pirkei DeRabbi Eliezer 39

When they came to the border of Egypt, all the males were enrolled in genealogical lists to the number of sixty-six, Yosef with his two sons in Egypt, made the total of sixty-nine. And it is written, "With seventy persons thy fathers went down into Egypt" [Deuteronomy 10:22]. What did the Holy One, blessed be He, do? He entered into the number with them, and the total became seventy, to fulfill that which is said, "I will go down with thee into Egypt" [Genesis 46:4]. When Israel came up from Egypt all the mighty men were enrolled, [amounting to] 600,000, less one. What did the Holy One, blessed be He, do? He entered into the number with them, and their total amounted to 600,000, to fulfill that which is said, "I will go down with thee into Egypt, and I will also surely bring thee up again" [Genesis 46:4].

Rebbi Yishmael said: Ten times did the sons of Yaakov say to Yosef, "thy servant, our father." Yosef heard the word, and was silent. Silence gives consent; therefore, were ten years deducted from his life. Yosef heard that his father had come to the border of Egypt, and he took all the men who had intercourse with him, and he went to meet his father. All the people go forth to meet the king, but the king does not go forth to meet any man. But this teaches thee that the father of a man is like his king.

Rebbi Pinchas said: The Holy Spirit rested on Yosef from his youth; and it led him in all matters of wisdom like a shepherd who leads his flock, as it is said, "Give ear, O Shepherd of Israel, thou that leadest Yosef like a flock, thou that sittest upon the

Pirkei DeRabbi Eliezer 39

cherubim" [Psalms 80:1]. In all his wisdom a certain woman enticed him, and when he wished to accustom himself to sin, he saw the image of his father, and repented concerning it.

Three people conquered their passion before their Creator, and they were Yosef, Boaz, and Palte, son of Laish. It was fit that twelve tribes should have arisen from Yosef, as it is said, "And the seed of his hands was active" [Genesis 49:24], but there remained two tribes, Menashe and Ephraim. The woman brought grave charges against him to vex him, and he was confined in prison for ten years. There he interpreted the dreams of the servants of Pharaoh, he interpreted for each one according to his dream just as though the events were taking place before him, as it is said, "And it came to pass, as he interpreted to us, so it was" [Genesis 41:13].

And he interpreted the dream of Pharaoh when the Holy Spirit rested upon him, as it is said, "And Pharaoh said unto his servants, "can we find such a one as this, a man in whom the spirit of God is?" [Genesis 41:38].

All the nations came to Yosef to purchase food from him. And Yosef spoke to each people according to their different tongue. And he knew what they were speaking. Therefore, his name was called Yehoseph יהוסף, Hashem added the letter ה to his name as he knew all the languages of the people. Gabriel Hamelech taught him all the 70 languages the night before he was released from jail. As it is said, "For

Yosef understood them, for there was an interpreter between them" [Genesis 42:23].

Moreover, when he went into the market-place he saw the people forming themselves into various companies and groups, and each one would speak in his own tongue, and he knew what they were saying, as it is said, "He appointed it in Yosef for a testimony, when he went out over the land of Egypt, when I heard the speech of one that I knew not" [Psalms 81:5]. Further, when he was riding in the chariot, and passed through all the borders of the land of Egypt, the Egyptian girls were climbing up the walls for his sake, and they threw to him rings of gold, so that perchance he might look at them, and [they could] see the beauty of his figure, but nobody's eye degraded him, for he was highly esteemed in the eyes of everyone, as it is said, "Yosef is a fruitful bough… his daughters run over the wall" [Genesis 49:22].

All the nations came to purchase food. And they brought to Yosef their tribute and a present, and money to purchase food. And he spoke to each people according to their different tongue; therefore, was his name called **Turgeman** [Translator], as it is said, "For there was an interpreter between them" [Genesis 42:23], therefore was he speaking.

Some of them were buying grain on account of the famine in their houses, and they went forth, and others came to buy food; and one asked his fellow as to the price in the market. From their reply they

Pirkei DeRabbi Eliezer 39

opened the price of the market. When they came to Yosef, he said to them: Just as ye have heard, so it is; in order that the market should not be scarce and prices dear. Hence the sages said: He who makes a corner in the market will never see a sign of blessing.

Rebbi Tanchum said: Yosef commanded and they built the treasure-houses in each city, and he gathered all the produce of the lands into the treasure-houses. The Egyptians were scoffing at him, saying: Now the worms will eat the stores of Yosef. But no worm had any power over them; neither did the stores diminish until the day of his death. And he supported the land in the famine of bread, therefore was his name called **Kalkol** [Fed]. And Kalkol is Yosef, as it is said, "And Yosef nourished" [Genesis 47:12]. Moreover, he nourished his father, and his brethren, and all his father's house, in the famine with bread to their satisfaction. "And Yosef nourished his father, and his brethren, and all his father's household, with bread, according to their families" [Genesis 47:12].

Rebbi Eliezer said: In the hour of the death of Yaakov he called to his son Yosef, and said to him: O my son. Swear to me by the covenant of circumcision that thou wilt take me up to the burial-place of my fathers in the land of Canaan to the Cave of Machpelah. The ancients used to swear by the covenant of circumcision prior to the giving of the Torah, as it is said, "Put, I pray thee, thy hand under my thigh" [Genesis 24:5], and "he swore unto him" [Genesis 47:31]. He kept the oath and did accordingly,

Pirkei DeRabbi Eliezer 39

as it is said, "And he said, Swear unto me" [Genesis 47:31]. And all the mighty men of the kingdom went up with him to bury him, and to show loving-kindness to Yaakov his father, as it is said, "And Yosef went up to bury his father" [Genesis 50:7]. All the people of the land were bringing food on account of the famine to the camp of Yosef. The Holy One, blessed be He, said to them: Ye have shown loving-kindness to Yaakov, my servant, I also will give you your reward, and also unto your children in this world. When the Egyptians died in the Reed Sea they did not die in the water, but they were deemed worthy to be buried in the earth. The Holy One, blessed be He, said to them: Ye have submitted yourselves to the divine punishment; I also will give you a place of burial, as it is said, "Thou stretchedst forth thy right hand, the earth swallowed them" [Exodus 15:12].

When they came to the **Cave of Machpelah**, Esav came against them from Mount Horeb to stir up strife, saying: The Cave of Machpelah is mine. What did Yosef do? He sent Naphtali to subdue the constellations, and to go down to Egypt to bring up the perpetual deed which was between them, therefore it is said, "Naphtali is a hind let loose" [Genesis 49:21]. **Chushim**, the son of Dan, had defective hearing and speech, and he said to them: Why are we sitting here? He was pointing to Esav with his finger. They said to him: Because this man will not let us bury our father Yaakov. What did he do? He drew his sword and cut off Esav's head with the sword, and took the head into the Cave of

Pirkei DeRabbi Eliezer 39

Machpelah. And they sent his body to the land of his possession, to Mount Seir.

What did Yitzhak do? He grasped the head of Esav and prayed before the Holy One, blessed be He, and said: Sovereign of all the universe. Let mercy be shown to this wicked one, for he had not learnt all the precepts of the Torah, as it is said, "Let favour be shewed to the wicked, yet will he not learn righteousness" [Isaiah 26:10]. He was speaking in iniquity concerning the land of Israel and the Cave of Machpelah, as it is said, "In the land of uprightness will he deal wrongfully" [Isaiah 26:10].

The Holy Spirit answered him, saying: As I live. He shall not see the majesty of God.

Chapter 40

The fifth descent was when He came down to the thorn-bush, as it is said, "And I am come down to deliver them out of the hand of the Egyptians" [Exodus 3:8]. He abandoned the entire mountain, and descended into the thorn-bush, and He abode therein. And the thorn-bush was an emblem of grief and distress, and it was full of thorns and thistles. Why did He abide in the midst of the thorn-bush which was an emblem of grief and distress? Because He saw Israel in great grief and He also dwelt with them, thus fulfilling that which is said, "In all their affliction He was afflicted" [Isaiah 63:9].

Rebbi Levi said: That ROD which was created in the twilight was delivered to the **ADAM** [first man] out of the Garden of Eden. Adam delivered it to Enoch, and Enoch delivered it to Noah, and Noah handed it on to Shem. Shem passed it on to Avraham, Avraham transmitted it to Yitzhak, and Yitzhak gave it over to Yaakov, and Yaakov brought it down into Egypt and passed it on to his son Yosef, and when Yosef died and they pillaged his household goods, it was placed in the palace of Pharaoh. And Yitro was one of the magicians of Egypt, and he saw the rod and the letters which were upon it, and he desired in his heart to have it, and he took it and brought it, and planted it in the midst of the garden of his house. No one was able to approach it any more.

Pirkei DeRabbi Eliezer 40

When Moshe came to his house of Yitro, he went into the garden of Yitro's house, and saw the rod and read the letters which were upon it, and he put forth his hand and took it. Yitro watched Moshe, and said: This one in the future will redeem Israel from Egypt. Therefore, he gave him Zipporah his daughter to wife, as it is said, "And Moshe was content to dwell with the man; and he gave Moshe Zipporah, his daughter" [Exodus 2:21].

Moshe was keeping the sheep of Yitro for forty years, and the beasts of the field did not consume them, but they increased and multiplied exceedingly, and concerning them the Scripture saith, "As the flock of holy things" [Ezekiel 36:38].

And he led the flock until he came to **Horeb** [Mountain of Sinai], as it is said, "And he led the flock to the back of the wilderness, and came to the mountain of God, unto Horeb" [Exodus 3:3]. There the Holy One, blessed be He, was revealed unto him from the midst of the thorn-bush. Moshe saw the bush burning with fire, and the fire did not consume the bush, and the bush did not extinguish the flames of fire. Now the bush does not grow in the earth unless it has water beneath it. Moshe saw and was wondering very much in his heart, and he said: What kind of glory is there in its midst? He said: I will now turn aside and see this great sight, why the thorn-bush is not burnt. The Holy One, blessed be He, said to him: Moshe. Stand where thou art standing, for there in the future will I give the Torah to Israel, as it is said, "And he said, Draw not nigh hither; put off thy shoes from off thy feet, for the place whereon thou standest is holy ground" [Exodus 3:5]. The Holy One, blessed be He, said to him: Go. Hence [the sages] said: Anyone who enters the Temple must remove his shoe, for thus spake the Holy One, blessed be He, to Moshe: "Put off thy shoes from off thy feet" [Exodus 3:5].

The Holy One, blessed be He, said to him: "Come and I will send thee unto Pharaoh" [Exodus 3:10]. He answered before Him: Sovereign of all worlds. Have I not spoken thus to Thee three or four times, that I have no power, for I have a defective tongue, as it is said, "And Moshe said unto the Hashem, O Hashem, I am not eloquent" [Exodus 4:10]. Not only this, but moreover Thou dost send me into the power of my enemy who seeks my hurt. For this reason, I fled from him, as it is said, "But Moshe fled from the face of Pharaoh" [Exodus 2:15]. He answered him: Do not fear him, for all the men who sought thy life are already dead.

Were they dead? Were they not alive? Only they had diminished their wealth. Hence, thou mayest learn that all who lose their wealth are as though they were dead, therefore it is said, "For all the men are dead who sought thy life" [Exodus 4:19]. God said to him: "Come and I will send thee unto Pharaoh" [Exodus 3:10]. He replied to Him: Sovereign of all worlds. "Send by the hand of him whom thou wilt send" [Exodus 4:13] - that is to say, by the hand of that man whom Thou wilt send in the future. He said to him: I have not said, "Come and I will send thee to

Pirkei DeRabbi Eliezer 40

Israel," but "Come and I will send thee unto Pharaoh" [Exodus 3:10]. And as for that man of whom thou sayest that I should send him to Israel in the future that is to come, so it is said, "Behold, I will send you Eliyahu the prophet before the great and terrible day of the Hashem come" [Malachi 3:23]. "And he shall turn the heart of the fathers to the children, and the heart of the children to their fathers" [Malachi 3:24].

Moshe spake before Hashem: Sovereign of all worlds. Give me a wonder or a sign. He said to him: Cast thy staff to the ground. He cast his staff to the ground, and it became a fiery serpent. Why did the Holy One, blessed be He, show unto Moshe a sign with a fiery serpent, and why did He not show it to him with something else? But just as the serpent bites and kills the sons of man, likewise Pharaoh and his people bit and slew the Israelites. Afterwards it became again like a dry stick. Thus, He spake: Likewise, Pharaoh and his people shall become like this dry stick, as it is said, "And the Hashem said unto Moshe: Put forth thine hand, and take it by the tail" [Exodus 4:4]. He spake before Him: Sovereign of all worlds. Give me a wonder. He said to him: "Put now thine hand into thy bosom" [Exodus 4:6]. And he put his hand into his bosom, and he brought it out leprous like snow. Why did the Holy One, blessed be He, show unto Moshe a sign by means of an unclean thing, and why did He not show it by means of a clean thing? But just as the leper is unclean and causes uncleanliness, likewise Pharaoh and his people were unclean, and they caused Israel to be unclean. Afterwards Moshe became clean again, and He spake to him: Likewise, shall Israel become clean from the uncleanliness of the Egyptians, as it is said, "And he said, put now thine hand into thy bosom" [Exodus 4:7].

Why did He show unto Moshe the fire in the midst of the thorn bush? But the fire refers to Israel, who are compared to fire, as it is said, "And the house of Yaakov shall be a fire" [Obadiah 1:18]. The thorn-bush refers to the nations of the world, who are compared to thorns and thistles. He said to him: Likewise, shall Israel be in the midst of the nations. The fire of Israel shall not consume the nations, who are compared to thorns and thistles; but the nations of the world shall extinguish the flames of Israel -these flames are the words of the Torah. But in the future that is to come the fire of Israel will consume all the nations, who are compared to thorns and thistles, as it is said, "And the peoples shall be as the burnings of lime" [Isaiah 33:12].

Moshe said before the Holy One, blessed be He: Sovereign of all worlds. Make known to me Thy great and holy Name, that I may call on Thee by Thy Name, and Thou wilt answer me, as it is said, "And God said unto Moshe, I am that I am" [Exodus 3:14]. "And God said further to Moses, "Thus shall you speak to the Israelites: The LORD, the God of your fathers, the God of Abraham, the God of Isaac, and the God of Jacob, has sent me to you: This shall be My name forever, This My appellation for all eternity." [Exodus 3:15].

Pirkei DeRabbi Eliezer 40

The angels saw that the Holy One, blessed be He, had transmitted the secret of the Ineffable Name to Moshe, and they rejoined: Blessed art thou, O Hashem, who graciously bestoweth knowledge.

Chapter 41

The sixth descent was when He came down on Sinai, as it is said, "And the Hashem came down upon Mount Sinai" [Exodus 19:20]. On the sixth of Sivan the Holy One, blessed be He, was revealed unto Israel on Sinai, and from His place was He revealed on Mount Sinai, and the heavens were opened, and the summit of the mountain entered into the heavens. Thick darkness covered the mountain, and the Holy One, blessed be He, sat upon His throne, and His feet stood on the thick darkness, as it is said, "He bowed the heavens also, and came down; and thick darkness was under his feet" [Samuel-B 22:10].

Rebbi Ṭarphon said: The Holy One, blessed be He, rose and came from Mount Sinai and was revealed unto the sons of Esav, as it is said, "And he said, The Hashem came from Sinai, and rose from Seir unto them" [Deuteronomy 33:2]. And **Seir** means only the sons of Esav, as it is said, "And Esav dwelt in Mount Seir" [Genesis 36:8]. The Holy One, blessed be He, said to them: Will ye accept for yourselves the Torah? They said to Him: What is written therein? He answered them: It is written therein, "Thou shalt do no murder" [Exodus 20:13]. They replied to Him: We are unable to abandon the blessing with which Yitzhak blessed Esav, for he said to him, "By thy sword shalt thou live" [Genesis 27:40]. Thence He turned and was revealed unto the children of Yishmael, as it is said, "He shined forth from Mount

Pirkei DeRabbi Eliezer 41

Paran [Mount Sinai]" [Deuteronomy 33:2]. "Paran" means only the sons of Yishmael, as it is said, "And he dwelt in the wilderness of Paran" [Genesis 21:21]. The Holy One, blessed be He, said to them: Will ye accept for yourselves the Torah? They said to Him: What is written therein? He answered them: "Thou shalt not steal" [Exodus 20:15] is written therein. They said to Him: We are not able to abandon the usage which our fathers observed, for they brought Yosef down into Egypt, as it is said, "For indeed I was stolen away out of the land of the Hebrews" [Genesis 40:15]. Thence He sent messengers to all the nations of the world. He said unto them: Will ye receive for yourselves the Torah? They said to Him: What is written therein? He said to them: "Thou shalt have no other gods before me" [Exodus 20:3]. They said to Him: We have no delight in the Torah, therefore let Him give His Torah to His people, as it is said, "The Hashem will give strength unto his people; the Hashem will bless his people with peace" [Psalms 29:11]. Thence He returned and was revealed unto the children of Israel, as it is said, "And he came from the ten thousands of holy ones" [Deuteronomy 33:2]. The expression "ten thousand" means the children of Israel, as it is said, "And when it rested, he said, Return, O Hashem, unto the ten thousands of the thousands of Israel" [Numbers 10:36]. With Him were thousands twice-told of chariots, even twenty thousand of holy angels, and his right hand was holding the Torah, as it is said, "At his right hand was a fiery law unto them" [Deuteronomy 33:2].

Hence, thou mayest learn that the words of the

Pirkei DeRabbi Eliezer 41

Torah are like coals of fire, "His left hand was under my head" [song of sonds 2:6]. Why was it "at his right hand"? [Isaiah 62:8]. Whence do we know that it was given to them with expression of love? Because it is said, "The Hashem hath sworn by his right hand, and by the arm of his strength" [Isaiah 62:8].

Rebbi Eliezer said: From the day when the Israelites went forth from Egypt, they were journeying and encamping in smoothness, they were journeying in smoothness and they were encamping in smoothness, as it is said, "And they journeyed from Rephidim, and they came to the wilderness of Sinai, and they encamped in the wilderness" [Exodus 19:2]; until they all came to Mount Sinai, and they all encamped opposite the mountain, like one man with one heart, as it is said, "And there Israel encamped before the mount" [Exodus 19:2]. The Holy One, blessed be He, spake to them: Will ye receive for yourselves the Torah? Whilst the Torah had not yet been heard they said to Him: We will keep and observe all the precepts which are in the Torah, as it is said, "And they said, all that the Hashem hath spoken will we do, and be obedient" [Exodus 24:7].

Rebbi Elazar of Modein said: From the day when the heavens and the earth were created, the name of the mountain was Horeb. When the Holy One, blessed be He, was revealed unto Moshe out of the thorn-bush, because of the word for the thorn-bush **S'neh** [The burning bush] it was called Sinai, and that is Horeb. And whence do we know that Israel accepted the Torah at Mount Horeb? Because it is

Pirkei DeRabbi Eliezer 41

said, "The day that thou stoodest before the Hashem thy God in Horeb" [Deuteronomy 4:10].

Rebbi Pinchas said: On the eve of Sabbath the Israelites stood at Mount Sinai, arranged with the men apart and the women apart. The Holy One, blessed be He, said to Moshe: Go, speak to the **Beit Yaakov** [daughters of Israel], asking them whether they wish to receive the Torah. Why were the women asked first? Because the way of men is to follow the opinion of women, as it is said, "Thus shalt thou say to the house of "Yaakov" [Exodus 19:3]; these are the women. "And tell the children of Israel" [Exodus 19:3]; these are the men. They all replied [as] with one mouth, and they said: "All that the Hashem hath spoken we will do, and be obedient" [Exodus 24:7]. The Scripture also says, "They that sing as well as they that dance shall say, All my fountains are in thee" [Psalms 87:7].

Rebbi Chanina said: In the third month the day is double the night, and the Israelites slept until two hours of the day, for sleep on the day of the feast of Azereth is pleasant, the night being short. And Moshe went forth and came to the camp of the Israelites, and he aroused the Israelites from their sleep, saying to them: Arise ye from your sleep, for behold, your God desires to give the Torah to you. Already the bridegroom wishes to lead the bride and to enter the bridal chamber. The hour has come for giving you the Torah, as it is said, "And Moshe brought forth the people out of the camp to meet God" [Exodus 19:17]. And the Holy One, blessed be

He, also went forth to meet them; like a bridegroom who goes forth to meet the bride, so the Holy One, blessed be He, went forth to meet them to give them the Torah, as it is said, " Lord, when Thou didst go out of **Se'ir**, when Thou didst march out of the field of Edom, the earth trembled, and the heavens dropped, the clouds also dropped water" [Judges 5:4].

Rebbi Yehoshua ben Karha said: The feet of Moshe stood on the mount, and all his body was in the midst of the heaven, like a tent which is spread out, and the children of men stand inside it, but their feet stand on the earth, and all of them are inside the tent; so was it with Moshe, his feet stood on the mountain, and all his body was in the heavens, beholding and seeing everything that is in the heavens. The Holy One, blessed be He, was speaking with him like a man who is conversing with his companion, as it is said, "And the Hashem spake unto Moshe face to face" [Exodus 33:11]. The Holy One, blessed be He, said to Moshe: Go and sanctify the Israelites for two days, as it is said, "And the Hashem said unto Moshe, Go unto the people, and sanctify them to-day and to-morrow" [Exodus 19:10]. What then was the sanctity of Israel in the wilderness? There were no uncircumcised people in their midst; the manna descended from heaven for them; they drank water out of the Well; clouds of glory surrounded them. What then was the sanctity of Israel in the wilderness? It refers to their avoidance of sexual intercourse.

Moshe argued with himself. Moshe said: A man of

Pirkei DeRabbi Eliezer 41

Israel may have gone to his wife, and they will be found to be prevented from receiving the Torah. What did he do? He added one day more for them on his own account, so that if a man of Israel went to his wife, they would be found to be clean for two complete days; therefore, he added one day for them on his own account.

The Holy One, blessed be He, said to him: Moshe. How many souls of the children of men would have come forth from Israel in that night? What thou hast done has been rightly accomplished. The Holy One, blessed be He, approved his action.

The Holy One, blessed be He, said: Let Moshe descend to the camp, and afterwards will I cause My Torah to be proclaimed. He said to him: "Go down, charge the people" [Exodus 19:21]. Moshe was wishing to be there, and he said to Him: I have already charged the people. He said to him: Go, and call thy Rebbi. Moshe descended to the camp to call Aharon, and the Holy One, blessed be He, proclaimed His Torah unto His people, as it is said, "So Moshe went down unto the people, and told them" [Exodus 19:25]. What is written after this? "And God spake all these words, saying, I, the Hashem, am to be thy God, who brought thee out of the land of Egypt, out of the house of bondage" [Exodus 20:1-2].

The voice of the first commandment went forth, and the heavens and earth quaked thereat, and the waters and rivers fled, and the mountains and hills were moved, and all the trees fell prostrate, and the dead

Pirkei DeRabbi Eliezer 41

who were in **Sheol** [The lowest level of Gehinnom] revived, and stood on their feet till the end of all the generations, as it is said, "But with him that standeth here with us this day" [Deuteronomy 29:14]. and those [also] who in the future will be created, until the end of all the generations, there they stood with them at Mount Sinai, as it is said, "And also with him that is not here with us this day" [Deuteronomy 29:14]. The Israelites who were alive then fell upon their faces and died.

The voice of the second commandment went forth, and they were quickened, and they stood upon their feet and said to Moshe: Moshe, our teacher. We are unable to hear any more the voice of the Holy One, blessed be He, for we shall die even as we died now, as it is said, "And they said unto Moshe, Speak thou with us, and we will hear: but let not God speak with us, lest we die" [Exodus 20:15]. And now, why should we die as we died now? The Holy One, blessed be He, heard the voice of Israel, and it was pleasing to Him, and He sent for Michael and Gabriel the Angels, and they took hold of the two hands of Moshe against his will, and they brought him near unto the thick darkness, as it is said, "And Moshe drew near unto the thick darkness where God was" [Exodus 20:17].

It is only written here in the text concerning, Moshe that "he drew near." The rest of the commandments He spake through the mouth of Moshe, and concerning him the text says, "As the cold of snow in the time of harvest, so is a faithful messenger to

Pirkei DeRabbi Eliezer 41

them that send him" [Proverbs 25:13].

And it came to pass, "When ye hear the sound of the **SHOFAR** [Trumpet]" [Samuel-B 15:10]. Why did the Holy One, blessed be He, cause His voice to be heard out of the midst of the darkness, and not out of the midst of the light? A parable: to what is the matter to be likened? To a king who was having his son married to a woman, and he suspended in the wedding chamber of his son black curtains, and not white curtains. He said to them: I know that my son will not remain with his wife except for forty days; so that on the morrow they should not say the king was an astrologer, but he did not know what would happen to his son. So, with the King, who is the Holy One, blessed be He, and His son is Israel, and the bride is the Torah. The Holy One, blessed be He, knew that Israel would not remain loyal to the commandments except for forty days, therefore the Holy One, blessed be He, caused them to hear His voice out of the midst of darkness, and not out of the midst of light, therefore it is said, "And it came to pass, when ye heard the voice" [Deuteronomy 5:28].

Rebbi Yehuda said: When a man speaks with his companion, he hears the sound of his voice, but he does not see any light with it; the Israelites heard the voice of the Holy One, blessed be He, on Mount Sinai, and saw the voice going forth from the mouth of the Almighty in the lightning and the thunder, as it is said, "And all the people saw the thundering and the lightning" [Exodus 20:14]. "The blare of the horn grew louder and louder, As Moses spoke, God

Pirkei DeRabbi Eliezer 41

answered him in thunder" [Exodus 19:19]. All the precepts which are in the Torah number 611, and two, which the Holy One, blessed be He, spake, as it is said, "God has spoken once, two have I heard thus" [Psalms 62:11].

Rebbi Pinchas said: All that generation who heard the voice of the Holy One, blessed be He, on Mount Sinai, were worthy to be like the ministering angels, so that insects had no power over them. They did not experience pollution in their lifetime, and at their death neither worm nor insect prevailed over them. Happy were they in this world and happy will they be in the world to come, and concerning them the Scripture says, "Happy is the people, that is in such a case" [Psalms 144:15].

Chapter 42

"And it came to pass, when Pharaoh had let the people go" [Exodus 13:17]. This is what the Scripture says, "Thy shoots are a garden of pomegranates" [Song of Songs 4:13]. Just as this garden is full of [various] kinds of trees, each one bearing according to its kind, so the Israelites, when they went forth from Egypt, were full of all good, endowed with the various kinds of blessings, as it is said, "Thy shoots are like a garden of pomegranates" [Song of Songs 4:13].

Ramban Gamaliel said: The Egyptians pursued after the children of Israel as far as the Reed Sea, and encamped behind them. The enemy was behind them and the sea was in front of them. And the Israelites saw the Egyptians, and feared very greatly, and there they cast away from themselves all the Egyptian abominations, and they repented very sincerely, and called upon their God, as it is said, "And when Pharaoh drew nigh, the children of Israel lifted up their eyes" [Exodus 14:10]. Moshe beheld the anguish of Israel, and arose to pray on their behalf. The Holy One, blessed be He, said to him: "Speak unto the children of Israel that they go forward" [Exodus 14:15].

Moshe spake before the Holy One, blessed be He, saying: Sovereign of all worlds. The enemy is behind them, and the sea is in front of them, which way shall they go forward? What did the Holy One, blessed be He, do? He sent Michael, and he became

Pirkei DeRabbi Eliezer 42

a wall of fire between Yisrael and the Egyptians. The Egyptians desired to follow after Israel, but they are unable to come near because of the fire. The angels beheld the misfortune of Israel all the night, and they uttered neither praise nor sanctification to their Creator, as it is said, "And the one came not near the other all the night" [Exodus 14:20].

The Holy One, blessed be He, said to Moshe: Moshe. "Stretch out thine hand over the sea, and divide it" [Exodus 14:16]. "And Moshe stretched out his hand over the sea" [Exodus 14:21], but the sea refused to be divided. What did the Holy One, blessed be He, do? He looked at the sea, and the waters saw the face of the Holy One, blessed be He, and they trembled and quaked, and descended into the depths, as it is said, "The waters saw thee, O God; the waters saw thee, they were afraid: the depths also trembled" [Psalms 77:17].

Rebbi Eliezer said: On the day when The Holy One, blessed be He, said, "Let the waters be gathered together" [Genesis 1:9], on that very day were the waters congealed, and they were made into twelve valleys, corresponding to the twelve tribes, and they were made into walls of water between each path, and the people could see one another, and they saw the Holy One, blessed be He, walking before them, but the heels of His feet they did not see, as it is said, "Thy way was in the sea, and thy paths in the great waters, and thy footsteps were not known" [Psalms 77:19].

Pirkei DeRabbi Eliezer 42

Rabbi Akiva said: The Israelites advanced to enter the Reed Sea, but they turned backwards, and the tribe of Benjamin wanted to enter, as it said: "There is little Benjamin who rules them" [Psalms 68:28]. The tribe of Judah began to stumble, which is said: "The princes of Yehuda who command them" [Psalms 68:28]. Fearing lest the waters would come over them. The tribe of Yehuda sanctified His great Name, and entered the sea first, and under the dominion of the hand likewise of the sons of Yehuda did all Israel enter the sea after them, as it is said, "Yehuda became his sanctuary, Israel his dominion" [Psalms 114:2]. The Egyptians desired to follow after Israel, but they turned backwards, fearing lest the waters would return over them. What did the Holy One, blessed be He, do? He appeared before them like a man riding on the back of a mare, as it is said, "To a steed in Pharaoh's chariots" [Song of Songs 1:9]. The horse on which Pharaoh rode saw the mare of God, and it neighed and ran and entered the sea after it.

The Egyptians saw that Pharaoh had entered the sea, and all of them entered the sea after him, as it is said, "And the Egyptians pursued after them" [Exodus 14:23]. Forth-with the waters returned, and covered them, as it is said, "And the waters returned, and covered the chariots, and the horsemen" [Exodus 14:28].

Ben Azzai said: Everything is judged according to the principle of measure for measure; just as the Egyptians were proud, and cast the male children into the river, so the Holy One, blessed be He, cast them into the sea, as it is said, "I will sing unto the Hashem, for he hath triumphed triumphantly; the horse and his rider hath he thrown into the sea" [Exodus 15:21].

Rebbi Shela said: All the children of the Israelites whom the Egyptians cast into the river did not die, for the river cast them up, and threw them into the desert of Egypt. The Holy One, blessed be He, brought a rock to the mouth of each one, and a rock to the side of each one. The rock which was at his mouth was feeding him with honey and milk, and the rock which was at their side was anointing them with oil, like a lying-in woman who anoints her son, as it is said, "And he made him to suck honey out of the rock, and oil out of the flinty rock" [Deuteronomy 32:13]. When Israel came to the sea, they saw the Holy One, blessed be He, and they recognized Him, and praised Him, and sanctified Him, as it is said, "This is my God, and I will praise him" [Exodus 15:2].

Rebbi Levi the Son of Simon said: On the fourth day the Israelites encamped by the edge of the sea, and to the south of the sea. The Egyptians were floating like skin-bottles upon the surface of the waters, and a north wind went forth and cast them opposite the camp of Israel, and the Israelites went and saw them, and they recognized them, and they said: These here were the officials of the palace of Pharaoh, and those there were the taskmasters, and they recognized every one, as it is said, "And Israel saw the Egyptians dead upon the sea shore" [Exodus 14:30].

Pirkei DeRabbi Eliezer 42

Rebbi Reuven said: The entire body follows the head, and when the shepherd goes astray the sheep go astray after him, as it is said, "For the sins of Jeroboam which he sinned, and wherewith he made Israel to sin" [Kings-B 10:29]. When the shepherd is good, all follow after him. Moshe began to sing, and to utter praises before the Holy One, blessed be He, and all Israel followed him, as it is said, "Then sang Moshe and the children of Israel" [Exodus 15:1]. Miriam began to sing and to utter praises, before the Holy One, blessed be He, and all the women followed her, as it is said, "And Miriam the prophetess, the sister of Aharon, took a timbrel... and all the women went out after her" [Exodus 15:20]. Whence did they have timbrels and chorus in the wilderness? But the righteous always know and conciliate God, and are assured that the Omnipresent, blessed be He, performs for them miracles and mighty deeds. Before the time of their departure from Egypt they prepared for themselves timbrels and chorus.

Yisrael spake before the Holy One, blessed be He: Sovereign of all worlds. These Egyptians who have arisen to come against us to destroy us from Thy world, as well as all who rise up against us, are as though they had risen up against Thee. Let the majesty of Thy might and thy fierce anger consume them like stubble, as it is said, "And in the greatness of thine Excellency thou overthrowest them that rise up against thee: thou sendeth forth thy wrath, it consumeth them as stubble" [Exodus 15:7].

Pirkei DeRabbi Eliezer 42

Yisrael spake before the Holy One, blessed be He: Sovereign of all worlds. There is none like Thee among the ministering angels, and therefore all their descriptive names contain part of the word Elo him **God**; Michael and Gabriel. "Who is like unto thee among the divine creatures, O Hashem?" [Exodus 15:11]. Pharaoh replied after them with the tongue, saying: "Who is like thee, glorious in holiness, fearful in praises, doing wonders?" [Exodus 15:11]. "Fearful in praise" is not written here, but "fearful in praises"; for the praises of the ministering angels are on high, and the praises of Israel are uttered on earth below. "Fearful in praises, doing wonders" [Exodus 15:11], and thus Scripture says, "But thou art holy, O thou that inhabitest the praises of Israel" [Psalms 22:4].

"**Thou** stretchedst out thy right hand, the earth swallowed them" [Exodus 15:12]. The Holy One, blessed be He, told the earth to bury the slain. The earth said unto Him: Sovereign of all worlds. The waters have killed them, let the waters swallow them. He answered the earth saying: On this occasion receive them; on another occasion such that be killed by thee in the future will I cast into the sea, namely, Sisera and all his host, these will I cast into the sea, as it is said, "The river Kishon swept them away, that ancient river" [Judges 5:21]. The earth continued, saying to Him: Give me the oath by Thy right hand, that Thou wilt not claim them at my hand. The Holy One, blessed be He, put forth His right hand, and swore to the earth that He would not claim them, as it is said, "Thou stretchedst out thy right hand, the earth swallowed them" [Exodus 15:12].

Pirkei DeRabbi Eliezer 42

All the kings of the earth heard of the departure from Egypt, and the dividing of the Reed Sea; they trembled and feared, and fled from their place, as it is said, "The peoples have heard, they tremble" [Exodus 15:14].

Moshe spake before the Holy One, blessed be He: Sovereign of all worlds. Put Thy dread and Thy fear upon them, that their heart may be as stone, until Israel has passed through the Jordan, as it is said, "Till thy people pass over" [Exodus 15:16].

"**Thou** shalt bring them in, and plant them in the mountain of thine inheritance" [Exodus 15:17]. Thou shalt bring them in to Thy holy mountain. The Holy One, blessed be He, said to Moshe: Moshe. Thou hast not said, "Bring us in and plant us," but thou hast said, "Thou shalt bring them in and plant them." The One who brings in, He also brings out. By thy life. According to thy words so shall it be. In this world I shall bring them in, and in the world to come I will plant them as a true plant which shall not be plucked up out of their land, as it is said, "And I will plant them upon their land, and they shall no more be plucked up out of their land which I have given them, saith the Hashem thy God" [Amos 9:15]; and it also says, "The Hashem shall reign for ever and ever" [Exodus 15:18].

Chapter 43

Repentance and good deeds are a shield against punishment. Rebbi Yishmael said: If repentance had not been created, the world would not stand. But since repentance has been created, the right hand of the Holy One, blessed be He, is stretched forth to receive the penitent every day, and He says, Repent, ye children of men. "Repent, ye children of men" [Jeremiah 3:21]. Know thou the power of repentance. Come and see from Ahab, king of Israel, for he had robbed, coveted, and murdered, as it is said, "Hast thou killed, and also taken possession?" [Kings-A 21:19]. He sent and called for Jehoshaphat, king of Yehuda, who gave him thrice daily forty stripes, and in fasting and with prayer he rose up early and retired late, before the Holy One, blessed be He, and he did not return any more to his evil deeds. His repentance was accepted, as it is said, "Seest thou how Ahab humbleth himself before me? Because he humbleth himself before me, I will not bring the evil in his days" [Kings-A 21:29].

Rebbi Abbahu said: Know thou the power of repentance. Come and see from David, king of Israel. For the Holy One, blessed be He, had sworn to the forefathers that He would multiply their seed like the stars of the heavens. And David came to count their number. The Holy One, blessed be He, said to him: David. I have sworn to the forefathers that I would multiply their seed as the stars of the heavens. And thou comest to annul my word. For

Pirkei DeRabbi Eliezer 43

thy sake the flock is given over to destruction; and in three hours there fell seventy thousand men, as it is said, "And there fell of Israel seventy thousand men" [Chronicles-A 21:14]. Rebbi Shimon said: Only Abishai, son of Zeruiah, fell amongst the Israelites, for he was equal in his good deeds and his knowledge of the Torah to the seventy thousand men, as it is said, "And there fell of Israel seventy thousand men" [Chronicles-A 21:14]. "Men" is not written here, only "man." And David heard and rent his garments, and clothed himself in sackcloth and ashes, and he fell upon his face to the ground before the ark of the covenant of God.

He sought to do penitence, and spake before the Holy One, blessed be He: Sovereign of all worlds. It is I who have sinned; forgive me, I beseech Thee, my sin. His repentance was accepted, and He said to the angel who had destroyed **RAV** [many] among the people: "Stay thine hand" [Chronicles-A 21:15]. What is the meaning of **RAV** [many]? He said to him: RAV-the teacher, has fallen in Israel. What did the angel do? He took his sword and cleaned it with the garment of David. David saw the sword of the angel, and he trembled in all his limbs until his death as it is said, "But David could not go before it to inquire of God; for he was afraid because of the sword of the angel of the Hashem" [Chronicles-A 21:30].

Rebbi Yehoshua said: Know thou the power of repentance. Come and see from Menashe, son of Hezekiah, who perpetrated all the evil abominations much more than all the nations. He made his son to pass through the fire to Baal outside Yerushalayim, causing [doves] to fly, and sacrificing to all the host of heaven. The princes of the troops of the king of Babylon came, and they caught him by the hair of his head, and brought him down to Babylon, and they put him in a pan over a fire, and there he called upon all the other gods to whom he had sacrificed, and not one of them either answered him or saved him. He said: I will call on the God of my fathers with all my heart; perhaps He will do unto me according to all His wonders which He did unto my father. And he called on the God of his fathers with all his heart, and He was entreated of him, and He heard his supplication, as it is said, "And he prayed unto him; and he was intreated of him, and heard his supplication… then Menashe knew that the Hashem he was God" [Chronicles-B 33:13]. In that hour Menashe said: There is both judgment as well as a judge.

Ben Azzai said: Know thou the power of repentance. Come and see from the story of Rebbi Shimon, son of Laḳish. He with two of his friends in the mountains, were robbing all who passed them on the way. What did he do? He forsook his two companions who were plundering on the mountains, and he returned to the God of his fathers with all his heart. Fasting and praying he arose early and retired late, before the Holy One, blessed be He, and he was studying the Torah all the rest of his days, and giving gifts to the needy. He did not return any more to his evil deeds, and his repentance was accepted. On the day when he died, his two companions, who were plundering on the mountains, also died. And they

Pirkei DeRabbi Eliezer 43

gave a portion in the treasury of the living to Rebbi Shimon, son of Laḵish, but his two companions were put in the **lowest Sheol** [Hell].

The two companion's spake before the Holy One, blessed be He: Sovereign of all the universe. There is before Thee respect for certain persons. This one was plundering with us on the mountains, and he is in the treasury of the living, whilst the other men are in the **lowest Sheol** [Hell]. He said to them: This one repented in his lifetime, but ye have not repented. They said to Him: Give us the opportunity, and we will repent very sincerely. He said to them: Repentance is only possible until one's death.

A parable to what is the matter comparable? To a man who wished to take a voyage at sea? If he did not take with him bread and water from an inhabited land, he will not find anything to eat or to drink on the sea. Again, if a man wish to go to the end of the wilderness, unless he take from some inhabited place bread and water, he will not find anything to eat or to drink in the wilderness. Likewise, if a man did not repent in his lifetime, after his death he cannot repent. But God gives to a man according to his ways, as it is said, "I the Hashem search the heart, I try the reins, even to give every man according to his ways, according to the fruit of his doings" [Jeremiah 17:10].

Rebbi Nechunia, son of Haḵḵanah, said: Know thou the power of repentance. Come and see from Pharaoh, king of Egypt, who rebelled most

Pirkei DeRabbi Eliezer 43

grievously against the Rock, the Most-High, as it is said, "Who is the Hashem that I should hearken unto his voice?" [Exodus 5:2]. In the same terms of speech in which he sinned, he repented, as it is said "Who is like thee, O Hashem, among the mighty?" [Exodus 15:11]. The Holy One, blessed be He, delivered him from amongst the dead. Whence do we know that he died? Because it is said, "For now I had put forth my hand, and smitten thee" [Exodus 9:15]. He went and ruled in Nineveh. The men of Nineveh were writing fraudulent deeds, and everyone robbed his neighbour, and they committed sodomy, and such-like wicked actions. When the Holy One, blessed be He, sent for Yonah, to prophesy against [the city] its destruction, Pharaoh hearkened and arose from his throne, rent his garments and clothed himself in sackcloth and ashes, and had a proclamation made to all his people, that all the people should fast for two days, and all who did these wicked things should be burnt by fire. What did they do? The men were on one side, and the women on the other, and their children were by themselves; all the clean animals were on one side, and their offspring were by themselves. The infants saw the breasts of their mothers, and they wished to have suck, and they wept. The mothers saw their children, and they wished to give them suck. By the merit of 123,000 children more than twelve hundred thousand men were saved, as it is said, "And should not I have pity on Nineveh, that great city; wherein are more than six score thousand persons that cannot discern between their right hand and their left hand; and also, much cattle?" [Yonah 4:11]; "And the Hashem

Pirkei DeRabbi Eliezer 43

repented of the evil, which he said he would do unto them". For forty years was the Holy One, blessed be He, slow to anger with them, corresponding to the forty days during which He had sent Yonah. After forty years they returned to their many evil deeds, more so than their former ones, and they were swallowed up like the dead, in the lowest Sheol, as it is said, "Out of the city of the dead they groan" [Job 24:12].

The Holy One, blessed be He, sent by the hand of His servants, the prophets, to Israel saying, "O Israel, return unto the Hashem thy God" [Hosea 14:1]. Even unto Him whose voice ye heard at Mount Sinai, saying, "I, the Hashem, am to be thy God" [Exodus 20:2].

"**For** thou hast fallen by thine iniquity" [Hosea 14:2]. "And thy wealth" is not written here, but "For thou hast fallen by thine iniquity." It is not written here, "Take with you silver and gold," but "Take with you words" [Hosea 14:3]. It is not written here, "And we will render silver and gold," but "And we will render as bullocks the offering of our lips" [Hosea 14:3].

Rebbi Yehuda said: If Israel will not repent, they will not be redeemed. Israel only repents because of distress, and because of oppression, and owing to exile, and because they have no sustenance. Israel does not repent quite sincerely until Eliyahu comes, as it is said, "Behold, I will send you Eliyahu, the prophet, before the great and terrible day of the Hashem come. And he shall turn the heart of the

Pirkei DeRabbi Eliezer 43

fathers to the children, and the heart of the children to their fathers" [Malachi 3:23-24].

Blessed art thou, O Hashem, who delightest in repentance.

Chapter 44

Rebbi Yochanan, son of Nuri, said: After all the mighty deeds and wonders which the Holy One, blessed be He, did unto Israel in Egypt, and at the Reed Sea, they repeatedly tempted the Omnipresent ten times, as it is said, "Yet have they tempted me these ten times" [Numbers 14:22]. Moreover, they slandered the Holy One, blessed be He, saying: He has forsaken us in this wilderness, and His **Shekhinah** [divine presence] is not in our midst, as it is said, "Is the Hashem among us, or not?" [Exodus 17:7].

Rebbi Yishmael said: After this section what is written? "Then came Amalek" [Exodus 17:8]. Amalek came against them to punish them. He who comes from a journey should be met on the way with food and drink. **Amalek** [A nation of the sons of Esav] saw them faint and weary, owing to the Egyptian bondage and the affliction of the journey, and he did not take to heart the precept of **Honour**, but he stood by the way like a she-bear, bereaved by man and eager to slay mother and children, as it is said, "How he met thee by the way" [Deuteronomy 25:18].

Rebbi Azariah said: Amalek was a descendant of Esav, and because of his ancestor's enmity he came against them to punish them. The cloud was surrounding the camp of Israel like a city surrounded by a wall. The adversary and enemy were unable to touch them, but when anyone needed a ritual bath

Pirkei DeRabbi Eliezer 44

the cloud excluded him from the camp of Israel, because the camp of Israel was holy, as it is said, "Therefore shall thy camp be holy" [Deuteronomy 23:14], and then Amalek was smiting and slaying the hindmost of those who were beyond the cloud, as it is said, "And he smote the hindmost of thee, all that were feeble behind thee" [Deuteronomy 25:18].

Moshe said to Yehoshua: Choose men for us, houses of the fathers, men who are mighty in strength and valour, and go forth and do battle with Amalek. Moshe, Aharon, and Hur stood on a high place, in the camp of Israel, one on his right hand, and one on his left. Hence, thou mayest learn that the precentor is prohibited to officiate unless there are two men standing with him, one on his right hand and one on his left.

All the Israelites were standing outside their tents; they had gone forth from their tents, and saw Moshe kneeling on his knees, and they were kneeling on their knees. He fell on his face to the ground, and they fell on their faces to the ground. He spread out the palms of his hands towards the heavens, and they spread out their hands to heaven. Just as the precentor officiates, in like manner all the people answer after him.

The Holy One, blessed be He, caused Amalek and his people to fall into the hand of Yehoshua, as it is said, "And Yehoshua discomfited Amalek and his people with the edge of the sword" [Exodus 17:13].

Pirkei DeRabbi Eliezer 44

Rebbi Shela said: The Holy One, blessed be He, wished to destroy, to cut off all the seed of Amalek. What did the Holy One, blessed be He, do? He put forth His right hand and took hold of the throne of His glory, and swore that He would destroy and cut off all the seed of Amalek, as it is said, "And he said, because there is a hand against the throne of the Hashem, the Hashem will wage war against Amalek" [Exodus 17:16].

Rebbi Pinchas said: After forty years Moshe wished to say to Israel: Do ye remember that which ye said in the wilderness - "Is the Hashem among us, or not?" [Exodus 17:7]. But Moshe said: If I speak thus to Israel, behold I will put them to shame, and whosoever puts his fellow to shame will have no portion in the world to come.

A parable to what is the matter to be compared? To a king who had a garden and a dog chained at the entrance to the garden. The king was sitting in his upper room, watching and looking at all that transpired in the garden. The friend of the king entered to steal fruit from the garden, and he incited the dog against him, and it tore his garments. The king said: If I say to my friend, why didst thou enter my garden? Behold I will put him to shame; therefore, behold, I will say to him: Didst thou see that mad dog, how it tore thy clothes? And he will understand what he has done. Likewise, spake Moshe: Behold, I will tell Israel the story of Amalek, and they will understand what is written before it; therefore, Moshe said: "Remember what Amalek

Pirkei DeRabbi Eliezer 44

did unto thee by the way, as ye came forth out of Egypt" [Deuteronomy 25:17].

The Israelites said to our teacher Moshe: Moshe. One Scripture text says, "Remember what Amalek did unto thee" [Deuteronomy 25:17]. and it is written, "Remember the Sabbath day, to keep it holy" [Exodus 20:8]; How can these two texts be fulfilled? He said to them: The cup of spiced wine is not to be compared to the cup of vinegar. This **Remember** is in order to observe and to sanctify the Sabbath day, and the other **Remember** is in order to destroy and to cut off all the seed of Amalek, as it is said, "Therefore it shall be, when the Hashem thy God hath given Thee rest from all thine enemies… thou shalt not forget" [Deuteronomy 25:19]. Israel forgot to destroy and to cut off all the seed of Amalek, but the Holy One, blessed be He, did not forget. When Shaul reigned, Samuel said to him: "Thus saith the Hashem of hosts, I have marked that which Amalek did to Israel…. Now go and smite Amalek, and utterly destroy all that they have" [Samuel-A 15:2-3]. What is the meaning of "all that they have"? Even all the living male creatures. "Spare them not, but slay" [Samuel-A 15:3]. Shaul took the men of war, and he went out to meet Amalek. When Shaul came to the crossing of the ways, he stood still, and thought in his heart, as it is said, "And Shaul came to the city of Amalek, and argued in the valley" [Samuel-A 15:5]. Shaul said: If the men have sinned, what have the beasts done amiss? A **Bath Ḳol** [A voice from heaven] came forth, saying to him: Shaul. Be not more righteous than thy Creator, as it is said, "Be not

Pirkei DeRabbi Eliezer 44

righteous overmuch" [Ecclesiastes 7:16].

Rebbi said: When Shaul came to the camp of Amalek he saw the children of Israel tarrying in the midst of Amalek. He said to them: Separate yourselves from the midst of Amalek, as it is said, "And Shaul said unto the Kenites, Go, depart, you go down from among the Amalekites, lest I destroy you with them" [Samuel-A 15:6]. Did Yitro show loving-kindness to all Israel? But did he not show loving-kindness to Moshe our teacher alone? Hence, thou mayest learn that whosoever shows loving-kindness unto one of the great men of Israel is considered as though he had shown loving-kindness unto Israel. Because of the loving-kindness which he showed, his children were saved from among the Amalekites.

Rebbi Yosef said: When Sennacherib came to the land of Israel, all the nations who were in the regions round about the land of Israel saw the camp of Sennacherib, and feared greatly, and every man fled from his place, as it is said, "I have removed the bounds of the peoples, and have robbed their treasures" [Isaiah 10:13]. They went into the wilderness, and intermixed with the children of Yishmael, and all of them were composed of ten peoples, as it is said, "The tents of Aram, and the Yishmaelites; Moav, and the Hagarenes; Gebal, and Ammon, and Amalek; Philistia, with the inhabitants of Tyre; Assyria also is joined with them" [Psalms 83:6, 7-9]. All of them are destined to fall by the hand of the Son of David, as it is said, "O my God, make

Pirkei DeRabbi Eliezer 44

them like the whirling dust" [Psalms 83:13]. "As the fire that burneth the forest, and as the flame that setteth the mountains on fire" [Psalms 83:14]. "So, pursue them with thy tempest, and terrify them with thy storm" [Psalms 83:15].

Chapter 45

Rebbi Simeon Ben Yochai said: When the Holy One, blessed be He, was revealed to Moshe out of the thorn-bush, in order to send him to Egypt, Moshe spake before the Holy One, blessed be He saying: Sovereign of all the worlds. Swear to me that all things which I desire to do, thou wilt do, so that I should not speak words before Pharaoh, and Thou wilt not fulfill them, for then will he slay me. And He swore unto him that "whatsoever thou desirest to do, I will do, except with reference to two things," namely, to let him enter the land of Canaan, and to postpone the day of his death. Whence do we know that He swore unto him? Because it is said, "By myself have I sworn, saith the Hashem, the word is gone forth from my mouth in righteousness" [Isaiah 45:23]. When Israel received the commandments, they forgot their God after forty days, and they said to Aharon: The Egyptians were carrying their god, and they were singing and uttering hymns before it, and they saw it before them. Make unto us a god like the gods of the Egyptians, and let us see it before us, as it is said, "Up, make us a god" [Exodus 32:1].

They betook themselves to the one who carried out the words of Moshe, to Aharon his brother, and Hur, the son of his sister. Whence do we know that Hur was the son of Moshe's sister? Because it is said, "And Caleb took unto him **Ephrath**, which bare him Hur" [Chronicles-A 2:19]. Why was Miriam's name called Ephrath? Because she was a daughter of the

Pirkei DeRabbi Eliezer 45

palace, a daughter of kings, one of the magnates of the generation; for every prince and great man who arose in Israel had his name called an Ephrathite, as it is said, "And Yeroboam, the son of Nebat, an Ephrathite" [Kings-A 11:26]; and it says, "And David was the son of that Ephrathite" [Samuel-A 17:12]. Was he then an Ephrathite? Was he not of the tribe of Yehuda? But he was a nobleman, a son of kings, one of the magnates of the generation. But since Hur was of the tribe of Yehuda, and one of the magnates of the generation, he began to reprove Israel with harsh words, and the plunderers who were in Israel arose against him, and slew him.

Aharon arose and saw that Hur, the son of his sister, was slain; and he built for them an altar, as it is said, "And when Aharon saw this, he built an altar before it" [Exodus 32:5].

Aharon argued with himself, saying: If I say to Israel, give ye to me gold and silver, they will bring it immediately; but behold I will say to them, give ye to me the earrings of your wives, and of your sons, and forthwith the matter will fail, as it is said, "And Aharon said to them, Break off the golden rings" [Exodus 32:2]. The women heard this, but they were unwilling to give their earrings to their husbands; but they said to them: Ye desire to make a graven image and a molten image without any power in it to deliver. The Holy One, blessed be He, gave the women their reward in this world and in the world to come. What reward did He give them in this world? That they should observe the New

Pirkei DeRabbi Eliezer 45

Moons more stringently than the men, and what reward will He give them in the world to come? They are destined to be renewed like the New Moons, as it is said, "Who satisfieth thy years with good things; so that thy youth is renewed like the eagle" [Psalms 103:5].

The men saw that the women would not consent to give their earrings to their husbands. What did they do? Until that hour the earrings were also in their own ears, after the fashion of the Egyptians, and after the fashion of the Arabs. They broke off their earrings which were in their own ears, and they gave them to Aharon, as it is said, "And all the people brake off the golden rings which were in their ears" [Exodus 32:3]. "Which were in the ears of their wives" is not written here, but "which were in their ears." Aharon found among the earrings one plate of gold upon which the Holy Name was written, and engraven thereon was the figure of a calf, and that plate alone did he cast into the fiery furnace, as it is said, "So they gave it me: and I cast it into the fire, and there came out this calf" [Exodus 32:24]. It is not written here, "And I cast them in," but "And I cast it in the fire, and there came out this calf." The calf came out lowing, and the Israelites saw it, and they went astray after it.

Rebbi Yehuda said: Sammae"l [The angel of death] entered into it, and he was lowing to mislead Israel, as it is said, "The ox knoweth his owner" [Isaiah 1:3].

The Holy One, blessed be He, said to Moshe: Israel

has forgotten the might of my power, which I wrought for them in Egypt and at the Reed Sea, and they have made an idol for themselves. He said to Moshe: Go, get thee down from thy greatness. Moshe spake before the Holy One, blessed be He: Sovereign of all the worlds. Whilst Israel had not yet sinned before Thee, Thou didst call them "My people," as it is said, "And I will bring forth my hosts, my people" [Exodus 7:4]. Now that they have sinned before Thee, Thou sayest unto me, "Go, get thee down, for thy people have corrupted themselves" [Exodus 32:7]. They are Thy people, and Thine inheritance, as it is said, "Yet they are thy people and thine inheritance" [Deuteronomy 9:29].

Moshe took the tables of the law, and he descended, and the tables carried their own weight and Moshe with them; but when they beheld the calf and the dances, the writing fled from off the tables, and they became heavy in his hands, and Moshe was not able to carry himself and the tables, and he cast them from his hand, and they were broken beneath the mount, as it is said, "And Moshe anger waxed hot, and he cast the tables out of his hands, and brake them beneath the mount" [Exodus 32:19].

Moshe said to Aharon: What hast thou done to this people? Thou hast made them unruly, like a woman who is unchecked owing to immorality. He said to Moshe: I saw what they did to Hur, and I feared very greatly.

Rebbi said: All the princes were not associated in

Pirkei DeRabbi Eliezer 45

the affair of the calf, as it is said, "And upon the nobles of the children of Israel he laid not his hand" [Exodus 24:11]. [The word **AZILE** means the princes] therefore they were accounted worthy to gaze upon the glory of the **Shekhinah** [divine presence], as it is said, "And they saw the God of Israel" [Exodus 24:10].

Rebbi Yehuda said: The tribe of **Levi** also did not associate itself in the affair of the calf, as it is said, "Then Moshe stood in the gate of the camp, and said, whoso is on the Hashem's side let him come unto me. And all the sons of Levi gathered themselves together unto him" [Exodus 32:26]. Moshe saw that the tribe of Levi was with him. He became strengthened with his might, and he burnt the calf with fire, and powdered it, like the dust of the earth, and he cast its dust upon the face of the waters, as it is said, "And he took the calf which they had made" [Exodus 32:20]. He made Israel drink the water with the dust of the calf. Everyone who had kissed the calf with all his heart, his upper lip and his bones became golden, and the tribe of Levi slew him, until there fell of Israel about three thousand men, as it is said, "And the sons of Levi did according to the word of Moshe" [Exodus 32:28].

The Holy One, blessed be He, sent five angels to destroy Israel. The angels were Wrath, Anger, Temper, Destruction, and Glow of Anger. Moshe heard, and he went to invoke Avraham, Yitzhak, and Yaakov at the Cave of Machpelah, and he said: If ye be of the children of the world to come, stand ye

Pirkei DeRabbi Eliezer 45

before me in this hour, for behold your children are given over like sheep to the slaughter. Avraham, Yitzhak, and Yaakov stood there before him. Moshe spake before the Holy One, blessed be He saying: Sovereign of all the worlds. Didst Thou not swear to these forefathers thus to increase their seed like the stars of the heaven, as it is said, "Remember Avraham, Yitzhak, and Israel, thy servants, to whom thou sworest by thine own self, and saidst unto them, I will multiply your seed as the stars of heaven" [Exodus 32:18].

By the merit of the three patriarchs, the three angels, Wrath, Anger, and Temper, were restrained from doing harm to Israel. But two angels remained. Moshe spake before the Holy One, blessed be He: Sovereign of all the universe. For the sake of the oath which Thou didst swear unto them, keep back the angel Destruction from Israel, as it is said, "To whom thou sworest by thine own self" [Exodus 32:18]; and Destruction was kept back from Israel, as it is said, "But he, being full of compassion, forgave their iniquity, and destroyed them not" [Psalms 78:88]. Moshe spake before the Holy One, blessed be He: Sovereign of all worlds. For the sake of Thy great and holy Name, which Thou didst make known unto me, hold back from Israel, the angel called Glow of Anger, as it is said, "Turn away from thy fierce anger" [Exodus 32:12]. What did Moshe do? He dug in the earth in the possession of Gad, as though for the foundation of a large dwelling, and he buried "Fierce Anger" in the earth, like a man who is bound in the prison. Every time Israel sins it arises and opens its

Pirkei DeRabbi Eliezer 45

mouth to bite with its breath, and to destroy Israel. Moshe pronounced against it the divine Name, and brought it down beneath the earth. Therefore, is its name called Peor the one who opens? When Moshe died, what did the Holy One, blessed be He, do? He put his burial-place opposite to it. Every time Israel sins it opens its mouth to bite with its breath, and to destroy Israel, but when it sees the burial-place of Moshe opposite to it, it returns backward, as it is said, "And he buried him in the valley, in the land of Moav, over against the house of Peor" [Deuteronomy 34:6].

Chapter 46

Rebbi Elazar, son of Azariah, said: On Friday, on the 6th of the month, at the sixth hour of the day, Israel received the Commandments. At the ninth hour of the day, they returned to their tents, and the Manna was prepared for them for two days, and Israel rested on that Sabbath full of joy as with the joy of the festival, because they were worthy to hear the voice of the Holy One, blessed be He, as it is said, "For who is there of all flesh, that hath heard the voice of the living God speaking out of the midst of the fire, as we have, and lived?" [Deuteronomy 5:22]. The Holy One, blessed be He, said to Moshe in a pure expression of speech: Go, tell the children of Israel, that for my sake they should return to their tents, as it is said, "Go, say to them, Return ye to your tents" [Deuteronomy 5:26]. It is possible that even thou Moshe shouldst return. Hence, thou mayest learn that from the hour when Moshe brought down the Torah to Israel, he did not approach his wife, as it is said, "But as for thee, stand thou here by me" [Deuteronomy 5:27].

Rebbi Yehoshua, son of Karha, said: Forty days was Moshe on the mountain, reading the Written Law by day, and studying the Oral Law by night. After the forty days he took the tables of the Law and descended into the camp on the 17th of Tammuz, and he broke in pieces the tables, and slew the sinners in Israel. He then spent forty days in the camp, until he had burnt the calf, and powdered it

Pirkei DeRabbi Eliezer 46

like the dust of the earth, and he had destroyed the idol worship from Israel, and he instituted every tribe in its place. And on the New Moon of Elul the Holy One, blessed be He, said to him: "Come up to me on the mount" [Exodus 24:12], and let them sound the Shofar trumpet throughout the camp, for, behold, Moshe has ascended the mount, so that they do not go astray again after the worship of idols. The Holy One, blessed be He, was exalted with that Shofar, as it is said, "God is exalted with a shout, the Hashem with the sound of a trumpet" [Psalms 47:6]. Therefore, the sages instituted that the Shofar should be sounded on the New Moon of Elul every year.

Rebbi Kahane said: The tables of the Law were not created out of the earth but out of the heavens, the handicraft of the Holy One, blessed be He, as it is said, "And the tables, the work of God were they " [Exodus 32:16]. They are the tables which were of old, "and the writing" was divine writing; that was the writing which was of old, "graven upon the tables." Do not read Charuth, **Graven**, but read Cheruth, **Liberty**. When the Holy One, blessed be He, said to Moshe: "Hew thee two tables of stone like unto the first" [Exodus 34:1]. a quarry of sapphires was created for Moshe in the midst of his tent, and he cut them out thence, as it is said, "And he hewed two tables of stone like unto the first" [Exodus 34:4]. Moshe descended with the tables, and spent forty days on the mountain, sitting down before the Holy One, blessed be He, like a disciple who is sitting before his teacher, reading the Written Law, and repeating the Oral Law which he had learnt.

Pirkei DeRabbi Eliezer 46

The ministering angels said to him: Moshe. This Torah has been given only for our sakes. Moshe replied to them: It is written in the Torah, "Honour thy father and thy mother" [Exodus 20:11]. Have ye then father and mother? Again, it is written in the Torah, "When a man dieth in the tent" [Numbers 19:14]. Does death happen among you? They were silent, and did not answer anything further.

Hence the sages say: Moshe went up to the heavenly regions with his wisdom, and brought down the might of the trust of the ministering angels, as it is said, "A wise man scaleth the city of the mighty, and bringeth down the strength of the confidence thereof" [Proverbs 21:22]. When the ministering angels saw that the Holy One, blessed be He, gave the Torah to Moshe, they also arose and gave unto him presents and letters and tablets for healing the sons of man, as it is said, "Thou hast ascended on high, thou hast led thy captivity captive; thou hast received gifts among men" [Psalms 68:19].

The Son of Bethera said: Moshe spent forty days on the mount, expounding the meaning of the words of the Torah, and examining its letters. After forty days he took the Torah, and descended on the tenth of the month, on the Day of Atonement, and gave it as an everlasting inheritance to the children of Israel, as it is said, "And this shall be unto you an everlasting statute" [Leviticus 16:34].

Rebbi Zechariah said: They read in the Torah and found written therein, "And ye shall afflict your

Pirkei DeRabbi Eliezer 46

souls" [Leviticus 23:32]. and on the Day of Atonement, they caused a Shofar to be sounded throughout all the camp and proclaimed a fast for all Israel, old and young. Were it not for the Day of Atonement the world could not stand, because the Day of Atonement is in this world and in the world to come, as it is said, "It is a Sabbath of Sabbaths unto you" [Leviticus 16:31]. **A Sabbath** refers to this world, **Sabbath's** refers to the world to come. Moreover, if all the festivals pass away, the Day of Atonement will not pass away, for the Day of Atonement effects reconciliation for serious offences as well as for slight offences. Whence do we know that the Day of Atonement effects reconciliation? Because it is said, "For on this day shall atonement be made for you, to cleanse you; from all your sins shall ye be clean" [Leviticus 16:30]. "From your sins" is not written here, but "from all your sins shall ye be clean before the Hashem" [Leviticus 16:30].

Sammae"l [The angel of death] said before the Holy One, blessed be He: Sovereign of all the universe. Thou hast given me power over all the nations of the world, but over Israel Thou hast not given me power. He answered him, saying: Behold, thou hast power over them on the Day of Atonement if they have any sin, but if not, thou hast no power over them. Therefore, they gave him a present on the Day of Atonement, in order that they should not bring their offering, as it is said, "One lot for the Hashem, and the other lot for Azazel" [Leviticus 16:8].

The lot for the Holy One, blessed be He, was the

Pirkei DeRabbi Eliezer 46

offering of a burnt offering, and the lot for Azazel was the goat as a sin offering, for all the iniquities of Israel were upon it, as it is said, "And the goat shall bear upon him all their iniquities" [Leviticus 16:22]. Sammae"l [The angel of death] saw that sin was not to be found among them on the Day of Atonement. He said before the Holy One, blessed be He: Sovereign of all the universe. Thou hast one people like the ministering angels who are in heaven. Just as the ministering angels have bare feet, so have the Israelites bare feet on the Day of Atonement. Just as the ministering angels have neither food nor drink, so the Israelites have neither food nor drink on the Day of Atonement. Just as the ministering angels have no joints, in likewise the Israelites stand upon their feet. Just as the ministering angels have peace obtaining amongst them, so the Israelites have peace obtaining amongst them on the Day of Atonement. Just as the ministering angels are innocent of all sin on the Day of Atonement, so are the Israelites innocent of all sin on the Day of Atonement. The Holy One, blessed be He, hears the prayers of Israel rather than the charges brought by their accuser, and He makes atonement for the altar, and for the sanctuary, and for the Ha-Kohen's, and for all the people of the congregation both great and small, as it is said, "And he shall make atonement for the holy place" [Leviticus 16:33].

Moshe said: On the Day of Atonement, I will behold the glory of the Holy One, blessed be He, and I will make atonement for the iniquities of Israel. Moshe spake before the Holy One, blessed be He:

Pirkei DeRabbi Eliezer 46

Sovereign of all the universe. "Shew me, I pray thee, thy glory" [Exodus 33:18]. The Holy One, blessed be He, said to him: Moshe. Thou art not able to see my glory lest thou die, as it is said, "For men shall not see me and live" [Exodus 33:20]; but for the sake of the oath which I have sworn unto thee I will do thy will. Stand at the entrance of the cave, and I will make all the angels who move before me pass before thy face. Stand in thy might, and do not fear, as it is said, "And he said, I will make all my goodness pass before thee" [Exodus 33:19]. When thou dost hear the Name which I have spoken to thee, there am I before thee, as it is said, "And he said, I will make all my goodness pass before thee" [Exodus 33:19].

The ministering angels said: Behold, we serve before Him by day and by night, and we are unable to see His glory, and this one born of woman desires to see His glory. And they arose in wrath and excitement to slay him, and his soul came nigh unto death. What did the Holy One, blessed be He, do? He revealed Himself unto him in a cloud, as it is said, "And the Hashem descended in the cloud" [Exodus 34:5]. This was the seventh descent.

The Holy One, blessed be He, protected him with the hollow of His hand that he should not die, as it is said, "And it shall come to pass, while my glory passeth by, that I will put thee in a cleft of the rock, and I will cover thee with my hand" [Exodus 33:22]. When the Holy One, blessed be He, had passed by, He removed the hollow of His hand from him, and he saw the traces of the **Shekhinah** [divine

Pirkei DeRabbi Eliezer 46

presence], as it is said, "And I will take away mine hand, and thou shalt see my back" [Exodus 33:22]. Moshe began to cry with a loud voice, and he said: "O Hashem, O Hashem, a God full of compassion and gracious ..." [Exodus 34:6].

Moshe said before the Holy One, blessed be He: Sovereign of all worlds. Pardon now the iniquities of this people. He said to him: Moshe. If thou hadst said, Pardon now the iniquities of all Israel, even to the end of all generations He would have done so. It was an acceptable time. But thou hast said: Pardon, I beseech Thee, the iniquities of this people with reference to the affair of the calf. He said to him: Moshe. Behold, let it be according to thy words, as it is said, "And the Hashem said, I have pardoned according to thy word" [Numbers 14:20].

Chapter 47

Rebbi Elazar, son of Arakh, said: When the Holy One, blessed be He, descended upon Mount Sinai to give the Torah to Israel, sixty myriads of the ministering angels descended with Him, corresponding to the sixty myriads of the mighty men of Israel, and in their hands were swords and crowns, and they crowned the Israelites with the Ineffable Name. All those days, whilst they had not done that deed, they were as good as the ministering angels before the Holy One, blessed be He. The Angel of Death did not hold sway over them, and they did not discharge any excretions like the children of man; but when they did that deed the Holy One, blessed be He, was angry with them, and He said to them: I thought that ye would be like the ministering angels, as it is said, "I said, Ye are angels, and all of you sons of the Most-High" [Psalms 82:6]. But now, "Nevertheless, ye shall die like men" [Psalms 82:7].

Rebbi Yehuda said: As long as a man is dressed in his garments of glory, he is beautiful in his appearance and in his honour; so were the Israelites when they apparelled themselves with that Name, they were good before the Holy One, blessed be He, like the ministering angels. But when they did that deed of the golden calf, the Holy One, blessed be He, was angry with them. In that night the same sixty myriads of ministering angels descended, and they severally took from each one of them what they had put upon them, and they became bare, not according to their own wish, as it is said, "And the children of Israel stripped themselves" [Exodus 33:6]. It is not written here, "the children of Israel took away," but "the children of Israel stripped themselves." Some say by itself their adornment was stripped off.

Rebbi said: At every place where Israel sat down in the wilderness, they made idols for themselves, as it is said, "And the people sat down to eat and to drink" [Exodus 32:6]. What is written here? "And they rose up to play" [Exodus 32:6]; they commenced to worship idols. One verse says, "And Israel abode in Shittim" [Numbers 25:1]. What is written here? "And the people began to commit whoredom with the daughters of Moav" [Numbers 25:1]. They commenced to be immoral.

Rebbi Yehuda said: "The counsel of the wicked is far from me" [Job 21:16]. This text refers to the counsel of Balaam, the wicked, who advised Midian, and there fell of Israel twenty-four thousand men. He said to them: You will not be able to prevail against this people, unless they have sinned before their Creator. They made for themselves booths outside the camp of Israel, and they sold all kinds of merchandise of the market. The young men of Israel went beyond the camp of Israel and they saw the daughters of Midian, who had painted their eyes like harlots, and they took wives of them, and went astray after them, as it is said, "And the people began to commit whoredom with the daughters of Moav"

[Numbers 25:1].

Shimon and Levi were exceedingly zealous because of the immorality, as it is said, "And they said, as with a harlot should he deal with our sister?" [Genesis 34:81]. Each man took his sword and they slew the men of Shechem. The prince of the tribe of Shimon did not remember that which his ancestor had done, and he did not rebuke the young men of Israel, but he himself came publicly to the Midianitish woman for an immoral purpose, as it is said, "Now the name of the man of Israel that was slain, who was slain with the Midianitish woman, was Zimri… a prince of a fathers house among the Shimonites" [Numbers 25:14].

All the princes with Moshe, Eleazar, and Pinchas saw the angel who was to destroy the people, and they sat down and wept, and they did not know what to do. Pinchas saw how Zimri went publicly to the Midianitish woman for an immoral purpose, and he was moved by a great zeal, and he snatched the spear out of the hand of Moshe, and ran after Zimri and pierced him through the back, through the pudenda, and the spear went into the belly of the woman. Therefore, the Holy One, blessed be He, gave a good reward to him and to his sons with the food of the shoulder. And the jaws were separated, the jaws of the man [from] the jaws of the woman; therefore, the Holy One, blessed be He, gave him and his sons a good reward with the food of the cheeks, as it is said, "And they shall give unto the Ha-Kohen the shoulder, and the two cheeks, and the maw"

Pirkei DeRabbi Eliezer 47

[Deuteronomy 18:3].

He arose like a great spiritual leader and he judged Israel, as it is said, "Then stood up Pinchas, and he executed judgment" [Psalms 106:30]. What is the meaning of this expression, "And he executed judgment"? Like a great judge. Just as thou dost say, "And he shall pay as the judges determine" [Exodus 21:22]. And he smote the young men of Israel so that all Israel should see and fear, as it is said, "And all Israel shall hear, and fear" [Deuteronomy 21:21]. The Holy One, blessed be He, saw what Pinchas had done, and forthwith was He filled with compassion; the plague was stayed, as it is said, "And so the plague was stayed" [Numbers 16:50].

Rebbi Eliezer said: He called the name of Pinchas by the name of Eliyahu - Eliyahu of blessed memory, who was of those who repented in Gilead, for he brought about the repentance of Israel in the land of Gilead. The Holy One, blessed be He, gave him the life of this world and the life of the world to come, as it is said, "My covenant was with him of life and peace" [Malachi 2:5]. He gave to him and to his sons a good reward, in order that [he might have] the everlasting Ha-Kohenhood, as it is said, "And it shall be unto him, and to his seed after him, the covenant of an everlasting Ha-Kohenhood" [Numbers 25:13].

Rebbi Elazar of Modein said: Pinchas arose, and pronounced the ban upon Israel by the mystery of the Ineffable Name, and with the script which was written on the tables of the Law, and by the ban of the celestial Court of Justice, and by the ban of the terrestrial Court of Justice, that a man of Israel should not drink the wine of the nations unless it had been trodden by the feet, as it is said, "And as for my sheep, that which ye have trodden with your feet they eat, and they drink that which ye have fouled with your feet" [Ezekiel 34:19]. Because all the wine of the nations was devoted to idolatry and immorality, for they took the first of their new wine for idolatry and immorality, as it is said, " whoredom and wine and new wine take away the heart" [Hosea 4:11]. And it is said: Do not be of those who guzzle wine, Or glut themselves on meat [Proverbs 23:20].

Rebbi Pinchas said: The Holy One, blessed be He, said to Moshe: Do ye remember what those Midianites did to you, for twenty-four thousand men fell in Israel? But before "thou art gathered in," arise, execute vengeance, as it is said, "Avenge the children of Israel of the Midianites; afterwards shalt thou be gathered unto thy people" [Numbers 31:2].

What did Moshe do? He took a thousand men and a prince from each tribe of the tribes of Israel. Behold, there were twelve thousand men, and he who had been zealous because of the immorality, was the prince over them. The holy vestments and the trumpets of alarm were in his hand, and they went, and they took captive the daughters of Midian, and they brought them to the camp. Moshe said to Pinchas: Because of these did not twenty-four thousand men of Israel fall? As it is said, "Behold,

Pirkei DeRabbi Eliezer 47

these caused the children of Israel, through the counsel of Balaam, to commit trespass against the Hashem in the matter of Peor" [Numbers 31:16]; and he began to be angry with them, as it is said, "And Moshe was wroth with the officers of the host" [Numbers 31:14]. During his anger the Holy Spirit departed from him. Hence, thou mayest learn that the impetuous man destroys his wisdom. Eleazar saw and he heard the voice behind Moshe, as it is said, "And Eleazar the Ha-Kohen said unto the men of war… This is the statute of the Law which the Hashem hath commanded Moshe" [Numbers 31:21]. He said to them: He commanded Moshe and He did not command me.

Chapter 48

Rabban Yochanan, son of Zakkai, opened his exposition with the text: "In that day the Hashem made a covenant with Abram, saying, unto thy seed will I give this land, from the river of Egypt unto the great river, the river Euphrates" [Genesis 15:18]. Abram said before the Holy One, blessed be He, Sovereign of all the universe. Thou hast not given me seed, yet dost Thou say, "Unto thy seed will I give this land" [Genesis 15:18]. He said: "Whereby shall I know that I shall inherit it?" [Genesis 15:8]. The Holy One, blessed be He, said to him: Abram. The entire world stands by my word, and thou dost not believe in my word, but thou sayest, "Whereby shall I know that I shall inherit it?" [Genesis 15:8]. By thy life. In two ways shalt thou surely know, as it is said, "And he said to Abram, know of a surety that thy seed shall be a stranger in a land which is not theirs… and they shall afflict them" [Genesis 15:18].

Rebbi Elazar, son of Azariah, said: Is it not so that the Israelites did not dwell in Egypt except for 210 years? But in order to teach thee, know that this is so, come and see; for when Yosef went down to Egypt, he was seventeen years old, and when he stood before Pharaoh, he was thirty years old, as it is said, "And Yosef was thirty years old when he stood before Pharaoh, king of Egypt" [Genesis 41:46]. And the seven years of plenty, and the two years of famine, behold, they are nine-and-thirty years in all. And Levi, the son of Yaakov, was six years older

Pirkei DeRabbi Eliezer 48

than Yosef, and when he went down to Egypt, he was forty-five years, and the years of his life in Egypt were ninety-two years; behold, all of them amount to 137 years, as it is said, "And the years of the life of Levi were a hundred thirty and seven years" [Exodus 6:16]. On his going down to Egypt, his wife bare unto him Yocheved, his daughter, as it is said, "And the name of Amram's wife was Yocheved" [Numbers 26:59], and she was 130 years when she bare Moshe, as it is said, "And Moshe was fourscore years old when he stood before Pharaoh" [Exodus 7:7]. Behold, the total is **210** years in all. And thus, it says, "And they shall serve them; and they shall afflict them four hundred years" [Genesis 15:13].

Rebbi Elazar, son of Arakh, said to them: The Holy One, blessed be He, said this to Avraham only at the hour when he had seed, as it is said, "Thy seed shall be a stranger in a land that is not theirs" [Genesis 15:13]. From the time when Yitzhak was born until Israel went forth from Egypt 400 years elapsed. Rabban Yohanan ben Zakkai, son of Zakkai said to him: Verily it is written, "Now the sojourning of the children of Israel, which they sojourned in Egypt, was four hundred and thirty years" [Exodus 12:40]. He answered him, saying: 210 years Israel abode in Egypt, and five years before Yaakov came to Egypt there were born unto Yosef the fathers of two tribes, Menashe and Ephraim, and they belonged to the Israelites. Behold, we have 215 years of days and nights, this equals 430 years; for the Holy One, blessed be He, reduced the time for the sake of the merit of the Patriarchs, for they are the mountains of

Pirkei DeRabbi Eliezer 48

the world, and for the sake of the merit of the mothers, for they are the hills of the world, and concerning them the Scripture says, "The voice of my beloved. Behold, he cometh, leaping upon the mountains, skipping over the hills" [Song of Songs 2:8].

Rebbi Eliezer said: During all those years, when the Israelites abode in Egypt, they dwelt securely and peacefully at ease until **Ganoon**, one of the grandchildren of Ephraim, came and said to them, The Holy One, blessed be He, has revealed Himself to me, to lead you out of Egypt. The children of Ephraim, in the pride of their heart, for they were of the royal seed, and mighty men in battle, took their wives and their sons, and they went forth from Egypt. The Egyptians pursued after them, and slew of them 200,000, all of them mighty men, as it is said, "The children of Ephraim, being armed and carrying bows, turned back in the day of battle" [Psalms 78:9].

Rebbi Yannai said: The Egyptians did not enslave the Israelites but for one hour of the day of the Holy One, blessed be He, that is to say, for 83⅓ years. Whilst yet Moshe was not born, the magicians said to Pharaoh: In the future a child will be born, and he will take Israel out of Egypt. Pharaoh thought, and said: Cast ye all the male children into the river, and he will be thrown in with them, and thereby the word of the magicians will be frustrated; therefore, they cast all the male children into the river.

Three years elapsed until the birth of Moshe. When

Moshe was born, they said to Pharaoh: Behold, he is born, and he is hidden from our vision. Pharaoh said to them: Since he is born, henceforth ye shall not cast the male children into the river, but put upon them a hard yoke to embitter the years of their lives with hard labour, as it is said, "And they made their lives bitter" [Exodus 1:14].

Rebbi Natanel said: The parents of Moshe saw the child, [for] his form was like that of an angel of God. They circumcised him on the eighth day, and they called his name **Yekuthiel**.

Rebbi Shimon said: They called him **Tob** [good], as it is said, "And when she saw him that he was good" [Exodus 2:2]. They concealed him in a house of the earth for three months. After three months she put him in an ark of bulrushes, and she cast him upon the bank of the river. All things are revealed before the Holy One, blessed be He. Now Batya, the daughter of Pharaoh, was smitten sorely with leprosy and she was not able to bathe in hot water, and she came to bathe in the river, and she saw the crying child. She put forth her hand and took hold of him, and she was healed. She said: This child is righteous, and I will preserve his life. Whosoever preserves a life is as though he had kept alive the whole world. Therefore, was she worthy to inherit the life in this world and the life in the world to come.

All the household of Pharaoh's palace were helping to educate Moshe, as it is said, "And it came to pass

Pirkei DeRabbi Eliezer 48

in those days, when Moshe was grown up, that he went out unto his brethren" [Exodus 2:11]. Moshe went into the camp of Israel, and saw one of the taskmasters of Pharaoh smiting one of the sons of Kohath, the Levites, for they were his brethren, as it is said, "And he saw an Egyptian smiting an Hebrew, one of his brethren" [Exodus 2:11]. He began to rebuke him with the sword of his lips, and he slew him, and buried him in the midst of the camp, as it is said, "And he smote the Egyptian, and hid him in the sand" [Exodus 2:12]. The word **Chol** [sand] signifies here Israel only, as it is said, "Yet the number of children of Israel shall be as the sand of the sea" [Hosea 2:1].

He went forth on the second day, and saw two Hebrew men striving. Who were they? **Dathan and Abiram**, as it is said, "And he said to him that did the wrong, wherefore smitest thou, thy fellow?" [Exodus 2:14]. Dathan said to him: What Dost, thou wish to kill me with the sword of thy mouth as thou didst kill the Egyptian yesterday, as it is said, "Who made thee a prince and a judge over us? Speakest thou to kill me, as thou killedst the Egyptian?" [Exodus 2:14]. "Seekest thou to kill me" is not written [in the Scripture] here, but "Speakest thou to kill me."

When Moshe and Aharon came to Pharaoh, they said to him: "Thus saith the Hashem, the God of Israel, and Let my people go" [Exodus 7:26], that they may serve Me. He said: I know not the Hashem. "Who is the Hashem that I should hearken unto his

Pirkei DeRabbi Eliezer 48

voice to let Israel go? I know not the Hashem, and moreover I will not let Israel go" [Exodus 5:2]. Aharon cast down his rod, and it became a fiery serpent. The magicians also cast down their rods, and they became fiery serpents. The rod of Aharon ran and swallowed them up with their rods, as it is said, "And Aharon's rod swallowed up their rods" [Exodus 7:12].

Moshe put his hand into his bosom, and brought it forth leprous like snow, and the magicians also put their hands in their bosoms, and brought them forth leprous like snow. But they were not healed till the day of their death. Every plague which the Holy One, blessed be He, brought upon them, they also produced every plague until He brought upon them the boils, and they were not able to stand and to do likewise, as it is said, "And the magicians could not stand before Moshe because of the boils" [Exodus 9:11].

Rabbi Akiva said: The executioners of Pharaoh used to strangle the Israelites in the walls of the houses, and the Holy One, blessed be He, heard their cry, as it is said, "And God heard their groaning, and God remembered his covenant with Avraham, with Yitzhak, and with Yaakov" [Exodus 2:24]. Further, they burnt their children in the furnace of fire, as it is said, "But the Hashem hath taken you, and brought you forth out of the iron furnace, out of Egypt" [Deuteronomy 4:20]. And measured them equally, as it is said: "Who struck Egypt through their first-born" [Psalms 136:10].

Pirkei DeRabbi Eliezer 48

When Israel went forth, what did the Holy One, blessed be He, do? He cast down all the idols of their abominations, and they were broken, as it is said, "Upon their gods also the Hashem executed judgments" [Numbers 33:4].

Rebbi Yossi said: The Egyptians defiled the Israelites and their wives with them. **Bedijah**, the grandson of Dan, married a wife from his tribe, **Shelomith, daughter of Dibri**, and in that night the taskmasters of Pharaoh came in unto her, for they slew him and came in unto her, and she conceived and bare a son. In every case the offspring follows the nature of the seed: if it be sweet, it will be due to the sweet seed; if it be bitter, it will be due to the bitter seed. And when Israel went forth from Egypt, he began to blaspheme and revile the Name of the God of Israel, as it is said, "And the son of the Israelitish woman blasphemed the Name, and cursed" [Leviticus 24:11].

Rebbi Yishmael said: The five fingers of the right hand of the Holy One, blessed be He, all of them appertain to the mystery of the Redemption. He showed the **little finger** of the hand to **Noah**, pointing out how to make the ark, as it is said, "And this is how thou shalt make it" [Genesis 6:15]. With the **second finger**, which is next to the little one, He smote the firstborn of the Egyptians, as it is said, "The magicians said unto Pharaoh, this is the finger of God" [Exodus 8:19]. With how many plagues were they smitten with the finger? With ten plagues. With the **third finger**, which is the third starting from the little finger, He wrote the **Tables** of the Law, as it is said, "And he gave unto Moshe, when he had made an end of communing with him… tables of stone, written with the finger of God" [Exodus 31:18]. With the **fourth finger**, which is next to the thumb, the Holy One, blessed be He, showed to Moshe what the children of Israel should give for the redemption of their souls, as it is said, " This they shall give… half a shekel for an offering to the Hashem" [Exodus 30:13]. With the **thumb and all the hand**, the Holy One, blessed be He, will smite in the future all the children of Esav, for they are His foes, and likewise will He smite the children of Yishmael, for they are His enemies, as it is said, "Let thine hand be lifted up above thine adversaries, and let all thine enemies be cut off" [Micah 5:9].

Rebbi Eliezer said: The five letters of the Torah:
ך ר ם מ ן נ ף פ ץ צ
Which alone of all the letters in the Torah are of double shape, all appertain to the mystery of the Redemption. With "Khaph" "Khaph" [100] our father Avraham was redeemed from Ur of the Chaldees, as it is said, **Lekh Lekha** לך לך "Get thee out of thy country, and from thy kindred… unto the land that I will shew thee" [Genesis 12:1]. With Mem Mem ם מ our father Yitzhak was redeemed from the land of the Philistines, as it is said, "Go from us: for thou art much mightier **Memennu M'od** than we" [Genesis 26:16]. With Nun Nun ן נ our father Yaakov was redeemed from the hand of Esav, as it is said, "Deliver me, I pray thee, **Hazile nena** from the hand of my brother, from the hand of Esav"

Pirkei DeRabbi Eliezer 48

[Genesis 32:11]. With Pe Pe פ פIsrael was redeemed from Egypt, as it is said, "I have surely visited you, **Pakod Pakadti** and seen that which is done to you in Egypt, and I have said, I will bring you up out of the affliction of Egypt" [Exodus 3:16]. With Zaddi Zaddi the Holy One, blessed be He, in the future will redeem Israel from the oppression of the kingdoms, and He will say to them, I have caused a branch to spring forth for you, as it is said, "Behold, the man whose name is **Zemach** the **Branch**; and he shall grow up yizmach out of his place, and he shall build the temple of the Hashem" [Zechariah 6:12]. These letters were delivered only to our father Avraham. Our father Avraham delivered them to Yitzhak, and Yitzhak [delivered them] to Yaakov, and Yaakov delivered the mystery of the Redemption to Yosef, as it is said, "But God will surely visit **Pa**kod yi **Ph**kod you" [Genesis 50:24]. Yosef his son delivered the secret of the Redemption to his brethren. Asher, the son of Yaakov, delivered the mystery of the Redemption to Serach his daughter. When Moshe and Aharon came to the elders of Israel and performed the signs in their sight, the elders of Israel went to Serach, the daughter of Asher, and they said to her: A certain man has come, and he has performed signs in our sight, thus and thus. She said to them: There is no reality in the signs. They said to her: He said "Pakod yi phkod" - "God will surely visit you" [Genesis 50:24]. She said to them: He is the man who will redeem Israel in the future from Egypt, for thus did I hear, **Pakod Pakadti**" - "I have surely visited you" [Exodus 3:16]. Forthwith the people believed in their God and

Pirkei DeRabbi Eliezer 48

in His messenger, as it is said, "And the people believed, and when they heard that the Hashem had visited the children of Israel" [Exodus 4:31].

Rabbi Akiva said: The taskmasters of Pharaoh were beating the Israelites in order that they should make the tale of bricks, and it is said, "And the tale of the bricks, which they did make heretofore, ye shall lay upon them" [Exodus 5:8]. The Israelites were gathering the straw of the wilderness, and they were carrying it on their asses and also on their wives, and their sons. The straw of the wilderness pierced their heels, and the blood was mingled with the mortar. Rachel, the granddaughter of Shuthelach, was near childbirth, and with her husband she was treading the mortar, and the child was born there and became entangled in the brick mould. Her cry ascended before the Throne of Glory. The angel Michael descended and took the brick mould with its clay, and brought it up before the Throne of Glory. That night the Holy One, blessed be He, descended, and smote the firstborn of the Egyptians, as it is said, "And it came to pass at midnight that the Hashem smote all the firstborn in the land of Egypt" [Exodus 12:29].

Rebbi Yehuda said: All that night the Israelites were eating and drinking, rejoicing and taking wine and praising their God with a loud voice, whilst the Egyptians were crying with a bitter soul, because of the plague which came upon them suddenly, as it is said, "And there was a great cry in Egypt; for there was not a house where there was not one dead"

Pirkei DeRabbi Eliezer 48

[Exodus 12:30].

The Holy One, blessed be He, said: If I bring forth the Israelites by night, they will say, He has done His deeds like a thief. Therefore, behold, I will bring them forth when the sun is in his zenith at midday, as it is said, that very day the LORD freed the Israelites from the land of Egypt, troop by troop [Exodus 12:51]

By the merit of three things Israel went forth from Egypt:
1. They did not change their language;
2. they did not change their names;
3. and they did not slander one another.

In the unity of God's Name Israel went forth from Egypt full of all good things, comprising all blessings, because He remembered the word which He spake to our father Avraham, as it is said, "And also that nation, whom they shall serve, will I judge, and afterwards shall they come out with great substance" [Genesis 15:14].

Chapter 49

Rebbi Simeon, son of Yochai, said: The Holy One, blessed be He, wished to destroy and to cut off all the seed of Amalek. He sent to Shaul, the son of Kish, to destroy and to cut off all the seed of Amalek. Shaul and the people heard, and did not spare any vile man except Agag, as it is said, "But Shaul and the people spared Agag, and the best of the sheep, and of the oxen" [Samuel-A 15:9]. Samuel heard thereof, and he went to meet them, and he said to them: Ye have spared Amalek, and ye have left over a remnant of him. They said to him: The sheep and the oxen are for sacrifices unto thy God. Samuel said to Shaul: The Omnipresent hath no delight in burnt offerings and sacrifices, but only in obeying His voice and in doing His will, as it is said, "And Samuel said, hath the Hashem as great delight in burnt offerings and sacrifices, as in obeying the voice of the Hashem? Behold, to obey is better than sacrifice, and to hearken than the fat of rams" [Samuel-A 15:22].

Rebbi Pinchas said: The Holy One, blessed be He, saw that in the future there would arise from Agag a man, a great enemy and adversary of the Jews. Who was this? This was Haman, as it is said, "Because Haman, the son of Hammedatha, the Agagite, the enemy of all the Jews" [Esther 9:24]. From the seed of Shaul arose an avenger and a redeemer for Israel, who delivered them out of the hand of Haman. Who was this? This was Mordecai, as it is said, "There

Pirkei DeRabbi Eliezer 49

was a certain Jew in Shushan, the capital, whose name was Mordecai... the son of Kish, a Benjamite" [Esther 2:5].

And there stood Samuel before the Holy One, blessed be He, and he said: Sovereign of all the Universe. Do not forget the sin which **Esav** did to his father, for he took strange women for his wives, as it is said, "And they were a source of bitterness to Ytzhak and Rebekah" [Genesis 26:36]. Who offered sacrifices and burnt incense to idols, to embitter the years of the life of his parents. Remember his sin unto his sons and unto his grandsons unto the end of all generations, as it is said, "Let the iniquity of his fathers be remembered with the Hashem" [Psalms 109:14]. Samuel heard the voice of Agag muttering with his mouth, saying: Perhaps the bitterness of the evil death has passed from me, as it is said, "And Agag said, surely the bitterness of death is past" [Samuel-A 15:32]. Samuel said to him: Just as the sword of Amalek thy ancestor consumed the young men of Israel who were outside the cloud, so that their women dwelt as childless women and widows, so by the prayer of the women all the sons of Amalek shall be slain, and their women shall dwell as childless women and widows. And by the prayer of Esther and her maidens all the sons of Amalek were slain and their women remained childless and widowed, as it is said, "And Samuel said, as thy sword hath made women childless, so shall thy mother be childless among women" [Samuel-A 15:33].

The prayer of Samuel destroyed the power of the

children of Agag against Israel, as it is said, "And Samuel broke Agag before the Lord in Gilgal" [Samuel-A 15:33].

The Holy One, blessed be He, said: He has made his attack against the heavenly beings, and God will send against them insignificant things, to teach them that the power of their might is nought. When Titus, the wicked, entered the Holy of Holies, he said: No adversary or enemy can prevail against me. What did the Holy One, blessed be He, do to him? He sent a single gnat, and it went into his nostril, and it ate its way into his brain. That gnat became like a young pigeon, weighing two pounds, to teach him that there was nothing at all in the might of his power. When Israel walked in the Holy of Holies with a proud heart, and said: No adversary or enemy is able to stand before us. What did the Holy One, blessed be He, do to them? He sent against them a man, proud and like one sifting the sea, Nebuchadnezzar, whose name was **Kabbir Mayim** [like one sifting the sea], to teach; "For by strength shall no man prevail" [Samuel-A 2:9].

Rebbi Chakhinai said: The Holy One, blessed be He, set no limit to the kingdoms, except to the Egyptian bondage, and to the kingdom of Babylon. Whence do we know this about the Egyptian bondage? Because it is said, "And they shall serve them; and they shall afflict them four hundred years" [Genesis 15:13]. The Holy One, blessed be He, dealt according to the abundance of His tender mercy, and He shortened this time limit by its half, 210 years.

Pirkei DeRabbi Eliezer 49

Whence do we know about the Babylonian kingdom? Because it is said, "For thus saith the Hashem, after seventy years be accomplished for Babylon, I will visit you, and perform my good word toward you, in causing you to return to this place" [Jeremiah 29:10].

Rebbi Abbahu said: Forty-five years did Nebuchadnezzar reign. Know that it is so. In the year when he began to reign, he went up to Yerushalayim, and conquered Jehoiakim, king of Yehuda, as it is said, "In the third year of the reign o Jehoiakim, king of Yehuda, came Nebuchadnezzar, king of Babylon, unto Yerushalayim, and besieged it" [Daniel 1:1]. For eight years he ruled over the kingdom of Jehoiakim, and eleven years Zedekiah ruled. Behold, nineteen years before he destroyed the Temple. Thereafter he ruled twenty-six years. Know that it is so. Come and see from the exile of Jehoiachin until his son Evil-Merodach reigned thirty-seven years elapsed, as it is said, "And it came to pass in the seven and thirtieth year of the captivity of Jehoiachin, king of Yehuda, in the twelfth month, on the seven and twentieth day of the month, that Evil-Merodach, king of Babylon, in the year that he began to reign, did lift up the head of Jehoiachin, king of Yehuda, out of prison" [Kings-B 25:27].

Rebbi Yehonaton said: The last of the kings of Media was Artaxerxes, king of Babylon, and he reigned thirty-two years, as it is said, "But in all this time I was not in Yerushalayim; for in the two and thirtieth year of Artaxerxes, king of Babylon, I went

Pirkei DeRabbi Eliezer 49

unto the king" [Nehemiah 13:6].

Rebbi Tachanah said: Come and see how wealthy Ahasuerus was, for he was wealthier than all the kings of Media and Persia, and concerning him the Scripture saith, "And the fourth shall be far richer than they all" [Daniel 11:2]. What was the wealth of Ahasuerus? He erected couches of gold and silver in the streets of the city, to show all the peoples how rich he was, as it is said, "The couches were of gold and silver" [Esther 1:6]. All the vessels used by Ahasuerus were not vessels of silver, but vessels of gold. He brought the vessels of the Temple, and all the vessels of his palace were changed in appearance, so that they became like lead, as it is said, "The vessels being diverse one from another" [Esther 1:7].

All the pavement of his palace consisted of precious stones and pearls, as it is said, "Upon a pavement of porphyry, and white marble, and alabaster, and stone of blue colour" [Esther 1:6].

Rebbi Eliezer said: For half the year Ahasuerus made great banquets for all the peoples, as it is said, "Many days, even a hundred and eighty days" [Esther 1:4]. Every people who ate its food in impurity, had its food provided in impurity, and every people who ate its food in purity had its food provided according to the regulations of purity, as it is said, "That they should do according to every man's pleasure" [Esther 1:8].

Pirkei DeRabbi Eliezer 49

Rebbi Shimon said: It was the universal custom of the kings of Media when they were eating and drinking to cause their women to come before them stark naked, playing and dancing, in order to see the beauty of their figures. When the wine entered the heart of Ahasuerus, he wished to act in this manner with Vashti the queen. She was the daughter of a king, and she was not willing to do this. He decreed concerning her, and she was slain. When the wine had passed from the heart of Ahasuerus, he sought after Vashti, but he did not find her. They told him of the deed which had been done, and also of the decree which had been ordained concerning her. Why was the decree passed against her? Because she used to make the daughters of Israel come and toil for her on Sabbaths, therefore was the decree ordained against her that she should be slain naked on the Sabbath, as it is said, "He remembered Vashti, and what she had done, and what was decreed against her" [Esther 2:1].

Rebbi Zechariah said: Merit is transmitted by the hand of the worthy. By the hand of Daniel, the sovereignty was transferred to Esther, because he said to the king, let not the king weep, since all that thou hast done thou hast done according to the Torah. And whosoever keeps the Torah, the Holy One, blessed be He, preserves his kingdom; for thus the Torah says that the man shall rule his wife, as it is said, "And he shall rule over thee" [Genesis 3:16]. The king sent in all the provinces to do according to his words, as it is said, "That every man should bear rule in his own house" [Esther 1:22]. He also said to the

Pirkei DeRabbi Eliezer 49

king: "Let there be sought for the king fair young virgins" [Esther 2:2]. Not "all young virgins," but "fair young virgins." "And let the maiden which pleaseth the king be queen instead of Vashti" [Esther 2:4]; and it is written elsewhere, "And the maiden pleased him" [Esther 2:9]. This refers to Esther. The Holy One, blessed be He, invested her with grace and love in the eyes of all who saw her. "And Esther obtained favour in the sight of all them that looked upon her" [Esther 2:15].

Chapter 50

"**There** was a certain Jew in Shushan, the capital, whose name was Mordecai" [Esther 2:5]. Rebbi Shema'iah said: Was there then no other Jew in Shushan, the capital, except Mordecai alone? Lo. It is written, "And the Jews that were in Shushan" [Esther 9:18]. But because he was a Jew, and a direct descendant of the patriarchs and also of the royal seed, and he was engaged in [the study of] the Torah all his days, and he was not defiled by any forbidden food in his mouth, therefore was his name called "a Jew."

"**Whose** name was Mordecai" [Esther 2:5]. because his prayer ascended before the Holy One, blessed be He, like the scent of pure myrrh מר דרור. "The son of Yair" [Esther 2:5]. [Yair means to give light]. because he enlightened Mair the faces of the scholars in Halacha. "The son of Shimei" [Esther 2:5]. who went forth to curse David. "The son of Kish" [Esther 2:5]. of the seed of those who could use both the right hand and the left, as it is said, "The children of Ephraim, being armed and carrying bows" [Psalms 78:9].

Rebbi Shimon said: Come and see the wisdom of Mordecai, for he knew seventy languages, as it is said, "Who came with Zerubbabel, Jeshua, Nehemiah, Azariah, Raamiah, Nahamani, Mordecai, Bilshan, Mispereth, Bigvai, Nehum, Baanah. The number of the men of the people of

Israel Yehoshua… Mordecai, Bilshan" [Nehemiah 2:2]. and he sat in the gates of the king to see that Esther and her maidens should not become defiled by any kind of unclean food. He heard the two eunuchs of the king speaking in the language of the Chaldees, saying: Now will the king take the afternoon sleep, and when he arises, he will say, give me a little water; let a deadly poison be given to him in the golden vessel, and he will drink thereof and die. Mordecai went in and told Esther. Now Esther told the king in the name of Mordecai, as it is said, "And Esther told the king in Mordecai's name" [Esther 2:22]. Hence the Wise Men have said: Whosoever tells a matter in the name of its author brings redemption into the world.

When the king arose from his sleep, he said to his servants, his eunuchs, who were wont to give him something to drink: Give me a little water. They brought him the golden jug, and a deadly poison was therein. He said to them: Pour out the water before me. They said to him: O our Hashem, O king, this water is excellent, good, and even choice. Why should we pour it out before thee? He said to them: Thus, have I resolved to have it poured out before me. They poured it out before him, and he found therein the deadly poison, and he commanded that they should be hanged, as it is said, "They were both hanged on a tree" [Esther 2:23]. They were both hanged on one tree, one after the other, as it is said, "Upon a tree" [Esther 2:23]; it is not written, "Upon trees." All affairs which were enacted before the king they wrote before him, and they placed it in the king's

Pirkei DeRabbi Eliezer 50

box, and when the king wished to discover what had happened to him, they read the documents, and he knew what had happened to him. So, they wrote in the book the word which Mordecai had told, as it is said, "And it was written in the book of the chronicles" [Esther 2:23].

Rebbi Pinchas said: Two wealthy men arose in the world, one in Israel and one among the nations of the world, Korach in Israel, and Haman among the nations of the world, who took the treasures of the kings of Yehuda. When the king saw his wealth and his ten sons keeping guard before him, he exalted him, and aggrandized him, as it is said, "After these things did king Ahasuerus promote Haman, the son of Hammedatha" [Esther 3:1]. The king commanded concerning him that all the people should bow down and show reverence to him. What did Haman do? He made for himself an image of an idol, and had it embroidered upon his dress, above his heart, so that everyone who bowed down to Haman also bowed down to the idol which he had made. Mordecai saw this, and did not consent to bow down to the idol, as it is said, "But Mordecai bowed not down, nor did him reverence" [Esther 3:2]; and Haman was full of wrath against him, and said: These Jews hated my forefathers from of old, and now will I say to the king that he should destroy them from the world. Haman entered before Ahasuerus, and said to him: O my Hashem, O king, "There is a certain people scattered abroad and dispersed among the peoples in all the provinces of thy kingdom" [Esther 3:8], and they are of no benefit to thee and do not obey thee,

Pirkei DeRabbi Eliezer 50

and they do not perform thy will, and it is not for the king's profit to suffer them. If it please the king, accept half of my wealth and give me power over them, as it is said, "If it please the king, let it be written that they be destroyed" [Esther 3:9]. The king said to him: Behold, they are given into thy hand for nought, as it is said, "And the king said to Haman, the silver is given to thee, the people also" [Esther 3:11]. The Holy Spirit cried out, saying: "Thus saith the Hashem, Ye were sold for nought, and ye shall be redeemed without money" [Isaiah 52:3].

Rebbi Yossi said: Haman was an astrologer, and he wrote letters on slips, and cast lots by the constellations to know the distinction between one day and another, and between one month and another, and between one constellation and another, as it is said, "They cast Pur, that is, the lot, before Haman from day to day, and from month to month" [Esther 3:7]. He wrote and sent throughout all the provinces to destroy and to slay and to exterminate all the Jews on the thirteenth day of the month Adar, on the third day in the constellation Leo. Mordecai heard thereof, and rent his garments, and put on sackcloth with ashes, and he went forth into the midst of the city, as it is said, "And Mordecai knew all that was done" [Esther 4:1]; and he cried before the Holy One, blessed be He, saying: Sovereign of all the worlds. Thou didst swear to our fore-fathers to multiply their seed like the stars of the heaven, and now hast Thou given them like sheep to the slaughter. "Remember Avraham, Yitzhak, and Israel... to whom thou sworest... I will multiply

Pirkei DeRabbi Eliezer 50

your seed as the stars of heaven" [Exodus 32:13]. Esther heard thereof, and her strength failed, as it is said, "And the queen was exceedingly enfeebled" [Esther 4:4]. She sent and called for Hathach, the trusty servant of her household, to know what had been done to Mordecai. Hathach went forth to Mordecai, who told him the words. Hathach went in and told Esther. Haman saw Hathach coming and returning, and he slew him, and Esther did not find another man faithful enough to send to Mordecai. She said that it was her desire to return answer to Mordecai. She said to him, "Go, gather together all the Jews that are present in Shushan, and fast ye for me, and neither eat nor drink three days" [Esther 4:16]. These days were the thirteenth, the fourteenth, and the fifteenth of Nissan. Mordecai said to her: Is not the third day [of the fast] the day of Passover? She said to him: Thou art the elder in Israel. If there be no Israel, wherefore is the Passover? Mordecai hearkened to her words, and he agreed with her. "So, Mordecai transgressed" [Esther 4:17]. What is the meaning of the expression, "So he transgressed"? That he transgressed the festivals and Sabbaths. On the third day [of the fast] Esther put on the royal apparel, and sent and invited the king and Haman to the banquet which she had prepared on the fifteenth of Nissan. When they had eaten and drunk, Haman said: The king exalts me, and his wife aggrandizes me, and there is none greater than I am in all the kingdoms; and Haman rejoiced very much in his heart, as it is said, "Then went Haman forth that day, joyful and glad of heart" [Esther 5:9].

Pirkei DeRabbi Eliezer 50

"**On** that night the king's sleep fled" [Esther 6:1]. That night the throne of the King who is King of kings, the Holy One, blessed be He, became unsteady, because He saw that Israel was in great distress. The sleep of the king on earth fled, for he had seen in his dream Haman taking the sword to slay him; and he became agitated and arose from his sleep, and he told the sons of Haman, the scribes, to read in the books so as to see what had happened to him. They opened the books, and found the incident which Mordecai had told, but they did not wish to read this, and they rolled up the scrolls. The king said to them: Read ye what is written before you. But they were unwilling to read, and the writing was read [of its own account] by itself, as it is said, "And they were read before the king" [Esther 6:1]. It is not written here, "They were reading," but "They were read." The king spake to his servants: Call ye Haman to me. They said to him: Behold, he is standing outside. The king said: The thing is true which I saw in my dream; he has come only in this hour to slay me. He said: Let him come in. He entered before the king. The king said to him: I wish to exalt and aggrandize a certain man; what shall be done to him? Haman said in his heart, for the seed of Esav speak in their hearts, but never reveal their secret with their mouths, as it is said, "And Haman said in his heart" [Esther 6:6]. Haman said in his heart: He does not desire to exalt any other man except me. I will speak words so that I shall be a king just as he is. He said to him: Let them bring the apparel which the king wore on the day of the coronation, and let them bring the horse upon which the king rode on the

Pirkei DeRabbi Eliezer 50

coronation day, and the crown which was put upon the head of the king on the day of coronation. The king was exceedingly angry because of the crown. The king said: It does not suffice this villain, but he must even desire the crown which is upon my head. Haman saw that the king was angry because of the crown; he said: "And let the apparel and the horse be delivered to the hand of one of the king's most noble princes" [Esther 6:9]. The king said to him: Go, and do thus to Mordecai. As soon as Haman heard this he became greatly agitated, and he said to him: My Hashem, O king. There are very many named Mordecai. The king answered: "The Jew." Haman said to him: There are very many Jews. The king said to him: "He who sits at the king's gate" [Esther 6:10].

Haman took the apparel and the horse and went to Mordecai. Haman said to him: Arise, and put on the purple of the king. Mordecai said to him: Villain. Dost thou not know that for three days I have put on sack-cloth with ashes, sitting on the ashes, because of that which thou hast done to me? Now take me to the bath-house, and afterwards will I put on the purple of the king. And he washed him and dressed him. Haman said to him: Mount and ride upon the horse. He said to Haman: On account of the affliction of the fast I have no strength to mount and ride upon the horse. What did Haman do? He lowered himself, and Mordecai put his foot upon his neck, and he mounted and rode upon the horse. Mordecai said: Blessed be the Omnipresent, who hath not let aught of His words fall to the earth, to

Pirkei DeRabbi Eliezer 50

fulfill that which is said, "But thou shalt tread upon their high places" [Deuteronomy 33:29]. Mordecai betook himself to his seat of honour at the king's gate, whilst Haman was hurried along, and he went "to his house mourning and having his head covered" [Esther 6:12], because of that which had happened to him.

Zeresh his wife and all his astrologers said to him: Hast thou not heard what was done unto Pharaoh? as it is said, "And Zeresh his wife said unto him, If Mordecai, before whom thou hast begun to fall, be of the seed of the Jews, thou shalt not prevail against him" [Esther 6:13].

In that hour the pages of Esther came and took Haman to the banquet which she had prepared on the sixteenth of Nissan. When they had eaten and taken [wine] the king said to Esther: "What is thy petition, Queen Esther? And it shall be granted thee; and what is thy request?" [Esther 7:2]. She said to him: My Hashem, O king. I ask nought of thee, except my life, and my people. Because one man has come and has bought us to destroy, to slay, and to cause to perish. "But if we had been sold for bondmen and bondwomen, I had held my peace" [Esther 7:4]. The king said to her: Who is this man? She answered him: This one is the wicked Haman, as it is said, "And Esther said, an adversary and an enemy, even this wicked Haman" [Esther 7:6]. "The king arose in his wrath" [Esther 7:7]. What did the angel Michael do? He began to cut down the plants in his presence. Intense wrath was kindled within him, and the king

Pirkei DeRabbi Eliezer 50

returned from the palace garden to the place of the banquet of wine. What did the angel Michael do? He lifted up Haman from Esther. The king exclaimed: As for this villain, he is not satisfied with having purchased the people of Esther to destroy, to slay, and to cause to perish, but he must needs come upon her. "Will he even force the queen before me in the house?" [Esther 7:8]. Haman heard this word and his countenance fell, as it is said, "They covered Haman's face" [Esther 7:8]. And the king commanded that he should be hanged on the gallows. What did Eliyahu, his memory be a blessing, do? He assumed the guise of Harbonah, one of the chamberlains of the king. He said to him: My Hashem, O king. There is a tree in Haman's house taken from the Holy of Holies, fifty cubits high. Whence do we know that it was from the Holy of Holies? Because it is said, "And he built the house of the forest of Lebanon" [Kings-A 7:2]. Forthwith the king commanded that he should be hanged thereon, as it is said, "And the king said, Hang him thereon" [Esther 7:9], so as to fulfill that which is said, "Let a beam be pulled out from his house, and let him be lifted up and fastened thereon; and let his house be made a dunghill for this" [Ezra 6:11]. And it says, "So they hanged Haman on the gallows that he had prepared for Mordecai" [Esther 7:10]. The king took all that belonged to Haman and gave it to Mordecai and to Esther. He said to them: Write concerning the Jews as seems good in your eyes in the name of the king. They wrote official letters, and they sent throughout all the provinces to destroy, to slay, and to cause all the enemies of the Jews to perish on the thirteenth of the month of Adar, on the third day in the constellation of Leo. Just as the lion is the king over all the beasts, and he turns his gaze towards any place as he wishes; likewise, did he think fit, and he turned his face to destroy and to slay all the enemies of Israel, as it is said, "In the day that the enemies of the Jews hoped to have rule over them" [Esther 9:1].

Rebbi Eliezer said: Haman had forty sons; ten of them were the scribes of the books of the king, and thirty were ruling in all the provinces, as it is said, "And the ten sons of Haman, in the rest of the king's provinces" [Esther 9:12]. They were all hanged upon the gallows of their father, as it is said, "And they hanged Haman's ten sons" [Esther 9:14] upon the gallows. Another Scripture text says, "And they hanged Haman's ten sons" [Esther 9:14].

Rebbi Pinchas said: Mordecai ruled over the Jews. Just as the king is dressed in purple, so was Mordecai dressed in purple, as it is said, "And Mordecai went forth from the presence of the king in royal apparel" [Esther 8:15]. Just as the king has a crown upon his head, so Mordecai had a crown upon his head, as it is said, "And Mordecai went forth… with a great crown of gold" [Esther 8:15]. Just as the king's fear obtains in all the land, so was the fear of Mordecai upon them, as it is said, "Because the fear of Mordecai was fallen upon them…" [Esther 9:3]. Just as the king's money is current throughout the land, so was Mordecai's money current in all the land, as it is said, "For Mordecai was great" [Esther 9:4]. What was the money of Mordecai? On the one side was

Pirkei DeRabbi Eliezer 50

the face of Mordecai and on the other the face of Esther. Wherefore? Because he was a good man, and a man of peace and seeking the peace of his people, as it is said, "For Mordecai the Jew was next unto king Ahasuerus, and great among the Jews" [Esther 10:3]; concerning him the Scripture saith, "Mark the perfect man, and behold the upright: for the latter end of [that] man is peace" [Psalms 37:37].

Chapter 51

Rabban Gamaliel said: Just as the New Moons are renewed and sanctified in this world, so will Israel be sanctified and renewed in the future world just like the New Moons, as it is said, "Speak unto all the congregation of the children of Israel, and say unto them, Ye shall be holy: for I the Hashem your God am holy" [Leviticus 19:2]. The sages say: The heavens and the earth are destined to pass away and to be renewed. What is written concerning them? "And all the host of the heaven shall be dissolved, and the heavens shall be rolled together as a scroll" [Isaiah 34:4]. Just as when a man reads in a scroll of the Torah and he rolls it, and again he opens it to read therein and he rolls it together, likewise in the future will the Holy One, blessed be He, roll together the heavens like a scroll, as it is said, "And the heavens shall be rolled together as a scroll" [Isaiah 34:4]; "And the earth shall wax old like a garment" [Isaiah 51:6]; just as a man spreads out his garment and folds it up, and again he unfolds it and puts it on and renews it [thereby], likewise the Holy One, blessed be He, in the future will fold up the earth and again will He spread it out and put it in its place like a garment, as it is said. "And the earth shall wax old like a garment" [Isaiah 51:6].

All its inhabitants shall taste the taste of death for two days, when there will be no soul of man or beast upon the earth, as it is said, "And they that dwell therein shall die in like manner" [Isaiah 51:6]. On the

Pirkei DeRabbi Eliezer 51

third day He will renew them all and revive the dead, and He will establish it before Him, as it is said, "On the third day he will raise us up, and we shall live before him" [Hosea 6:2].

Rebbi Eliezer said: All the host of heaven in the future will pass away and will be renewed. What is written concerning them? "And all the host of heaven shall be dissolved" [Isaiah 34:4]. Just as the leaves fade from off the vine and the fig tree, and the latter remain standing as a dry tree, and again they blossom afresh and bear buds and produce new leaves and fresh leaves. Likewise in the future will all the host of heaven fade away like a vine and a fig tree, and they will again be renewed before Him to make known that there is passing away which does not really pass away. No more shall there be evil, and no more shall there be plague, and there shall not be the former misfortunes, as it is said, "For, behold, I create new heavens" [Isaiah 65:17].

Rebbi Yannai said: All the hosts of heaven pass away and are renewed every day. What are the hosts of heaven? The sun, the moon, the stars, and the constellations. Know that it is so. Come and see, for when the sun turns in order to set in the west, it bathes in the waters of the Ocean and extinguishes the flames of the sun, and no light is left, and it has no flame all night long until it comes to the east. When it arrives at the east it washes itself in the river of fire, like a man who kindles his lamp in the midst of the fire. Likewise, the sun kindles its lamps and puts on its flames and ascends to give light upon the

Pirkei DeRabbi Eliezer 51

earth, and it renews every day the work of the Creation. And thus, it is until even comes. At evening-time the moon and the stars and the constellations wash themselves in the river of hail, and they ascend to give light upon the earth. In the future that is to come, the Holy One, blessed be He, will renew them and add to their light a sevenfold light, as it is said, "Moreover, the light of the moon shall be as the light of the sun, and the light of the sun shall be sevenfold, as the light of seven days" [Isaiah 30:26]. "In the day" [Isaiah 30:26]. Like which day? In the day of the redemption of Israel, as it is said, "In the day that the Hashem bindeth up the hurt of his people" [Isaiah 30:26].

Rabban Gamaliel said: The Sabbath burnt offering which they brought every Sabbath consisted of two he-lambs, and the burnt offering for the New Moon which they brought every New Moon consisted of two young bullocks. Two for each occasion, corresponding to what? Corresponding to the two worlds, this world and the world to come. "One ram and one he-goat": just as they are a single nation, their God is likewise one. "Seven he-lambs of the first year without blemish" [Numbers 28:11], corresponding to those who bring their offerings, to Him who renews them like the New Moons, as it is said, "This is the burnt offering of every month throughout the months of the year" [Numbers 28:14].

Rebbi Zechariah said: After the words "the burnt offering of every month throughout the months of the year" [Numbers 28:14]. what is written? "And one

Pirkei DeRabbi Eliezer 51

he-goat for a sin offering unto the Hashem" [Numbers 28:15]. For what purpose was the sin offering? When the Holy One, blessed be He, created His world, He created two great luminaries, as it is said, "And God made the two great lights" [Genesis 1:16]. The one He made larger and the other smaller, and the moon obstinately refused to do the will of its Creator so as to be made smaller; therefore, Israel offered on its behalf the he-goat for a sin offering heavenwards as one of the burnt offerings of the New Moon, as it is said, "And one he-goat for a sin offering unto the Hashem" [Numbers 28:15]. What is the meaning of "unto the Hashem"? The Holy One, blessed be He, said: This he-goat shall be an atonement for me, because I have diminished the size of the moon.

Rebbi Eliezer said: In the future the Temple will be raised up and renewed, as it is said, "Behold, I will do a new thing; now shall it spring forth; shall ye not know it?" [Isaiah 43:19]. And its gates which are buried in the earth will be renewed in the future and arise everyone in its place, and the gate of the inner court which turned to the east. On the six days of work its doors shall be closed, and on the Sabbath day they are opened by themselves, as it is said, "Thus saith the Hashem God: The gate of the inner court that looketh toward the east shall be shut the six working days; but on the Sabbath day it shall be opened, and in the day of the new moon it shall be opened" [Ezekiel 46:1].

Rebbi Yehuda said: On Sabbath and New Moons Israel stood there, and they perceived that the

Sabbath day had come, and they sanctified the Sabbath day; and so also on the New Moons the Israelites were standing there and saw the doors opening by themselves, and they knew that in that hour it was New Moon, and they sanctified the New Moon, and afterwards this was done among the heavenly ones. Therefore, Israel sanctifies the New Moons first in the lower regions on earth and afterwards [it is sanctified] in the heavenly regions, because they have defined the beginning of the Molad of the Moon in the presence of Israel, who saw the doors open by themselves, and they knew that the **Shekhinah** [divine presence] of the Holy One, blessed be He was therein, as it is said, "For the Hashem, the God of Israel, hath entered in by it" [Ezekiel 44:2]. Forthwith they fall down and prostrate themselves before their God. So, it was in the past and so will it be in the future that is to come, as it is said, "And the people of the land shall worship at the door of that gate before the Hashem in the Sabbaths and in the New Moons" [Ezekiel 46:3].

Rebbi said: Is it not written, "There is no new thing under the sun" [Ecclesiastes 1:9]? The sages said to him: The righteous and all their works will be renewed, but the wicked will not be renewed and "no new thing" shall be given to them, even to all who worship and trust under the sun, therefore it is said, "There is no new thing under the sun" [Ecclesiastes 1:9].

Rebbi Pinchas said: In the future the waters of the well will ascend from under the threshold of the Temple, and they will overflow and bubble over and

Pirkei DeRabbi Eliezer 51

issue forth and become twelve streams corresponding to the twelve tribes, as it is said, "And he brought me back unto the door of the house; and behold, waters issued out from under the threshold of the house eastward, for the forefront of the house was toward the east: and the waters came down from under, from the right side of the house, on the south of the altar" [Ezekiel 47:1]. Three streams towards the south to pass through them up to the ankles, and three streams towards the west to pass through them up to the knees, as it is said, "When the man went forth eastward with the line in his hand, he measured a thousand cubits, and he caused me to pass through the waters, waters that were to the ankles. Again, he measured a thousand, and he caused me to pass through the waters, waters that were to the knees" [Ezekiel 47:3]. And three streams towards the east to pass through them up to the neck, for the neck is the extremity of the body, as it is said, "And he measured a thousand cubits, and he caused me to pass through the waters that were to the extremity" [Ezekiel 47:3]. And the waters descended to the brook of Kidron, and they rose higher than in "the stream, that I could not pass through" [Ezekiel 47:5], as it is said, "For the waters were risen, waters to swim in, a stream that could not be passed through" [ibid.]. And the waters are drawn thence, and they flow down to the fords of the Jordan, as it is said, "And they shall go down into the swarmeth" [Ezekiel 47:8].

Every field and vineyard which did not yield fruit, people water them with those waters and they yield fruit, as it is said, "And it shall come to pass, that

Pirkei DeRabbi Eliezer 51

every living creature which swarmeth, in every place whither the rivers come, shall live... for these waters are come thither, that all things may be healed and live" [Ezekiel 47:9]. Then the waters enter the Salt Sea and they heal it. And the waters "shall go towards the sea... and the waters shall be healed" [Ezekiel 47:8]. And there they generate all kinds of fish. The Scripture text here gives a general rule concerning the fish, that they will be as sweet as Manna. They ascend in the stream as far as Yerushalayim, and there they are caught in its nets, as it is said, "And it shall come to pass that fisher shall stand by it" [Ezekiel 47:10]. It is written, "They shall stand by it."

There upon the bank of the stream grow all kinds of trees bearing according to their kind. By the river they shall stand, "upon the banks thereof on this side and on that side" [Ezekiel 47:12]. Every month they bring forth new fruit, as it is said, "It shall bring forth new fruit every month" [Ezekiel 47:12]. Some of them are for food and others are growing, as it is said, "Because the waters thereof issue out of the sanctuary: and the fruit thereof shall be for meat, and the leaf thereof for healing" [Ezekiel 47:12].

Every man who is ill and bathes in those waters, will be healed, as it is said, "In every place whither the rivers come, he shall live... and everything shall live whithersoever the river cometh" [Ezekiel 47:9]. Every man who has a wound will be healed by taking of their leaves and applying them to his wound, as it is said, "And the fruit thereof shall be for meat, and the

Pirkei DeRabbi Eliezer 51

leaf thereof for healing" [Ezekiel 47:12]. What is the meaning of "for healing"? Rabban Yohanan ben Zakkai said: For a laxative; suck its leaves and one's food is digested.

Chapter 52

Seven wonderful things have been done in the world, the like of which have not been created.

The first wonder. From the day when the heavens and the earth were created no man was ever saved from the fire until our father Avraham came and was delivered from the fiery furnace. All the kings of the earth heard thereof and they were astonished, for they had not seen anyone like him from the day when the world was created. And whence do we know that he was delivered from the fiery furnace? Because it is said, "And he said unto him, I am the Hashem that brought thee out of the furnace of the Chaldees" [Genesis 15:7]. Another text says, "Thou art the Hashem the God, who didst choose Abram, and broughtest him forth out of the furnace of the Chaldees" [Nehemiah 9:7].

The second wonder. was about the wives of the sons of Noah. From the day when the heavens and the earth were created there never was a woman who at ninety years of age had a child, until Sarah came and bare a son when she was ninety years old. All the kings of the earth heard thereof, and they did not believe. What did the Holy One, blessed be He, do to them? He dried up the breasts of their wives, as it is said, "And all the trees of the field shall know that I the Hashem have brought down the high tree, have exalted the low tree, have dried up the green tree, and have made the dry tree to flourish" [Ezekiel 17:24].

Pirkei DeRabbi Eliezer 52

"**All** the trees of the field shall know" [Ezekiel 17:24]; this expression refers to the nations of the world. "That I the Hashem have brought down the high tree" [Ezekiel 17:24]. This refers to **Nimrod**. "I have exalted the low tree" [Ezekiel 17:24]; this is Avraham our father. "I have dried up the green tree," refers to the breasts of the wives of the nations of the world. "I have made the dry tree to flourish"; this refers to the breasts of Sarah, for they brought their children to be suckled by Sarah's breasts, for Sarah gave suck to all their children in peace, as it is said, "And she said, Who would have said unto Avraham, that Sarah should give children suck?" [Genesis 21:7].

The third wonder. Was from the day when the heavens and the earth were created there never was a man upon whom grey hairs were sprinkled until Avraham came. The people were astonished because they had not seen any one like him from the day when the world was created. Whence do we know that grey hairs were sprinkled upon him? Because it is said, "And Avraham was old, well stricken in age" [Genesis 24:1]. Rebbi Levitas, a man of Jamnia, said: Like a diadem which belongs to the head of the king, so are grey hairs beauty and glory to old men, as it is said, "The glory of young men is their strength, and the beauty of old men is the hoary head" [Proverbs 20:29].

The fourth wonder. Was from the day when the heavens and the earth were created no man was ill, who sneezed and lived, but in every place where he happened to be, whether on the way or in the market,

Pirkei DeRabbi Eliezer 52

and when he sneezed, his soul went out through his nostrils; until our father Yaakov came and prayed for mercy concerning this, and he said before the Holy One, blessed be He: Sovereign of all the worlds. Do not take my soul from me until I have charged my sons and my household; and He was entreated of him, as it is said, "And it came to pass after these things, that one said to Yosef, Behold, thy father is sick" [Genesis 48:1]. All the kings of the earth heard thereof, and they wondered because there had been no one like him from the days when the heavens and earth had been created. Therefore, a man is in duty bound to say to his fellow: Life. When the latter sneezes, for the death of the world was changed into light, as it is said, "His neesings flash forth light" [Job 41:18].

The fifth wonder. Was from the day when the heavens and the earth were created, the waters of the sea had not been changed into dry land until Israel went forth from Egypt and passed over on dry land in the midst of the sea, as it is said, "But the children of Israel walked on dry land in the midst of the sea" [Exodus 15:29]. All the kings of the earth heard thereof and trembled, because there had been nothing like it from the day when the world had been created, as it is said, "The people heard, they trembled" [Exodus 15:14].

The sixth wonder. Was from the day when the heavens and earth were created, the sun, the moon, and the stars and the constellations were ascending to give light upon the earth, and they did not come

Pirkei DeRabbi Eliezer 52

into contact with one another until Yehoshua came and fought the battles of Israel. It was the eve of the Sabbath, and he saw the plight of Israel lest they might desecrate the Sabbath, and further, he saw the magicians of Egypt compelling the constellations to come against Israel. What did he do? He stretched forth his hand to the light of the sun and to the light of the moon, and he invoked upon them the Divine Name, and each one stood for thirty-six hours in its place until the termination of the Sabbath day, as it is said, "And the sun stood still, and the moon stayed" [Yehoshua 10:13]. All the kings of the earth heard thereof and they wondered, because there had been none like him from the day when the world had been created, as it is said, "And there was no day like that before it or after it, that the Hashem hearkened unto the voice of a man" [Yehoshua 10:14].

The seventh wonder. Was from the day when the heavens and earth had been created there had never been a sick man who had recovered from his sickness, until Hezekiah, king of Yehuda, came and fell sick, as it is said; "Please, O LORD, he said, remember how I have walked before You sincerely and wholeheartedly, and have done what is pleasing to You" [Isaiah 38:3]. and yet he recovered, as it is said, "The writing of Hezekiah, king of Yehuda, when he had been sick, and was recovered of his sickness" [Isaiah 38:9]. He began to pray before the Holy One, blessed be He, saying: Sovereign of all worlds. "Now, O Hashem, remember, I beseech thee, how I walked before thee in truth and with a perfect heart, and have done that which is good in thy sight" [Kings-

Pirkei DeRabbi Eliezer 52

B 20:3]; and He was entreated of him, as it is said, "Behold, I will add unto thy days fifteen years" [Isaiah 38:8]; and He was entreated of him, as it is said, "Behold, I will add unto thy days fifteen years" [Isaiah 38:5]. Hezekiah said before the Holy One, blessed be He: Sovereign of all worlds. Give me a sign, as it is said, "And Hezekiah said unto Isaiah, what shall be the sign that the Hashem will heal me, and that I shall go up unto the house of the Hashem?" [Kings-B 20:8]. He answered him: Ahaz thy father compelled the constellations, and he bowed down to the sun, and the sun fled before him and went down in the west ten steps alms If thou desirest, it shall go down ten steps, or it shall ascend ten stePsalms Hezekiah spake before the Holy One, blessed be He: Sovereign of all worlds. Nay, but those ten steps which it has already gone down let it retrace and stand, as it is said, "Nay, but let the shadow return backward ten steps" [Kings-B 20:10]. And He was entreated of him, as it is said, "Behold, I will cause the shadow on the steps, which is gone down on the dial of Ahaz with the sun, to return backward ten steps" [Isaiah 38:8]. All the kings of the earth saw, and they were astonished, for there had been nothing like it from the day when the world was created, and they sent to behold the wonder, as it is said, "Howbeit in the business of the ambassadors of the princes of Babylon who sent unto him to inquire of the wonder that was done in the land" [Chronicles-B 32:31].

And Hezekiah saw the messengers, and his heart was puffed with pride, and he showed them all the treasures of the kings of Yehuda, and all the

Pirkei DeRabbi Eliezer 52

treasures of the Holy of Holies in the Temple, and further, he opened the Ark of the Covenant, and he showed them the tables of the Law, and he said to them: With this do we wage war and conquer, as it is said, "And Hezekiah was glad of them, and shewed them the house of his precious things" [Isaiah 39:2]. The Holy One, blessed be He, was angry with him, and He said to him: Was it not enough for thee to have shown them all the treasures of the kings of Yehuda and all the treasures of the Holy of Holies? Moreover, thou hast opened for them the Ark, and hast shown them the tables, the work of my hand. By thy life. They shall come up and take away all the treasures of the kings of Yehuda, and all the treasures of the Holy of Holies, as it is said, "Behold, the days come, that all that is in thine house, and that which thy fathers have laid up in store until this day, shall be carried to Babylon" [Isaiah 39:6]. Instead of the tables of the Law, they shall take of thy sons to be eunuchs in the palace of the king of Babylon, as it is said, "And of thy sons that shall issue from thee, which thou shalt beget, shall they take away; and they shall be eunuchs in the palace of the king of Babylon" [Isaiah 39:7]. These were Hananiah, Mishael, and Azariah, who were made eunuchs in the palace of the king of Babylon, and they did not beget children. Concerning them the Scripture says, "For thus saith the Hashem to the eunuchs that keep my sabbaths… Unto them will I give in mine house and within my walls a memorial and a name better than of sons and of daughters; I will give them an everlasting name, that shall not be cut off" [Isaiah 56:4].

Pirkei DeRabbi Eliezer 53

Chapter 53

Everyone who secretly slanders his fellows has no remedy, as it is said, "Whoso privily slandereth his neighbour, him will I destroy: him that hath a high look and a proud heart will I not suffer" [Psalms 101:5]. Another Scripture text says, "Cursed be he that smiteth his neighbour in secret" [Deuteronomy 27:24]. Know that it is so. Come and see from the narrative of the serpent which uttered slander concerning the Holy One, blessed be He, to Adam and his helpmate. The Holy One, blessed be He, cursed it, so that its food became the dust, as it is said, "And dust shalt thou eat all the days of thy life" [Genesis 3:14].

Rabban Gamaliel said: Israel also slandered the Holy One, blessed be He, by saying: Wilt thou say that He has power to feed us in the wilderness? As it is said, "And the people spoke against God and against Moshe" [Numbers 21:5]; they said, Can God prepare a table in the wilderness? Behold, he smote the rock that waters gushed out, and streams overflowed" [Psalms 78:19-20]. The Holy One, blessed be He, heard that they slandered His Glory, and from His Glory, which is a consuming fire, He sent against them a fire which consumed them round about, as it is said, "And the people were as murmurers… and the fire of the Hashem burnt among them, and devoured in the uttermost part of the camp" [Numbers 11:1]. The Israelites betook themselves to our teacher Moshe, and they said to him: Moshe, our Hashem. Let these be given like sheep to the slaughter, but not to the fire which is consuming fire. Moshe saw the plight of Israel, and he arose to pray on their behalf, and He was entreated of him, as it is said, "And the people cried unto Moshe" [Numbers 11:2].

Rebbi Yehuda said: That fire which descended from heaven settled on the earth, and did not again return to its former place in heaven, but it entered the Tabernacle. That fire came forth and devoured all the offerings which they brought in the wilderness, as it is said. "And there descended fire from heaven" is not written here, but "And there came forth fire from before the Hashem" [Leviticus 9:2]. This was the fire which came forth and consumed the sons of Aharon, as it is said, "And there came forth fire from before the Hashem" [Leviticus 9:2]. That fire came forth and consumed the company of Korach, as it is said, "And fire came forth from the Hashem" [Numbers 16:35].

No man departs from this world until some of that fire, which rested among the sons of man, passes over him, as it is said, "And the fire rested" [Numbers 11:2].

"**And** Miriam and Aharon spake against Moshe because of the Cushite woman whom he had married" [Numbers 12:1]. Was she then a Cushite woman? Was she not Zipporah? But just as this Cushite is different as regards his body from all other people, so was Zipporah different from all other women by her words and by her good deeds;

therefore, was she called a Cushite, as it is said, "For he had married a Cushite woman" [Numbers 12:1].

Rebbi Tachanah said: The Israelites also are called Cushites, as it is said, "Are ye not as the children of the Cushites unto me, O children of Israel?" [Amos 9:7]. Just as the body of this Cushite is different from all creatures, so do the Israelites differ from all the nations of the world in their ways and by their good deeds; therefore, are they called Cushites. One Scripture saith, "And Ebedmelech, the Cushite, said" [Yermiyahu 38:12]. Was it Ebed? Was he not Baruch, son of Neriah? But just as this Cushite is different in his body from all other people, so was Baruch, son of Neriah, different in his deeds and good ways from the rest of the sons of men. Therefore, was he called a Cushite?

One Scripture text says, "Then said Joab to the Cushite, Go, tell the king what thou hast seen" [Samuel-B 18:21]. Was he a Cushite? Was he not a Benjamite? But just as this Cushite is different from all creatures, so was the Benjamite different by his ways and his good deeds; therefore, was his name called **Cushite**.

Rebbi Eliezer said: Come and see the integrity and perfection of that man, for he said to Joab, even if thou wouldst give me gold and silver I would not transgress the king's commands which he commanded thee, as it is said, "And the man said unto Joab, Though I should receive a thousand pieces of silver in mine hand" [Samuel-B 18:12]. Joab

Pirkei DeRabbi Eliezer 53

said to him: I beseech thee, show me the place where Absalom is hanging. But he did not consent. Joab began to bend the knee, and to prostrate himself before him, as it is said, "Then said Joab, Shall I not entreat thee in this wise?" [Samuel-B 18:14]. Then he took Joab by his arm, and showed him the place where Absalom was hanging. Everyone who transgresses the commandment "Honour thy father" is accounted as though he had transgressed the Decalogue. Therefore, was Absalom pierced by ten spears, as it is said, "And ten young men that bare Joab's armour compassed about and smote Absalom; and slew him" [Samuel-B 18:15].

Six people were similar to the first man, and they were all slain. They were: **Samson** with his might, and he was slain; **Shaul** with his stature, and he was slain; **Asahel** with his swiftness, and he was slain; Josiah with his nostrils, and he was slain through his nostrils; **Zedekiah** with his eyes, and he was slain through his eyes; **Absalom** with his hair, and he was killed through his hair. Absalom was a mighty hero in battle, and his sword was bound upon his loins. Why did he not draw his sword and cut the hair of his head, and get down? But he saw that Gehinnom was open beneath him, and he said: It is better for me to hang by my hair and not to descend into the fire; therefore, he was hanging, as it is said, "Behold, I saw Absalom hanging in an oak" [Samuel-B 18:10].

Rebbi Yossi said: There are seven doors to Gehinnom. Absalom entered as far as the fifth door,

Pirkei DeRabbi Eliezer 53

and David heard thereof, and began to weep, to lament, and to mourn, and he called Absalom. My son. Five times, my son, my son, my son. "And the king was much moved, and he went up to the chamber over the gate, and wept: and as he went, thus he said, O my son Absalom, my son, my son Absalom. Would God I had died for thee, O Absalom, my son, my son." [Samuel-B 19:1]. And they brought him back from the five doors of Gehinnom, and he began to praise and laud and to glorify his Creator, saying: "Shew me a token for good; that they which hate me may see it, and be ashamed: because thou, Hashem, hast helped me, and comforted me" [Psalms 86:17]. "Thou hast helped me" out of the war of Absalom, and "thou hast comforted me" in my mourning for him.

Pirkei DeRabbi Eliezer 54

Chapter 54

The eighth descent was when He descended into the Tabernacle, as it is said, "And the Hashem came down in a pillar of cloud, and stood at the door of the Tent, and called Aharon and Miriam; and they both came forth" [Numbers 12:5]. The Holy One, blessed be He, said to them: Whosoever speaketh slander against his fellow in secret, hath no cure; if he slander his brother, the son of his father or the son of his mother, how much more so is this the case? The Holy One, blessed be He, was angry with them, and He departed from the Tent, as it is said, "And the anger of the Hashem was kindled against them; and he departed" [Numbers 12:9]. "And the cloud removed from over the Tent" [Numbers 12:10]. Forthwith Miriam became leprous. The Holy One, blessed be He, said: If Aharon also be leprous, the High Ha-Kohen, who is afflicted with a blemish, will not be able to bring an offering upon My altar; but he shall look upon his sister and become astonished, as it is said, "And Aharon looked upon Miriam, and, behold, she was leprous" [Numbers 12:10]. Aharon went to Moshe, and said to him: O our Hashem, Moshe. Brethren do not suffer themselves to be separated one from the other except through death, as it is said, "Though he be fruitful among his brethren" [Hosea 13:15]. Our sister, while still among the living, is separated from us, as it is said, "Let her not, I pray, be as one dead" [Numbers 12:12]. Not only this, but now all Israel will hear and say that the sister of Moshe and Aharon is leprous. Half of this infamous report concerns thee. Moshe was appeased by the words, and he arose and prayed for her, and He was entreated of him, as it is said, "And Moshe cried unto the Hashem, saying, Heal her, O God, I beseech thee" [Numbers 12:13].

Rebbi Levitas, a man of Jamnia, said: Unless the father of a leprous person spit in his face, he will not be healed, as it is said, "And the Hashem said unto Moshe, if her father had but spit in her face, would she not be ashamed seven days?" [Numbers 12:14]. Hence the sages say: A male afflicted with unclean issue needs seven days for his purification; a woman with an issue requires seven days' separation; a menstruant needs seven days of purification; one made unclean through a corpse needs seven days of purification; a mourner mourns for seven days; the wedding feast lasts seven days; and a leprous person requires seven days' separation. Whence do we know that a male with an unclean issue requires seven days for his purification? Because it is said, "And when he that hath an issue is cleansed of his issue, then he shall number to himself seven days for his cleansing" [Leviticus 15:13]. Whence do we know that a woman with an issue requires seven days of purification? Because it is said, "But if she be cleansed of her issue, then she shall number to herself seven days, and after that she shall be clean" [Leviticus 15:28]. Whence do we know that a menstruant requires seven days of separation? Because it is said, "She shall be in her separation seven days" [Leviticus 15:19].

Pirkei DeRabbi Eliezer 54

"**Her** separation" or impurity thou dost not read, but" in her impurity"; because Rebbi Ze'era said: The daughters of Israel have made the Law exceptionally stringent for themselves, so that if they see a blood stain of the size of a mustard seed they observe on its account seven days, after that they are cleansed of their issue of blood. Whence do we know that one made unclean through a corpse needs seven days of purification? Because it is said, "And whosoever in the open field toucheth one that is slain with a sword, or a dead body... shall be unclean seven days" [Numbers 19:16]. Whence do we know that the mourner mourns for seven days? Because it is said, "And he made a mourning for his father seven days" [Genesis 50.10]. Whence do we know that the bridal banquet lasts seven days? Because it is said, "Fulfill the week of this one.... And Yaakov did so, and fulfilled her week" [Genesis 29:27-28]. Whence do we know that a leper keeps seven days of purification? From Miriam, as it is said, "And Miriam was shut up without the camp seven days" [Numbers 12:15].

Rebbi said: They slandered God again and said, We were dwelling in the land of Egypt in ease and contentment, but the Holy One, blessed be He, and Moshe have brought us forth from Egypt to die in the wilderness, as it is said, "And the people spake against God, and against Moshe, Wherefore have ye brought us up out of Egypt to die in the wilderness?" [Numbers 21:5]. What did the Holy One, blessed be He, do unto them? He sent against them fiery serpents which bit and killed them, as it is said, "And the

Pirkei DeRabbi Eliezer 54

Hashem sent among the people fiery serpents, and they bit the people; and much people of Israel died" [Numbers 21:6]. Moshe beheld the misfortune of Israel, and he arose and prayed on their behalf. The Holy One, blessed be He, said to him: Moshe. Make thee a serpent of copper like that serpent which spoke slander betwixt Adam and his helpmate, and place it on a high place. Let every man who has been bitten direct his heart to his Father who is in heaven, and let him gaze at that serpent, and he will be healed. Moshe made a serpent of copper and set it up in a high place, and every man who had been bitten turned his heart to his Father who is in heaven, and gazed at that serpent, forthwith he became restored to health, as it is said, "And it came to pass, that if a serpent had bitten any man, when he looked at the serpent of copper, he lived" [Numbers 21:9]; and it also says, "If the serpent bite without enchantment, then is there no advantage in the master of the tongue" [Ecclesiastes 10:11].

Rebbi Meir said: If a doctor visit one whom a serpent has bitten, and cure him, verily will goodness be shown to this one.

Rebbi Yossi said: If a man hire a workman who is zealous, and when he discharges him should he give him his wages in full; what favour does he give him? But if he hire a workman who is lazy, [when] he discharges him should he give him his wages in full, verily he is giving him a real favour. Likewise, spake Solomon before the Holy One, blessed be He: Sovereign of all the worlds. Avraham, Yitzhak, and

Pirkei DeRabbi Eliezer 54

Yaakov were zealous workmen. Thou gavest to them wages in full, of their own earnings Thou didst give them. But we are lazy workmen, and when Thou wilt give us our wages in full, and wilt heal us; verily, everyone will praise Thee and bless Thee.

It is finished. Praise be to God.

Pirkei DeRabbi Eliezer 54

www.ingramcontent.com/pod-product-compliance
Lightning Source LLC
Chambersburg PA
CBHW070126080526
44586CB00015B/1575